PROCESS & PRACTICE

Fifth Edition

Ronald Conrad

McGraw-Hill Ryerson Limited

Toronto Montreal New York Auckland Bogotá Caracas
Lisbon London Madrid Mexico Milan New Delhi
San Juan Singapore Sydney Tokyo

McGraw-Hill Ryerson Limited
A Subsidiary of The McGraw·Hill Companies

PROCESS AND PRACTICE
Fifth Edition

ISBN: 0-07-552760-X

1 2 3 4 5 6 7 8 9 10   MP 6 5 4 3 2 1 0 9 8 7

Printed and bound in Canada

Editor-in Chief: Dave Ward
Supervising Editor: Margaret Henderson
Production Editor: Gail Marsden
Developmental Editor: Laurie Graham
Production Co-ordinator: Nicla Dattolico
Text and Cover Design: Dianna Little
Cover Illustration: Icon Graphics Inc.
Typesetter: McGraphics Desktop Publishing Ltd.
Typeface: Giovanni Book
Printer: Maracle Press

Visit our Web Site: www.mcgrawhill.ca

Canadian Cataloguing in Publication Data

Conrad, Ronald, date–
    Process and practice

5th ed.
Includes index.
ISBN 0-07-552760-X

1. English language – Rhetoric.   2. English language –
Grammar.   I. Title.

PE1408.C583 1997   808 .042   C97-930310-9

Contents

Part Five: The Research Essay 211

To the Student

The world is changing much faster than ever before. Near the end of this book, our new sample research essay examines some of the effects on you and your classmates: in a world transformed by technology, with old categories of jobs falling right and left, how can today's students find success in the new workplace? By improving their writing, suggests one expert, Canadian demographer David Foot. "The decline of literacy," he points out, "has enhanced the value of the small minority who can write well...."

He is right, and if you need some help developing this key skill for the future, you are holding it in your hand. *Process and Practice* is meant to strengthen your writing, showing you techniques, tricks and strategies to make your work more relevant, better organized, more fully developed, and more polished. Our first section, on "short essays," takes you through the conception and planning stage, into warmups to overcome any writer's block, and through the "discovery draft." Then it demonstrates dozens of ways to fine-tune that first draft into more polished versions.

The next section, on word processing, checks to make sure you are using all the best tools of this technology. It also gives advice for new users, and concludes with some down-to-earth discussion of how to choose your own machine and how to afford it.

The paragraph chapter then shows major principles through examples. Then begins a large section on editing: that is, on polishing your early versions. This means both troubleshooting errors and also applying some useful principles of style, to heighten your power on the page. The exercises in this section are made of examples collected from student essays, so they will "ring true." (By the way, note that the answers to many of these exercises are given at the end of the book, so that you can check your work, whether you are taking a course or using this book on your own.)

Finally, if your class is also doing a research paper, near the end of the book this more scholarly art is examined, and the full sample essay already mentioned shows how the principles are applied.

Let's close by looking at our title: *Process and Practice*. Many teachers once believed that writing was planned out all in advance, with a detailed outline functioning something like a blueprint on a construction site. As the world has changed around us, though, so has our view of writing. Current research shows what most good writers have always known in their heart, that writing is a messy business — not a technology of any kind, but an art. When we set out on a writing task, we often don't even know the best ideas we'll end up with by the time we're done. This book recognizes, even celebrates, the reality of *thinking by writing*. That is the "process." The "practice," of course, is what you are about to do....

R. C.

To the Teacher

Editing a fifth edition — of anything — surely gives rise to two opposite thoughts. "If they've stuck with me this far," the author considers, "I'd better not change anything now!" But the next moment he or she is already thinking "How can the thing already be four editions old??? It's time to change it all!!"

Having had both these thoughts all year, now, I have come to think that, as with most controversies, the truth is somewhere in the middle. When I consider, for example, those teachers who have used all four editions so far, and who have told us the reasons why, I truly hesitate to rip out whole sections or to turn the methodology inside out or to seriously alter the balance of exposition vs. exercise, or of composition vs. editing. Why would those people, then, who clearly have been using the book for its present features, continue?

Yet when I see the changes turning our society inside out — for example the shift in values explored in this edition's new sample research essay, "Students and the New Workplace" — it seems clear that no textbook can speak to today's students without reflecting today's changes. The challenge is to move into the future without forgetting the past.

Process and Practice has always sought this middle path. The first edition was quite traditional in pedagogy, but brought in the then-rare quality of Canadian content, and presented exercises built of actual examples collected from student papers. The second edition began an evolution of organization, removing spelling from the first page and, towards the end, adding the first and second draft of a sample "short essay." The logic of process gathered force in the third edition, which put invention and composition at the beginning, then moved gradually from the "short essay" to the smaller aspects of editing. Then, major reorganizing having already been done, the fourth draft focused on replacing the sample "short essay" and renewing and upgrading the exercises.

So in the fifth edition what is new? We are offering a book that will be recognized by its present users, but that also looks to the future. For example, in our society where now even bankers wear jeans on Fridays, the book's style seemed overly formal — so it was updated with a colloquialism here and there, more irony and humour, more direct phrasing, and shortening of many sentences and paragraphs. For similar reasons, the number of photos and cartoons, as well as the amount of white space, has been increased.

New material on composing has been added, for example a heuristic exercise entitled "Using a Little Craziness to Overcome Writer's Block," and the section on audience is amplified with a similar activity for small groups to do in class.

About 30 to 40 percent of the exercise content has been replaced, keeping the better items, and a few exercises that seemed too long have been pruned. This time many sections of explication have been fine-tuned: some amplified, and many cast in new language and examples for new times. For example "Euphemisms" now examines the hypocritical new language of corporate "downsizing" and layoffs.

Finally, we know that not all classes have been using the "Research Essay" section, so we have attempted to make it more user-friendly. The new sample essay is shorter, is on a topic that should be of gut-wrenching importance to today's student, and has been cast in a language somewhat less formal and scholarly — yet still, we believe, appropriate. Details of documentation conform to the *MLA Handbook for Writers of Research Papers*, fourth edition.

If you are new to this book, here are a few overall suggestions:

- We advise starting right off with the "Short Essays" section, and basing a large part of any composition course on it. Until the actual writing begins, what good will editing exercises achieve? Writing should be the main and ongoing activity of the course.

  We also advise the system of drafts explored in the "Short Essays" section. The first can be checked but not evaluated, or can be treated in peer editing, or — if class size limits your marking time — can be handed in at the same time as a second draft; you then mark only the second, while glancing at the first to make sure some real revision has actually gone on.

- Meanwhile, as the needs of the students make themselves clear through what you see in their papers, select the appropriate editing materials from wherever they occur in the book (rather than marching a whole class through a prescribed set of activities). Do note that many of these sections have a "diagnostic" and a progression of two or more levels of exercises, so you can individualize work for different groups. (Answers to those exercises that are not open-ended are in the Key at the end of the book.) Another approach is to individualize: assign exercises as you are marking each person's paper. These can then be done at home, and either checked by the student against the answer key, or handed in (the exercises are detachable).

Finally, I wish to thank the many students, too numerous to name, whose suggestions helped define the shape of this edition. I also thank the reviewers who did the same, from the perspective of the teacher: Janet Baker, St. Mary's University; Barry Fox, St. Mary's University; Carol Fullerton, Mount Royal College; Janet Hill, Acadia University; Gary Lipschutz, Centennial College; Jim Maloney, Seneca College; Sally Nelson, Dawson College; and Joan Pilz, Humber College. Thanks also to librarians Diane Granfield, Don Kinder and Susan Patrick, of Ryerson Polytechnic University, who helped me fine-tune the section on research sources and CD-ROM. Finally and especially, I thank my wife, Mary, for her clear suggestions that have contributed so much to all five editions so far.

R. C.

Part One

Process in Short Essays

How do we write? Answers to this question have changed since your parents and grandparents were in school. Some widely believed folklore has been exposed as untrue, while research has more and more clearly shown what really happens when you sit down at the computer or writing desk. Let's examine some theories of the past that no longer make sense.

POPULAR MISCONCEPTIONS ABOUT WRITING

• *Misconception 1: Writing is just a matter of inspiration: I either hit it or miss it.* Most ideas, including this one, contain at least a grain of truth. We all hope for inspiration as we write. But now we know that most good writing does not just strike the paper like a lightning bolt, but is gradually developed through a process of revision. The first try is just a beginning; the second version is more developed; a third will be more developed still. As many practicing writers have believed all along, "writing is 10 percent inspiration and 90 percent perspiration."

• *Misconception 2: Writing is almost totally planned in advance.* Not so many years ago most teachers and students believed (or at least said they believed) that a beautifully reasoned outline was the main task in writing an essay. All the rest was a sort of filling in of blanks. Today we realize that this approach can in fact paralyze our thought process. Of course a short outline usually helps, but overplanning is a straitjacket that leads us to ignore the many good ideas that come to us *as we are writing*. We now see that writing is discovery! Some of our best thoughts emerge as we are engaged in the act of writing.

We take a compass on a journey through the wilderness, and we take an outline on a journey through our thoughts. But the compass cannot foretell every turn and twist of the path. If it could, most of the adventure would be gone. Do use an outline, especially in longer papers, but leave room for discovery as well. And if your discoveries overwhelm your outline, then your outline may have been weak to begin

with. Consider changing it, in the light of what you have learned while writing.

• *Misconception 3: If I just avoid enough errors, then my writing will be good.* We can see where this idea led in the past: we were so nervous about grammar and spelling that we paid too little attention to the main point of writing—the message. Reaching for the dictionary in the middle of writing a passage, we lost our train of thought and spent the next 10 minutes chewing our pencil in frustration—especially if we believed Misconception 1, that we either "hit it or miss it" the first time.

You do not have to write in this painful and unproductive way. The first draft should go fast. You should be free and open. After all, you are exploring: the goal is to get your ideas safely out on paper, without worrying about how "correct" you are. Then *later*, once the pressure is off, you tinker with grammar, spelling and style.

This whole book is organized to encourage writing as a *process*. The opening chapter deals with the big things: getting an idea, focussing it, trying it out in a quick first draft to see what you have to say, then revising your *thoughts*. Following chapters move on to secondary things: paragraphing, economy of words, clear sentence structure, agreement, clear pronoun reference, spelling, etc. These are all important, because without them the message might not get through. But they are "secondary" because, without a clear message in the first place, even the most clear and correct writing achieves nothing at all—like a pile of good bricks on the ground, waiting to be formed into a house.

WHAT IS AN ESSAY?

The word "essay" comes from a French term that means a "try" or "attempt." Our "attempts" to explore a topic in essay form can be as short as one or two handwritten pages or as long as 20, 30 or even 50 pages. They can be a brief and spontaneous treatment of a subject that we already know, or they can be the product of weeks spent researching in the library.

Since the form of an essay can vary so much, let's look separately at the two most common assignments: we will call them *short essays* and *research essays*. In this chapter we will explore short essays, because it is these that are most often practised in composition courses, and because the strategies behind them are the main strategies of research papers as well.

Then at the end of this book, after examining the whole process of writing, we will explore the more specialized tasks of research papers.

STARTING OUT: WHAT IS MY SUBJECT?

First of all, an essay has a subject. What will you write about? Teachers often answer that question by assigning a topic or choice of topics. Other times, you must think up your own.

Many kinds of writing you may do later in life will have similarities to the essay. Your employer may demand written analysis of projects at work. As a son or daughter, mother or father, or partner in a relationship, you might write a letter to explain or solve problems with a loved one. Or as a concerned citizen, you may write an "essay" of protest to your member of parliament, your mayor, or the editor of your newspaper. At crucial times in your life, you may even write out your private thoughts, as many people do, just to realize what you really think about your choices.

Whatever the subject and circumstances, the hardest part is to *begin*. If you need to choose from a list of topics, begin by comparing. Which topic do you already know something about? Which seems most important? Which do you *like*? Choose it, because you will do your best writing on topics that attract you. Some teachers of composition will ask you to produce your own topics. There are students who dread this, thinking they will have nothing to say; others love the challenge, for they can finally write what's on their minds.

In either case, choosing your own topic is an act that closely simulates your writing tasks in later life outside the classroom. Now let's explore a powerful approach to this challenge of creating a topic.

PRIMING THE PUMP: FREEWRITING

Have you ever tried to get water from an old hand pump, but nothing came out? Have you ever stared at a blank screen with your hands on the keyboard, but nothing came out? In the case of the pump, hardly ever is the well dry. The problem lies simply in getting the flow started. Old-timers will pour a jar of water down the pump to seal the chamber; now their efforts will create a suction that pulls up that cold, clear water.

In the case of the blank screen, the well is not dry either. What needs to be done is a kind of mental priming, so that your efforts will pull up ideas from the depths of your mind.

YOU ARE
HERE

Drawing by Chas. Addams. © 1974 The New Yorker Magazine, Inc.

One of the best priming exercises is **freewriting**. Put a piece of paper and a watch on the desk. Now for about five minutes, just write. Write *anything* that comes to mind, even if it seems like mental garbage. Get it down as swiftly as your hand and pen or computer will let you. Then rush on to the next thought that arrives.

Do not stop the physical process of writing or typing until the time is up. If the next thought does not come, keep repeating the last one till it does. At the beginning of it all, if not even the first thought will come, try this: write "The" on the paper. Some word will then pop into your mind to follow "The," and another will follow it, until soon your first idea is out in the open.

Why write what may seem like garbage? Because researchers have shown that thoughts tend to appear not in logical order but in sudden leaps of association. If we start with a few of these intuitive leaps, we get the juices of thought flowing; we pump those raw materials of writing out into the open where our more logical thought processes can now work on them, shaping them into the logical arguments we wanted in the first place.

Here is an actual, unedited piece of freewriting. It took about six minutes, not five, because the writer got so involved in the emerging subject that she couldn't stop. It is also fairly long, because the writer was racing away at the computer keyboard.

Note the carelessness of her sentence structure: some passages run on and on with "ands," while others are cut off into partial sentences. Note also the careless spelling and typos, such as "sweatay" for "sweaty" and "what it" for "what if." **In freewriting these are not errors, for the whole point is just to get thoughts out in the open.**

> There are always transit strikes and every year the fare goes up, and for a while a lot of people either quit taking transit or talk about not taking it, and the statistics actually say that fewer people take it. Why not take the car? But when you look at what it costs to operate a car in the big city, it is pretty appalling. Parking, maintenan e, insurance, gasoline. And then, we complain about standing in the subway during rush hour, like in the summer when everybody is sweating and you feel like a swim in a cold lakle but you are carrying your stuff and trying to hang 9onto the sweatay bar to keep from falling over as the train swings around a curve. Or the streetcar is even worse because the streets are choked with traffic, and you go so slowly you might get there faster walking. But what if We all took transit? What if they added more lines and more cars? What if the traffic on the streets disappeared? Well, it wouldn't disappear, but what it. . . How could we do it? Ir raising the fares drives people

away, how about lowering them? How about making it free? How about making car drivers pay for the operation of the transit system? Everybody would scream taxes, but what if the life in our city improved?

This writer was lucky to start with a subject already in mind. She did not have to write a page of free association—jumping from one thought or image to another—before hitting upon the idea of public transit and the private car.

Yet this early and spontaneous version of her thoughts is far from the argument she will produce by the end of her first draft or second draft. She does criticize cars, but mostly from the point of view of cost. That's a good enough beginning to get her started. It will get her into the discovery draft, where she will then go much further, for example into the area of air pollution.

The writer criticizes public transit, too, but even here in the freewriting has discovered a solution which she will later choose to place at the end of her essay: reduce traffic and improve transit by making car drivers pay. **It is surprising how often a piece of freewriting, like this one, reveals the main points of the essay that will follow—how much it "discovers" even before the "discovery draft" begins.**

Think of your own experience in starting to write essays: Have you been afraid of the blank page? Has "writer's block" paralyzed you? Freewriting can move you past these common problems. After all, what do you have to lose—five minutes of your time? By ignoring the old myth that writing is all planned in advance, you can take mental shortcuts that may save hours of time. The trick is to **think by writing**.

Even if a required topic leaves you cold, so that you feel you have nothing to say, you can avoid writer's block by freewriting. Launch into a few minutes of warmup by putting onto that blank screen or page *something, anything,* that relates to your topic. You will often be surprised at what comes out; you may sense that, even at this stage, *the writing has somehow begun.*

PRIMING THE PUMP: BRAINSTORMING

Brainstorming is like freewriting, with this main difference: it is not a piece of continuous writing but a list of ideas put down in short form.

Suppose the person whose freewriting we have just seen had done brainstorming instead. Thinking of public transit and the private car, she would jot down anything that came to mind, in any order. Even ideas that seemed irrelevant or silly could join the list. Some might seem random or illogical; but, as in freewriting, what is there to lose? Five minutes of time? And only she will see the list (except for us, looking over her shoulder right now).

PUBLIC TRANSIT

- strike

- costs keep going up

- no student rate

- crowded, hot - can't get a seat

- wait for bus in winter. Cold

- drive car instead

- comfortable

- insurance - parts - Dad paid $700 for new central computer for his car

- pollution. Air getting worse in Toronto

- greenhouse effect. Winters getting warmer

A writer who brainstorms casts a net into the sea: when the catch is pulled in, it may include fish no one would want to eat. So what? They are thrown back and the good ones are kept.

As you look at the author's page of brainstorming, note her progression of thought. She begins with the transit strike, goes on to the cost of transit, then the crowding and waiting. Now comes the alternative of the comfortable car, but also the cost (she remembers her father paying $700 to replace his car's central computer). Then she gets closer to the core of her eventual essay, as she begins to jot down notes about traffic and air pollution. She even specifies the greenhouse effect, which will get only a mention at the end of her discovery draft, but which in the second draft will suddenly expand to become her major point against the car and in favour of public transit.

In these few minutes of brainstorming, in short form, *the writing has already begun.*

PRIMING THE PUMP: A CLUSTER OUTLINE

A similar but more visual device is the cluster outline. As in brainstorming, note down the ideas as they come, but connect them in a diagram. On page 5 see the ideas we read in the brainstorming example, but expressed in much more graphic form. (Some people do think better visually. You may be one of them.)

Note how this diagram sorts ideas more easily into groups. The writer first puts down the key thought of "public transit" in a circle in the middle of the page. Then around it she jots down other words or ideas it brings to mind, such as "price keeps going up" or "hot, crowded, hang onto poles," and connects them with lines to show relationships.

Note especially how, toward the lower left, the thought "driving instead" leads to a great many other thoughts, some positive ("comfortable") and others negative ("expensive" and "creates air pollution"). These thoughts about driving, as in an outline, are connected in groups: all the comfort together, all the expense together, and all the pollution together.

As the writer looks these over, she can **see** where her argument is leading, and above all where her main focus will be: on the large group of ideas concerned with pollution. As in freewriting and brainstorming, *the writing has already begun.*

PRIMING THE PUMP: FIGHTING WRITER'S BLOCK WITH IMAGINATION

We have just looked at freewriting, brainstorming and the cluster outline. One or two of these may be enough,

freeing our mind to move inside a subject. Sometimes, though, the often-mentioned literary disease of *writer's block* refuses to let us through. We all know the symptoms: sitting at the computer or writing desk frozen in time, stealing glances at our watch, feeling the sweat on our face and body, and looking with rising emptiness at that object of fear in front of us—the blank screen or page.

It doesn't have to be this way. Don't let yourself be intimidated by, literally, *nothing!* If other approaches have not worked, try a little craziness. The following techniques operate on the reality that original thought is often irrational; that a strange link exists between madness and genius. Composition theorists call this activity "heuristics." Here's how it works:

1. First have in mind a possible subject or topic.

2. Now run your eyes down the right-hand column of suggested perspectives, applying each in turn to your topic. Let your mind run wild. If what comes out is zany or ridiculous, is that a problem? If you are contemplating a traffic jam from the point of view of a virus, so what??? After all, you are only getting ideas and finding motivation at this stage; no-one says these early thoughts have to end up in your final draft.

3. Record your new ideas now, using any of the three prewriting techniques just discussed: freewriting, brainstorming or the cluster outline.

4. When you are finished, see if this process has freed new insights, a new introduction, a first page, a way of seeing your topic, that *gets you writing.* There is a very good chance it will. Let this happen in a fast discovery draft. *Do it!*

5. Probably by the second or third page, the craziness you felt at the beginning will have resolved itself into your more usual factual and logical way of treating a topic. Let it happen: *this is what you were aiming for in the first place.*

6. When you reach the end of this first draft, let it lie. The next day, though, check out the weird parts you may have left at the beginning. If they go too far—if they make no sense at all—redo them now in the more logical mode you probably fell into on the second or third page. By now you are on your way to the final version....

These techniques are meant mainly for the short, informal essays often done in composition courses. While they may also have their place in kick-starting your response to a research essay topic, do keep in mind that the highly factual and logical nature of research has its own distinctive requirements (see pages 211 to 237 at the end of this book).

Using a Little Craziness to Overcome Writer's Block: Worksheet

Follow the directions just given, using this material to kick-start your imagination and motivation to write. The topics at the left are only examples to show how the exercise works: see how to pair one of them with each of the ideas at the right, to generate the "craziness" that gets you thinking. Now substitute your own topic(s), or the topic(s) assigned by your instructor. As number 3 on page 6 states, record your reactions to this material (on another page), using either freewriting, brainstorming or cluster outlines.

EXAMPLES OF TOPIC IDEAS	NEW PERSPECTIVES: IMAGINE YOUR TOPIC IN THESE WAYS
the problem of traffic in the city	– upside down – in slow motion – in black and white – under a microscope – a century ago or a century from now – turned inside out – with its parts disassembled
street people	– as a computer game – as a TV sitcom – as science fiction – in the time of the Neanderthals – looking from outer space, or down from a mountaintop, or up from under the ocean
effects of video games	– in a country at war – in the Third World – as music – as a virus – as a Gary Larson cartoon – in summer, in winter, or at night – as a crime
anorexia nervosa	– as a sport – as an earthquake, tornado, hurricane, blizzard or flood – as a college or university course – as a vehicle: motorcycle, car, truck or train
corporate downsizing	– from the point of view of an insect, bird, fish, cat or dog – from the point of view of a disabled person in a wheelchair – from the point of view of a baby or a very old person – from the point of view of Adam or Eve, Marx, Freud, Joan of Arc, George Orwell, Lucien Bouchard, Martin Luther King, Céline Dion, Homer or Marge or Bart Simpson, or a space alien

THE THESIS STATEMENT

Once you have determined your topic and unloosened some ideas through freewriting, brainstorming or a cluster outline, you need to limit the scope and focus the purpose of the essay. Although the first version is a "discovery draft," those discoveries take place within limits. If you kept wandering from one good thought to the next, you could write forever without reaching the heart of one chosen idea.

Instead, why not use what most writers use, a THESIS STATEMENT. **Usually one complete sentence (but if necessary two or three), and almost always near the beginning of the essay, a thesis statement will do two things very clearly:**

• **Limit the scope of the argument**

• **Focus the writer's purpose**

(*Note*: Some people think a title, such as "Pollution in the City," is a thesis statement. It is not. A title is just a label, like the words "Tomato Soup" on a tin can. It is usually not even a sentence. You do need a title, but you need a thesis statement even more.)

Limiting the Scope—or, "*Less is More*"

Do you realize how short an essay is? A book may contain 100 000 words or more, a magazine article 2000 to 5000, but a classroom essay as few as 500 or even 250. Logic suggests, therefore, that **we choose either a small topic or a small aspect of a larger one**.

One student who didn't think of this decided to analyze communism, socialism and capitalism—certainly a worthy project—but he crammed these three major economic systems of the world into a grand total of two pages! Thinking of the thousands of entire books written on each of these systems, we could have predicted what came out: a collection of generalizations everyone has already heard, with no analysis and not one example to bring the stuff alive. So what good did writing this essay do at all? How did it express the knowledge, insights and point of view of the writer?

Yet the author later confided to the teacher that he had real-life insights into one of these systems, for he had been a political prisoner in a country that practised it. Fascinated, the teacher made an immediate suggestion: if the writer had only *limited the scope* to a small part of the topic—say, his arrest or his trial or a day in his cell—he might have said far more about the system he had struggled against.

Think of writing as photography. Putting aside the wide-angle lens that includes so much that everything is far away, look through the telephoto lens that zooms you up close to a small part of the subject. Select the part most meaningful to you, the part most typical of the whole. Sharpen the focus. Then take the picture.

Focusing the Purpose

A thesis statement gives an opinion. It sets a direction for the main argument of the essay. It does not just state a fact, such as "Rumania was a communist country." We either knew that already or we learn it as we read the sentence. In either case the idea is self-contained, over with once it is stated, and as a result has no impact. If there is no real point, then the essay will be "pointless."

By contrast, a strong thesis statement is usually a *generalization*—that is, an *opinion*. The French philosopher Voltaire, a man feared by his own government, said "To hold a pen is to be at war." He may have been exaggerating; his shopping list or diary or letters to his family may not have argued or fought. But many of his public essays certainly did: they were attempts to convince readers of the author's opinions—for example on different problems of society and how to address them.

Remembering his own time in prison, our politically minded essay writer might have said something like this: "I discovered that in Rumania, life in a prison cell was not that different from life in the streets." Now his point of view could focus on the brutal guards, the dreary food, the sameness of the prison routine, perhaps even the rats and cockroaches—and through this close-up, in the short space of an essay, create an impression of the country in general as it suffered from its economic system. In making the cell represent the country, our writer would be saying *more with less*.

Thesis Statement: Where Does It Appear?

In most essays, especially long ones, the thesis is seldom the opening sentence. First we read a little background information so we can understand the thesis when it occurs. Or first we read a paragraph or two designed to trap our attention: perhaps a funny or tragic story related to the topic, a pertinent quotation, or a frightening statistic. But toward the end of this introduction we normally do find the thesis statement, which alerts us to the scope and purpose of the argument to come.

In very short essays, say of two or three or four pages, the writer may feel like just launching out with a thesis statement as the first words. But such a beginning may seem abrupt, even in a very short paper. Rather than starting off so bluntly, why not begin with at least a sentence or two of preparation, to tempt the reader? Give a bit of background information, a funny or tragic incident, a pertinent quotation or statistic. Warm your reader up a bit, rather than starting off cold with your main point. (See page 40 for more on how to write introductory paragraphs.)

NAME _____

Limiting the Scope: Worksheet

For each of the general subjects below, supply five "close-ups" that limit the scope to a size that might fit a short essay.

Example:

Computers

    a. *discussion groups on the Internet*

    b. *automatic banking*

    c. *computer games*

    d. *buying a computer*

    e. *surviving in the school computer lab*

1. Music

    a.

    b.

    c.

    d.

    e.

2. Crime

    a.

    b.

    c.

    d.

    e.

3. Television

    a.

    b.

    c.

    d.

    e.

4. Poverty

    a.

    b.

    c.

    d.

    e.

5. Quebec

    a.

    b.

    c.

    d.

    e.

NAME _____

Making Thesis Statements: Worksheet

*Develop each of your "close-ups" from the previous exercise into a generalization (an **opinion**) meant to interest your reader and set a direction for your essay. Remember that a thesis statement is a **complete sentence**.*

Example (from the general subject of "Computers"):

   a.   Discussion groups on the Internet

       For fanatics, Internet discussion groups are a substitute for life.

   b.   Automatic banking

       The main purpose of electronic banking is to reduce the number of bank employees.

   c.   Computer games

       The increasing violence of computer games contributes to violence in the schools.

   d.   Buying a computer

       The best way to select a computer is first to decide what software will be used, then what hardware is needed to run it.

   e.   Surviving in the school computer lab

       Starting projects early is the key to survival in the school computer lab.

1.   a.

     b.

     c.

     d.

     e.

2. a.

   b.

   c.

   d.

   e.

3. a.

   b.

   c.

   d.

   e.

4. a.

   b.

   c.

   d.

   e.

5. a.

   b.

   c.

   d.

   e.

AUDIENCE: WHO IS MY READER?

An absolutely essential thing to do before starting the first draft is to **visualize your reader or readers**. Who are they? What approach will work with them?

After all, you adjust the way you talk to your listeners: would you speak the same way and say the same things to a child and an old person? To a criminal and a judge? To your hockey coach and your member of parliament? Probably not. Neither would you write exactly the same things in the same way to these different people. To match your writing to your audience, ask three questions:

1. *What is my reader's level?* An essay for your professor is one thing; a letter to your school newspaper is another. If your reader is very thoughtful, you may use demanding vocabulary and complex arguments. But if your audience is at an average level of reading and thinking, restrain your vocabulary and explain ideas plainly.

2. *What does my reader know?* One look at the number of books in a library will convince us that we cannot learn everything. People specialize: not everyone can repair the faucet, write clear English and also calculate the income tax. As you plan an essay or report, recognize the differences between people: try to estimate your own reader's knowledge of the subject. Is he or she experienced in some areas—and inexperienced in others?

Some composition courses encourage essays on a wide variety of subjects. You might write on inflation, germ warfare, fibre optics or digital recording, with your English teacher as the audience. But watch out: if your own field is electronics, you might load your account of digital recording with terms this reader has never seen and may not find even in the dictionary. Have pity: if your reader is a nonspecialist, avoid most technical terms and define those you do use. Give background. Explain clearly. Use examples. Otherwise he or she will be lost. (For more on this, see "Jargon," p. 83.)

On the other hand, the same approach to a literature paper on, say, a novel by Rohinton Mistry, may cause problems. Your English teacher may be annoyed by explanation of terms she or he has used for 20 years, and may miss the challenge of a more complex argument. Therefore estimate, as well as you can, the reader's command over your subject—and write accordingly.

Are all these people really alike. . . ? *Roberts/Comstock.*

3.   *What does my reader believe?* Are you likely to communicate by quoting Marx to a banker, the Bible to an atheist, or Henry Morgentaler to a right-to-life activist? Probably not. Be realistic: do not send a message that is sure to be rejected.

Of course you must tell the truth, but in terms acceptable to your audience. For example, build on assumptions that you and your reader can share. Do not preach to a capitalist that socialism is better—but you can certainly claim that capitalism is not perfect, giving examples such as the Great Depression, inflation, massive corporate lay-offs while stock prices rise, etc. At the end of it all, even the banker may begin to understand another point of view.

One serious problem in composition courses is deciding who is the *real* audience. Though it is usually the teacher (and sometimes classmates) who will actually read your papers, a course in writing is only practice for writing in the real world. Your *real* readers will be everyone you write for for the rest of your life. For this reason, it may be a good thing to discuss the matter in class, to make sure the teacher does not see your choice of audience in overly personal terms. Once everyone involved agrees who the audience is, you will have a clearer idea of how to proceed.

Who Are They ...?

Do not think of your reader in the abstract. Instead, *visualize* the person or persons who will read your essay. You may be writing alone at a desk, but in thought you are communicating face to face.

The next worksheet explores this relationship, but also poses another challenge. In writing for a teacher you have a one-person audience, but in many other writing tasks you need to reach a variety of individuals within one group. Now you must think of them all: what arguments are universal enough to appeal to most people? What assumptions must be avoided because, although some people will agree, others will be alienated or even angry?

Relating to Your Audience: Worksheet for On-class Group Exploration

Form groups of three to five. From the left column, choose a topic and viewpoint that your group might want to argue in an essay. You know how readers are, though: they will agree or disagree with you, depending on how they already see things.

Now explore this challenge by examining all the readers at the right: what attitudes, what assumptions, will each probably hold about your chosen topic and point of view? (While we do not want to stereotype, reality tells us that things like profession, age, level of income, gender and other life experience do powerfully influence people's views.)

Finally, come up with at least one technique that should help your argument go over better with each potentially hostile member of your audience. (For example, the bank executive who may favour raising tuition fees might have postsecondary students in his or her own family.)

against: marijuana use	a high school principal
against: child labour in the Third World	a union member
	a member of the Reform Party
for: lowering the voting age	a social worker
against: social program cuts	a police officer
for: income tax cuts	a homeless person
against: raising tuition fees	a bank executive
against: U.S. ownership of Canadian companies	a logger in British Columbia
	a college or university student
for: Quebec separation	a wealthy investor
for: reducing the national debt	a retired widow
	a *Globe and Mail* subscriber
against: euthanasia	a single parent on welfare
for: spending more on a cure for AIDS	a very religious person
	a grade five student
for: closing tax loopholes	a recent immigrant
for: reducing violence on television	a feminist
	a subscriber to *Hot Rod* magazine
for: photo radar	a ballet dancer
against: clearcutting of our forests	a native person
for: establishment of year-round school	a farmer

THE DISCOVERY DRAFT

Now let's return to our writer who didn't appreciate the transit strike, who dislikes pollution, and who is looking for a better way to get around the city. She has done **freewriting** (pages 2–3), or **brainstorming** (pages 3, 4 and 6) or a **cluster outline** (pages 5 and 6), and perhaps a **heuristic** exercise (page 6) to start ideas flowing. Now she is ready to give those ideas preliminary shape in a thesis statement. Here is one she might formulate:

> The excitement of the strike soon turned to exasperation as the people drew their conclusion: public transit is essential to life in the city.

Notice what a "close-up" this statement is. It does not cover city life in general, or transportation in general, or even the strike in general. Instead, it focuses on *a small part of a large subject*: how the people of one city realized the value of public transit, through being deprived of it.

Note also how this thesis gives the topic a point of view, a *direction*. We already see what the writer thinks of public transit: she likes it. Now as we read the explanations and examples to come, we will be prepared to understand and react to the main idea.

But first our writer may be helped by one more planning step: an outline. We do all know people who plunge ahead with no outline at all. This may often work in a short essay, and sometimes even in a long one. But without at least some kind of plan, perhaps a few words to rough out the order of main points, a writer can end up like Stephen Leacock's famous horseman who "rode madly off in all directions."

Following the advice of researchers in composition, let's keep an outline short and *tentative*, because good new ideas will almost certainly strike *as we are writing* the first draft. If they do not fit the plan, we may even change the main point, despite what we have said in our thesis statement and outline. Remember that writing is discovery! You might recognize and promote this concept by calling your first version the "discovery draft."

Now here is our author's brief and tentative outline. Note that it includes the thesis statement.

THE BETTER WAY

I. Introduction
   A. Opening example: Toronto's transit strike
   B. Thesis statement: *The excitement of the strike soon turned to exasperation as the people drew their conclusion: public transit is essential to life in the city.*
II. Body: Public Transit vs. the Car
   A. Getting to school during the transit strike
   B. Disadvantages of public transit
   C. Disadvantages of the private automobile
      1. Expenses
      2. Pollution
III. Conclusion: Make the Car Drivers Pay for Public Transit
   A. To reduce traffic
   B. To make transit cheaper and better

With a tentative outline in front of you, you are ready for the discovery draft. Whether you use a computer or a pen, the tactics are similar. You keyboard or write rapidly, getting ideas out into the open without stopping the train of thought.

If the right word doesn't come, just leave a blank to fill in later. If a word or phrase seems wrong, don't fix it now: just leave it, or if you are writing by hand underline it, so later you can find it and revise. At the computer use visual markers, such as a row of ampersands (&&&&&&&&&&&&&&) or another method supplied by your software, to signal spots where you will return for troubleshooting.

If you sense a misspelled word or shaky grammar, underline or mark the spot electronically. Forget spell check for now, and *leave the dictionary and the handbook on the shelf—till later*. Write paragraphs naturally as they come: many will be good in your first draft, and the rest can be adjusted later.

> Finally, leaving room for later revision is essential. Do you want to cram new sentences into microscopic spaces between lines? If not, whether you write by hand or key into the computer, be sure to double-space now.

Here is the author's discovery draft:

DISCOVERY DRAFT: The Better Way

Last fall there was another transit strike. These 1
seem to happen every two or three years. People got
angry at first, because how would they get to work or get
to school in a city of this size? Then they worked out
their strategies. Employers organized car pools.
Neighbours and friends did the same. The GO train laid
on a lot more trains, with more cars. People put on
running shoes so they could walk a mile, or even three or
four, to work. It was almost exciting, as the emergency
gave people a sense of adventure. But the excitement of
the strike soon turned to exasperation as the people
drew their conclusion: public transit is essential to
life in the city.

The streets were choked with traffic. I tried car 2
pooling to get to class, but had to leave at 7:15 in the
morning because my friend starts work at 8:30. Then I
tried hitchhiking down Yonge Street. There were plenty
of rides, but nobody was going very far before they
turned off. And traffic was so slow, because everyone
was driving, that I actually saw people walking on the
sidewalk gaining on us block after block. One day I put
on my most comfortable running shoes and tried to walk
the five miles myself, but the pollution from all those
idling cars was so thick that my lungs were hurting and I
was dizzy by the time I got to my locker. There has to
be a better way, I thought to myself.

3   The Toronto Transit Commission, the TTC, calls itself "the better way." When we are trapped in a stuffed subway car in hot weather, during the height of rush hour, sweating like a pig and hanging onto the slippery bar to keep from falling over when the train starts and stops, we hardly think it is "the better way". We long to take a part-time job and get some money together to buy a car. Then we can speed to school, with our favourite tape on the stereo, and smoke and drink coffee and eat all we want to, without somebody's elbow in our face.

4   But is that actually the "better way"? Look at the economics of it. A decent car, even used, costs at least $8000. Insurance for people our age and in the big city costs $2000 if you're lucky, or up to $5000 a year if you have infractions and drive the kind of little red sports car everyone wants to drive. Then parking in Toronto runs $12 a day and up. Maintenance costs a few hundred a year if you're lucky, but with the older cars students can only afford, you may end up rebuilding or replacing a transmission, or doing other costly work. Then there are gasoline, oil, tires, and more. That makes the price of a TTC ticket, even with its annual increase, seem like pretty small stuff.

5   Then there's the environment. Many people my age have a greater concern than the generation of our parents. We've been exposed to the issues since grade one, and, after all, we are the ones who have to live our futures in this world polluted by all those who went

before us. My grandfather says that when he was a boy
he used to swim in the Don River. Now it's Toronto's
biggest sewer. Now you can't even swim in Lake Ontario
half the time. To think that our drinking water comes
right out of the lake takes away my thirst. If I could
afford it, I'd drink mineral water.

Air pollution is probably the worst problem in
Toronto though. A study came out a couple of years ago
that the very most polluted spot in all of Canada is
right along Yonge Street where I walk from the College
subway stop to my classes. On a bad day in warm weather
the haze just hangs in the air. It actually makes my
lungs hurt. Sometimes your eyes hurt and the tears come
just from the sulfuric acid in the air, from all the car
exhaust. You can hardly see the stars at night. Up in
the Bruce Peninsula where my friends and I went camping
last summer, you could see thousands, probably millions,
of stars twinkling all over the sky. You could see the
Milky Way, like a blanket of stars, across the middle.
You could see falling starts, and satellites moving
across the sky. They say there are a billion stars in
our galaxy and I felt like I was seeing them all. But
back in Toronto, nothing. A purplish haze covers the
sky at night, lit up from the lights all over town.

I this the kind of city we want? Public transit has
its problems, especially in rush hour. But the number
of people who drive their cars create much worse
problems. Do we want to choke ourselves to death with

6

7

pollution? Or is there a "better way"? I say that the old, much criticized Toronto Transit Commission is the "better way." It is the future.

8   How can we make it better? How can we get the drivers off the streets and into the buses, streetcars and subway trains? By sheer economics. By devising a system to make drivers pay for public transit, we will begin to clear the streets of traffic and upgrade the transit system at the same time. One there are more frequent transit vehicles, more people will use them. Most importantly for students, who can hardly pay all their expenses, the fare will be greatly reduced or even

9   gone. If our society can realize the true value of clean air to breathe, and of reducing the greenhouse effect that threatens to disrupt civilization across the world, the true cost of providing transit free of charge to the riders will seem very small indeed.

REVISING THE DISCOVERY DRAFT

Now put yourself in the place of our writer. After the prewriting, she has taken the plunge into a "discovery draft." Writing it gave a certain satisfaction: she got to complain about some things that were bothering her, and worked her feelings into a more or less coherent form.

In the moments after writing the last word, she may even consider the essay a masterpiece. She may have her family and friends read it, and consider them fools if they do not share her enthusiasm.

But a day later she has lost what we could call "the writer's high." As she looks over the draft more calmly, certain passages bother her. They don't seem as good as they did yesterday. Here is a "fact" that is wrong. And here is an idea that doesn't support the point.

But now another idea pops into her head. Why didn't she think of it yesterday? Our writer reaches again for the draft, and two hours later awakens from another "writer's high" to find the once-neat manuscript covered with messy revisions. In fact, the new section she just added on the greenhouse effect now seems to be the high point of her argument.

Now let's see exactly what she did. On the next pages is her second draft, with all changes and additions boxed so you can see them at once. Then right after that, on pages 27 to 29, a blow-by-blow analysis shows why each change was made, as a practical demonstration of what you can do as you develop one draft into the next draft.

Nowhere does word processing help the writer more than in the act of revising a draft.

Most experienced users key their discovery draft right into the machine. (Think of the time you waste writing all those words out first by hand!) Next it makes sense to do a quick spell check (see page 190), then print out "hard copy" to edit, because most people see words better on paper. Be sure to double-space, leaving room for handwritten changes. Print in "draft" mode, which is fast and uses less ribbon or ink. If your printer takes single-sheet feed, print early drafts on the backs of used paper (first removing any staples).

After the first version "cools off" for a day, edit your hard copy as our author has edited her second draft, which follows. (Some people do all their editing on screen, printing nothing but the final version. This more direct way may work for you, but if not go back to paper.)

Whether you edit on paper and transfer handwritten changes to the screen, or edit directly on screen, make sure you know all the commands that will speed your work: backspacing, deleting one letter, one word, a whole line, or all the rest of the page. Learn to move blocks of text, so that if you find, for example, that your key point is hidden in the middle of the paper, you can switch it to a more dramatic position at the end—without retyping.

While the draft is on screen, exploit the speed of your electronic thesaurus by using it on any word that is not exact enough or direct enough or strong enough or short enough. (See page 32.)

Finally, "save" each draft under a different "file name" (for example transit1, transit2, transit3, etc.), so you can go back to another version if you change your mind about what you revised or took out.

SECOND DRAFT: The Better Way

1   Last fall Toronto endured another transit strike.
People got angry at first, because how would they get to
work or get to school in a city of this size? Then they
devised their strategies. Employers organized car
pools. Neighbours and friends did the same. People put
on running shoes so they could walk a mile, or three or
four, to work. Some even got out their roller blades.
It was almost exciting, as the emergency gave people a
sense of adventure. But the excitement of the strike soon
turned to exasperation as the people drew their conclusion: public transit is essential to life in the city.

2   The day the strike began, traffic choked the streets.
I tried car pooling to get to class, but had to leave at
7:15 in the morning because my friend starts work at
8:30. Then I tried hitchhiking down Yonge Street,
a thing I would never do if the subway were running.
There were plenty of rides, but nobody was going very far
before turning off. And traffic was so slow, because
everyone was driving, that I actually saw people walking
on the sidewalk gaining on us block after block. One day
I too put on my most comfortable running shoes and tried
to walk the five miles myself, but the pollution from all
those idling cars was so thick that by the time I got to
my locker I was dizzy and my lungs were hurting. There
has to be a better way, I thought to myself.

3   The Toronto Transit Commission, the TTC, calls itself
"the better way." When we are trapped in a stuffed

subway car in hot weather, during the height of rush hour, sweating like pigs and hanging onto the slippery bar to keep from falling over when the train starts and stops, we hardly think it is "the better way." We long to take a part-time job and get some money together to buy a car. Then we could speed to school, with our favourite tape on the stereo, and smoke and drink coffee and eat candy bars all we wanted to, without somebody's elbow in our face.

But is that actually the "better way"? Look at the economics of it, for example. A decent car, even used, costs at least $6000. With luck, insurance for people our age in the big city costs $2000 a year, but if one has infractions and drives the kind of little red sports car everyone wants to drive, the bill can reach $5000 or more. Then parking in Toronto runs $12 a day and up. Maintenance costs a few hundred a year if the car is in decent condition. But if the vehicle is one of the oldies that students tend to buy, costly items such as the transmission or the central computer may have to be rebuilt or replaced. Then there are tires, oil and gasoline. Many students have worked so many hours to support the driving habit that they have failed out of school, missing their chance for a satisfying career and the salary that comes with it. That makes the price of a TTC ticket, even with its annual increase, seem like pretty small stuff.

Even more important than monetary costs of driving

are the environmental costs of driving. Many people my age have a greater concern for this planet than the generation of our parents has. We've been exposed to the issues since grade one, and, after all, we are the ones who have to live our futures in this world polluted by all those who went before us.

6 Air pollution, caused mostly by private vehicles, is one of Toronto's worst problems. A study published a couple of years ago in The Globe and Mail concluded that the very most polluted spot in all of Canada is right along Yonge Street where I walk from the College subway stop to my classes. On a bad day in warm weather the haze just hangs in the air. It actually makes my lungs hurt. Sometimes my eyes hurt and the tears come just from the sulfuric acid in the air.

7 Torontonians can hardly see the stars at night. Up in the Bruce Peninsula where my friends and I went camping last summer, thousands, probably millions, of stars twinkle all over the sky. We could see the Milky Way, like a blanket of stars, across the middle. We could see falling stars and satellites moving across the sky. The Milky Way is our galaxy. Astronomers say there are a hundred billion stars in it, and I felt like I was seeing them all. But back at Yonge and Bloor, the night sky was nothing but a purplish haze illuminated by lights all over town.

8 An even worse result of air pollution is the greenhouse effect, in which atmospheric carbon dioxide,

produced mostly by private vehicles, raises temperatures around the world by trapping the sun's heat. Toronto dwellers experience some of the results. Now in winter their sidewalks are covered with slush instead of proper snow, and those who once went cross-country skiing in parks and ravines can now do so only one or two days per year. Toronto summers have always been sultry, but lately for several weeks in July and August they are downright unbearable.

More serious are the greenhouse effects that drivers in cities such as Toronto cause elsewhere. As the increasingly warmed atmosphere melts polar ice, the oceans rise. Low-lying heavily populated coastal areas like Bangladesh experience more disastrous flooding every year, and will eventually disappear, causing a flow of environmental refugees such as the world has never seen. Meanwhile the same heat around the world is turning vast areas of marginal farmland into desert. In countries such as Ethiopia and Somalia, the desert is expanding at such a rate that famine kills ever larger numbers of men, women and especially children. The city dweller half a world away, in North America, contributes to this every time he or she takes the wasteful car instead of the more efficient streetcar, bus or subway train.

9

Is this how we want to live in our city? Public transit does have its problems, especially in rush hour. But the number of people who drive their cars creates

10

much worse problems. Do we want to sacrifice our school performance by working enough hours to support a car? Do we want to choke ourselves with pollution? Do we want to kill other people around the world by contributing to the greenhouse effect? Or is there a better way? I say that the old, much criticized Toronto Transit Commission is the "better way." It is the future.

11   But how can we make public transit truly "better"? How can we get the drivers off the streets and into the streetcars, buses and subway trains? By sheer economics. If we devise a system to make automobile drivers pay for public transit, we will begin to clear the streets of traffic and upgrade the transit system at the same time. Once there are more frequent transit vehicles, and once there is more room on them, more people will use them.

12   Students, who can hardly pay all their expenses, will find the fare greatly reduced or even gone. More importantly, if our society can realize the true value of clean air to breathe, and of reducing the greenhouse effect that threatens to disrupt civilization across the world, the true cost of providing transit free of charge to the riders will seem very small indeed.

REVISIONS: HOW AND WHY

"Revision" literally means "seeing again." Our writer has "seen again" at several points in the writing process. The short outline was a "re-seeing" of the freewriting and other prewriting activities. The discovery draft was then a "re-seeing" of all the thinking and planning that led up to it, and the second draft is a "re-seeing" of the discovery draft.

For example, not every remark in the cluster outline ends up in the discovery draft. Although it may be true that tourists are charmed by the city's picturesque streetcars, the author's real point became how public transportation solves problems.

On the other hand, though the cluster outline gives only one word to the transit strike, by the time the writer begins her first draft she chooses this dramatic event to attract the reader's attention and to lead into her thesis, the importance of public transit. In fact, even in the second draft she continues to develop this introduction, suddenly remembering the people roller blading and adding them to the hitchhikers and walkers.

More "re-seeing" occurs in the second draft. The closing of the discovery draft really bothered our author as she looked it over the next day: the remark about the greenhouse effect in the very last sentence was too sudden. It seemed to introduce a large new topic, only to drop it without developing it. Now, she realizes, this important point *should* be developed, so she goes ahead and does so. The result is a whole new section, paragraphs 8 and 9, which argues that public transit helps not only those who use it but others around the world as well.

By contrast, while looking over draft 1, the author realizes that the part she had liked so much, about her grandfather swimming in the Don River, is irrelevant to her topic. Since she has not been able to blame water pollution on private vehicles, she crosses the whole passage right out, and goes on to air pollution.

> Now let's look at the many smaller cases of "seeing again," to illustrate the range of improvements you can make when revising your own papers. (Paragraph numbers refer to the second draft, except where specified otherwise.)

- *Paragraph 1*: Compare the boxed revisions in the second draft to the original wording of the discovery draft. The weak "there was another transit strike" becomes the more direct "Toronto endured another transit strike." Now "devised" replaces "worked out," because "work" appeared also in the previous sentence. Repetition is annoying, thinks our author.

Now she considers her audience: will the average reader know what the "GO Train" of draft 1 is? First she writes another sentence explaining how this transit company serves the suburbs, and how its employees are *not* on strike. Then she wonders whether this example of public transit continuing to operate will just weaken her essay, making the TTC strike seem less important. Suddenly she crosses the whole passage out. But now she worries about concealing the truth, stacking the cards. Oh well, she thinks, I'll leave it for now and reconsider it if I have time for a third draft.

Finally, she adds the new sentence on roller blading, which is more vivid than the other examples from draft 1.

- *Paragraph 2*: In adding "The day the strike began," our author links this paragraph to what came before. The time signal also moves the argument forward. Now the active "traffic choked the streets" replaces the weak and passive "the streets were choked with traffic." Next the author points out how she normally does not hitchhike, so we know what an exceptional event a transit strike is.

Now she catches a grammar error in draft 1: ". . . nobody was going very far before they turned off." Since "nobody" is singular, "they turned" becomes "turning," to eliminate the faulty pronoun "they." Next she adds "too," to emphasize her action in joining the walkers. Finally, she shuffles the second-to-last sentence around, so the dizziness and hurting lungs stand out at the end, instead of the less important locker.

- *Paragraph 3*: Now "pig" becomes "pigs," to match the plural "we." The quotation mark after "the better way" now goes after the period, where most writers now would place it. "Could" and "wanted" are more accurate than "can" and "want," because the action is not yet taking place. Finally, the specific example of "candy bars" now develops the more general word "eat." Readers love to "see" the subject, our author thinks.

- *Paragraph 4*: Now revisions become so numerous that we will examine only the main ones. Note how "for example" helps us see what is coming: the present point about economics is not the whole argument in favour of public transit; there will be other points later. *Accuracy* is important: the car expenses drop from $8000 to $6000. I don't want to exaggerate, thinks our author; if readers don't believe this figure, they may not believe anything else I say either.

Another consideration is *tone*. Seeing words like "you" and "you're" in the discovery draft, our author decides to make the feeling more formal and objective, so her argument will seem serious. Therefore she removes all the "you"s. But the replacement pronoun "one" is a little stiff. Have I gone too far? she asks herself. Will this sound like a Ph.D. dissertation instead of an argument for the average person? She decides to keep the changes for now, then look them over later.

The biggest change, though, is the addition to the second-to-last sentence of students who may now miss their big chance in life by flunking out of school—all because of the time they spend working to support a car. I'll scare the readers, our author thinks, so they will heed my argument.

• *Paragraph 5*: As we said earlier, the grandfather and the Don River disappear from this paragraph because they seem irrelevant to the topic of transit. The vague words "Then there's the environment" from draft 1 now change to a proper transition that puts the "costs" of the private vehicle in a broader context: "Even more important than monetary costs of driving are the environmental costs of driving." In paralleling these two "costs," the whole paragraph is now a transition between major sections of the essay.

The thesaurus has long been a major editing tool. If a word is too vague, too long, too elementary or too scholarly for your audience, or too cheerful or too angry for its context, a thesaurus lists alternatives. If the right word exists, you will spot it and use it.

All major word processing systems have an electronic thesaurus, not as complete as the old hardbound *Roget's*, but so fast that the essayist can afford to use it constantly.

Suppose that five or ten words per page of your discovery draft do not feel quite right. Whatever your software, you give the command that calls up the thesaurus. Then for each word from your draft that you wish to test out, the screen fills with alternatives. You did, of course, already know these words, but the problem is that you just didn't think of them. Now with them all in front of you, it is easy to see if one is better than the word first used. If it is, choose it.

Once you get some practice, the electronic thesaurus is so fast that you will want to do much of your editing on screen.

See also page 191 on using the electronic speller.

• *Paragraph 6*: Our author cuts the original paragraph in two, because it looked forbiddingly long. Why discourage readers? she thinks.

Now she adds "private vehicles" to the first sentence, directly blaming them for the air pollution about to be discussed. Let's keep the readers aware of my overall point, she thinks.

Now she adds *The Globe and Mail*, to credit her source, but has no idea what issue she was reading. Should she go to the library tonight, do a search, and document the point? If this were a research essay she might have to. But it is not. Why not just double-check with my teacher tomorrow? she asks herself.

Finally, "you" becomes "my": after all, it is the writer, not the reader, whose eyes hurt.

• *Paragraph 7*: A number of little changes appear in this second half of old paragraph 6, many to heighten the formality. More "you"s are cut out, although some "we"s still appear, because they seem less conversational. Also the specific intersection "Yonge and Bloor" replaces "Toronto": let's help the reader "see" this city, thinks our author, in order to highlight its difference from the North.

• *Paragraphs 8 and 9*: As noted earlier, the words "greenhouse effect" in the closing of the discovery draft had really bothered our author. They would surely distract the reader's attention by mentioning a whole new point that was not even going to be covered. Well, *why not* cover it? suddenly thinks the writer. "Seeing again," she realizes that the thought of our killing other humans across the planet, just by driving cars, would strongly support her argument for mass transit. So now she writes these paragraphs, even though her outline had never mentioned the point.

She becomes excited, yet uneasy, producing phrases like "a flow of environmental refugees such as the world has never seen." Will the readers think I'm laying guilt on them? she asks herself. Will they resent me and even reject the argument? Yet this matter is crucial, she realizes. Maybe North Americans *do* need to change the way they travel. Let's take the chance, she thinks. Why write an essay at all if you don't have a point to make?

• *Paragraph 10*: One well-known kind of error is typos. Finding one in the first line, our author changes "I" to "Is." More importantly, she realizes that at this point in the argument, where she is reaching her summary, she has left out the point about personal economics and has been vague about "pollution" as well. Now she adds the economics and the greenhouse effect, so the reader takes the weight of the whole argument into the closing.

• *Paragraph 11*: Now our author splits this passage into two paragraphs, to make the closing more user-friendly. She makes a few other changes as well, for example adding "automobile" to "drivers," in case the reader might think transit drivers are also being criticized. Let's make it clear, thinks our author. She also adds the prospect of "more room" on transit vehicles, to counteract the common objection that transit is crowded.

• *Paragraph 12*: Here our author removes the words "most importantly" from the item about cost. Instead she puts "more importantly" in front of the item about *air pollution*, to emphasize what, only now in her second draft, she realizes is her strongest point.

FURTHER DRAFTS?

Our essayist sits back from her writing desk after all these revisions, with a sense of having finished the job. On the other hand, that's the same feeling she had after draft 1—and look at all the improvements made since then. Maybe tonight more passages will be wrong, more "facts" untrue, or more new ideas too good to leave out.

Come to think of it, just now while explaining the greenhouse effect, she had thought also of acid rain, another kind of air pollution caused in large part by the car. For a moment she almost began a section on it, too, but then held back. After all, is this a whole essay about pollution? Wouldn't the first point on the cost of driving a car seem off topic if followed by two big sections on two kinds of air pollution?

But now that she thinks of it, the economic costs already seem almost trivial compared to large numbers of Third-World citizens dying just because we drive cars. Why not go all the way? Why not forget the car expenses, and focus only on environmental arguments through the new greenhouse-effect point, and the point yet to be made on acid rain?

But what about my introduction? she asks. Does the transit strike make sense as an intro to acid rain? In fact, does it even make sense as an intro to the greenhouse effect? Maybe I should junk all the pollution and stay closer to the student (*myself*) just trying to get to class!

Wait a minute, she thinks to herself, this sounds like another draft. The essay's due tomorrow, and tonight I have to study economics. What if I just leave the essay? Sure, I could make changes forever, but it's a lot better than it was. I'm beginning to like it now.

She gets up from her writing desk, puts on her coat, and walks to the door. As she enters the park across the street and gazes up at the trees, she reflects on how complicated life is and how complicated writing is.

Process in the Short Essay: Assignments

Choose any one of the general subjects in the list below. Now apply the strategies of this chapter, developing your subject into a fairly short essay (your instructor may specify a length and depth of treatment). Complete the following steps of the writing process, or at least those specified by your instructor:

1. Get in touch with your ideas by **freewriting** (pages 2–3), or **brainstorming** (pages 3, 4 and 6) or making a **cluster outline** (pages 5 and 6) of your general subject chosen below.

2. **Limit your scope** and **focus your purpose** in a **thesis statement** (page 8).

3. **Visualize your reader** (pages 13–14). (You may be practising on your instructor, but who do you have in mind as the real readers in the outside world?)

4. Write a very short, tentative **outline** (page 16).

5. Write a **discovery draft** (pages 17–20). Be free, open and quick. Put off editing till later. Your instructor may collect this version and give written comments on it, or may have a short conference with you to discuss improvements, or may ask you to share reactions with a small group of classmates.

6. Write a **further draft or drafts** (pages 22–26), heightening your argument, and now editing to improve your style and form.

If you are using this book in a class, writing clinic or laboratory, your instructor may assign the above process of writing several times during the term (each time, of course, you begin with a different general subject). Or you may be asked to write on other subjects, or invent your own.

Now that you have studied this chapter, it is best to start right off with a first short essay, to get into the writing process, even though you haven't yet studied the editing skills discussed in later chapters. (If you waited till you had studied the whole book, how much time would be left for the actual writing???)

Then in later assignments you can apply all the rest of the book studied so far, or you can jump ahead to chapters that you especially need (see the table of contents and index). *But the key strategy is to start writing now, and keep on writing.*

GENERAL SUBJECTS

1. *aging*
2. *business*
3. *the city*
4. *culture*
5. *education*
6. *family life*
7. *the future*
8. *health*
9. *housing*
10. *language*
11. *leisure*
12. *mass media*
13. *nature*
14. *science*
15. *relationships*
16. *success*
17. *technology*
18. *travel*
19. *trends*
20. *work*

Note: Be sure to retitle the subject you have chosen, to reflect the smaller focus you are giving it. For example number 17, "technology," might become "Banking Machines as a Cause of Unemployment."

Part Two

Writing by Computer

Most of today's college and university students have grown up with computers. They played games at home, learned subjects electronically at school, began to do essays and spreadsheets at the keyboard, and researched materials on CD-ROM at the library or at home. Now more and more are travelling the "Information Highway" of the Internet to do everything from sending e-mail to friends across town or across the ocean, to arguing issues on "bulletin boards," to gathering facts online, to buying products or even finding a job.

If you already do these things, then stop reading now. You don't need the material that follows. On the other hand, if you have just begun computing, or especially if you have not yet begun at all, study this section. It does two things:

1. *It outlines the advantages and some neglected capabilities of word processing,* for people new to it or not yet doing it. (*Note*: these pages do not attempt to be a manual on use of software, because there are so many good programs and they change so rapidly.)

2. Avoiding overly specific data that would be obsolete by the time you read this, it lays out a *perspective on buying your own hardware and software*, so you can work conveniently and better at home.

HOW WORD PROCESSING GIVES THE WRITER SPEED AND FLEXIBILITY

Speed

• As in typing, you can key material in directly rather than writing by hand. If you are the average student, though, you have never taken a keyboarding course. You probably poke at the keys with two or three fingers, taking longer than if you used the ancient technology of pen and paper. One student, an ex-factory worker who had injured his back and was now on Workman's Compensation studying to be a public

health inspector, confessed to his English teacher that the four-page essay he was handing in had cost him six hours of typing.

Is this worth it? Do you realize that by learning "*touch typing*" (keyboarding with all your fingers, while not looking at the keys) you can double, triple or quadruple your speed of text production? Do you realize that this more closely matches the speed of your thoughts, so that your "discovery draft" comes out faster and better—rather than being choked off every time you look for the next key? If you don't have time for a keyboarding course, buy software instruction in this skill and learn at home. Whether at school or at home, though, *make this modest investment of time; it will pay off handsomely.*

• *Using the computer, you never again waste time retyping anything.* You produce a draft on the screen, then either edit it there or print a "hard copy" on paper to edit. Between sessions you store the document in the hard drive of your computer and/or on a floppy disk. Then at any time, you retrieve the essay to the screen for more revision and editing. (If you like to do these tasks on paper, do so and then transfer the changes to the screen.) After producing any number of "drafts" this way, whenever you are ready you just print out the good copy.

Finally, if a teacher is unsatisfied with your work, you no longer "rewrite" but only "revise," calling up the current version on screen and adjusting it. *Clearly word processing is ideal for the process approach to writing, which we follow in this book.*

• All popular word processing programs include a *speller*, which in a minute or two finds almost all spelling errors—except those caused by confusing two correct words such as "there" and "their," or "to" and "too." (See p. 191 for more details.) Some students computerize for this reason alone.

Another widespread feature, the electronic *thesaurus*, is so fast that writers can afford to use it often to sharpen word choice. (See p. 28 for more details.)

Photo courtesy of Ronald Conrad.

Most recent word processing software now includes a *style checker,* such as *Grammatik,* which some students find helpful. Be careful here, though: accept only the advice that is perfectly clear and seems right. (Many people find that only about half of what these programs say makes sense.)

• Major word processing systems also offer shortcuts called "*macros*": You can program a whole series of moves to be performed through only two or three keystrokes. With these you can then do things like pop your return address and today's date onto the top of all your letters, or move instantly into a favourite essay format with all margins, line spacing and choice of font ready to go. For some tasks, the savings in time can be significant.

Flexibility

• You can adjust format before, during or after keying in the essay. This includes choice of margins all around, choice of line spacing, choice of typeface, centring, and such variations as italics and boldface. Have you ever single-spaced an essay on a typewriter, only to be told by the instructor that it had to be double-spaced? Instead of retyping the whole thing, you can now change the line spacing in a few seconds.

• Finally, editing on screen provides a flexibility (and therefore speed) that can truly surprise a longtime pen, pencil or typewriter user:

  • On the screen you can instantly remove letters, words, lines or whole sections. *This encourages experimentation and exploration, which are qualities at the heart of the process model of writing.*

  • When you add words in the middle of a line, the rest moves to make room. You can insert a whole paragraph or more between parts already written. You can move a section of any size to another place, without retyping. In major software programs you can work with two or more documents at once, and can "import" charts or other graphics from another program into your essay or report.

Writing by computer, then, offers powerful advantages. Can you afford not to do it? This powerful tool not only helps you right now in school, but will almost certainly be needed later in the workplace. Can you imagine a successful resumé in the nineties that does not list computer skills?

LEARNING

Whether you are a complete beginner or have some computer experience from school, learning word processing may take time and strategy. Some advice:

• Start learning in summer or during a slow part of the school year—not the day before your major essay is due.

• Check out the student computer labs at your college or university. Does the equipment actually work? Are terminals free when you need them? Is instruction offered?

• If you are sitting at home in front of a new machine, opening your 600-page manual filled with terms that may or may not resemble English, you are probably biting your nails right now. Consider these strategies:

  • Rather than reading for hours before turning the machine on, read just enough to get going, then try it out. Learning to use a computer works best through a combination of three things: *study of the manual, trying things out on the machine,* and *advice from friends* (you almost certainly know a computer whiz who can get you out of almost any jam).

  • Don't be afraid of ruining the machine. It is less fragile than it seems. Try things out. Almost any move you make in most programs is reversible. Though it is possible to wipe out files that you, yourself, have keyed in, it is difficult to wreck the software or hardware. Remember that you can re-install a program from disk, if something you did has caused the program to malfunction. *If your hands are not on the machine, you are not learning.* If you do enjoy being careful, you can always watch the little things—like putting your coffee off to the side where it will not spill and fry your keyboard.

  • For most major software of any kind, several unofficial manuals have been published, and they are often better than the official one, which can be poorly organized or at the wrong level. If this is the case, go to the book store or library.

  • Most people can learn enough to run a piece of software in a couple of hours. If you have experience with other programs, just try the new one out even before spending real time on the manual; in fact, many computer users claim that if you can't figure out a program on your own, generalizing from other software you know, then the new program is not worth learning at all. Forget fine points for now. As the months and years go by, you can master them gradually.

THREE CAUTIONS FOR THOSE NEW TO THE COMPUTER

• Never work on a long document without "saving" it to disk (hard drive and/or floppy) at regular intervals, say every ten minutes. Some programs do this for you automatically. If it is not done, a power failure, a computer "crash," or even your cat jumping on the keyboard can wipe out hours of work.

Also never store an important document in your hard drive without saving a backup copy to a floppy disk—in case your hard drive "crashes." (The question is not *whether* but *when*, because every hard drive will someday crash.) Crucial documents, such as long theses, should be protected by three or even four copies, at least one stored in a different building—in case of theft or fire.

• Never plug your computer directly into the wall, because power surges caused by lightning, or by furnace fans, ovens, air conditioners and other large appliances could erase crucial data from your hard drive. Instead, buy a high quality "power bar" (multiple outlet) with built-in "surge suppressor."

• Do not even dream of putting someone else's floppy disk into your machine without checking it for computer "viruses." We hear a great deal these days about "safe sex"; now think about "safe computing." Thousands of computer viruses are on the loose, with names like "AIDS," "Blood-2," "Chaos," "Disk Killer," "Friday the 13th," "Holocaust," "Leprosy" and "Microbes." They do anything from insulting you on your own computer screen to destroying your software and even hardware. Practical jokers around the world are creating these malicious programs and imagining the expression on your face when one hits your screen. So are you going to be careless with your computer and your files?

Many schools are licensed to distribute protective virus-detecting software free to students. See about this important matter at your campus computer centre.

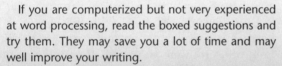

Throughout this book, whenever word processing gives the writer special tools to apply the skill under discussion, you will find a text box like this one.

If you are computerized but not very experienced at word processing, read the boxed suggestions and try them. They may save you a lot of time and may well improve your writing.

If you are writing by hand, though, just ignore these boxes. All the text outside them is meant both for those who write by hand and those who use a computer.

EQUIPMENT

In the previous edition, we tried to give current information about computer hardware. But before the book was even off the press, the specifics were becoming

obsolete. This time we do not even attempt to give technical specifics, since in the world of computers things are moving fast. For example we do not recommend a particular size of hard drive, for the cost of "memory" falls by an estimated one half every eighteen months—so that new software is designed to consume ever more of it, and the purchaser has to buy ever more of it.

Yet one thing does not change: in a time of governmental cutbacks and a weak economy, students have very little money. What follows, then, is an overview of the buyer's choices, with special emphasis on strategy: how to be computerized in the way that makes most sense for the amount of money you can afford.

First, *do you need to buy at all?* Every school has computers for student use, and many school computer labs offer instruction, or at least simplified manuals for beginners. Using this equipment can save you a great deal of money. Then by the time you graduate and get a real job, you can afford a much better system than you might have bought while still in school. In fact, the "dream machine" of two years back will be the entry-level machine of your graduation year.

Another question should be asked, though: will there be room in the computer lab the week you and everyone else are writing major projects? If not, you may want to buy your own machine.

Now you face many choices. One is whether to go for a *Macintosh system or an IBM-compatible system*. The advantage of "user-friendliness" that the Macintosh once had over the IBM compatibles is now gone, because software for all personal computers now offers graphic interfaces, intuitive commands, mouse support, and all the other features that make computing easier than it used to be.

Yet there are still pros and cons. One consideration is your field of study. For example, in many areas of design, the Macintosh and its software are standard. The president of one graphic arts firm in Toronto will not even hire anyone who does not own a Macintosh. Consult a teacher in your department as to this choice. On most other counts the IBM compatible is now ahead, though: it is usually cheaper, and in most fields more software is available for it.

Another choice is between *name brands* and *generic computers*. When personal computers first became popular, most people chose name brands, for fear of breakdown. Today, though, most go for a no-name machine at two-thirds the price, put together in a local factory, but containing most of the same standardized chips and other components as the brand-name machines. Of course any computer may break down, but today's machines, generics included, are surprisingly reliable. Most have a year guarantee, and if anything does go bad in the first few years it usually does so in the first weeks.

A further choice is size of computer. The standard *desktop* is large, relatively inexpensive, and easy to take apart for upgrading or repair. Another choice, the miniaturized *notebook,* can go with you to class or the library or home for the holidays, and is available with almost all the power and features of a good desktop. Because its insides are so cramped, though, it costs much more both to buy and repair.

At the other extreme of cost, with a price perhaps a fourth that of a desktop computer, is still another choice: the kind of *electronic typewriter* which, although its display is tiny and it lacks a hard drive, at least has a floppy disk drive. This gives you memory, which provides the key advantage of any computer: you may revise from draft to draft without retyping. If your finances are really hurting, consider it.

The customer must also decide whether to buy from a *small company* that offers good service, or an *electronics "supermarket"* with better prices but perhaps less service, and with sales staff who may or may not know their product. The first-time buyer might well find the personal help and security of the small dealer worth the extra cost. Has the store been in business a while? Unscrupulous firms have been known to close after a year or so, open again under a new name, and through this tactic make your guarantee worthless. Think also about location. Do you want to take your machine 20 miles for repairs, or carry it down to the corner dealer?

Still another perspective on your choice is based on two rapid and opposite changes always taking place: the first is a constant and remarkable lowering of price, as new manufacturing techniques and larger economies of scale occur. The second is a maintenance and even escalation of price as manufacturers and dealers load their models with increasingly elaborate and exotic features. This means that if you can find a really basic model (which, of course, is still more advanced than the top of the line from three years ago), you can buy fairly low. On the other hand, if you want today's and tomorrow's features, you are going to pay. The key, then, is to ask yourself *"What am I going to use this computer for?"* Once you know, then you will also know what kind of system to get. In summary, we suggest this strategy:

A. *If money is a problem,* get a used older machine (taking an experienced friend to check it over), or a cheap new basic desktop model, or even the kind of electronic typewriter with a floppy disk drive discussed above. Forget about exotic programs, but you can do essays and other writing assignments perfectly well.

B. *If money is not a problem,* look ahead. Will you be using huge new software programs supplied on CD-ROM? Is it important for you to use the Internet? Then clearly a CD-ROM drive and a modem or fax/modem are needed. Will you use powerful software for technical courses? Then you need a huge hard drive and large amounts of random access memory (RAM). *Choose your activities and especially your software first, then the machine that can run them.* Remember, though, that even if you buy a state-of-the-art machine today, in a few years it will sell for half the price—if it is sold at all. Unless you need big power now, strategy "A" may be best till you graduate.

One more necessary piece of hardware, the printer, is almost always sold separately from the rest of the system. Your choice will be one of these:

• *Laser printer:* the most expensive, though the cheapest models are now within reach of some students. The quality of print and graphics is razor sharp, a great many fonts may be included, and the cost of printing per page is relatively low. The machine is large and runs quietly.

• *Ink-jet printer:* half or a third as expensive as a laser printer, though the reproduction cost per page may then be twice as much because of the high cost of ink. Print quality is not as good as that of laser models, but is much better than that of dot matrix printers. Some models provide colour, which is desirable for anyone in design, or in business or technical areas which do graphing. The printer can be very compact (best for those who travel with their "notebook") and is quiet but slow.

• *Dot-matrix printer:* cheap, both in original cost and in cost of replacement ribbons. The 24-pin models may yield printing of near letter quality, but still not as good as that of the ink-jet and much worse than that of the laser. Dot-matrix printers are of medium size and are fast but loud.

So much for hardware; now how about software? Here discussing technical details is even trickier, because software changes even faster than the hardware that runs it. Rather than offer advice on brand names or versions this time, let's look at the more basic question of how to afford the stuff. *Major software can be very expensive, as much as a thousand dollars retail for large technical programs. What are your alternatives for obtaining it?*

• Some people consider illegal piracy to be the answer. While we recognize that this happens, we strongly counsel against it, not only for the obvious reason that those who are caught can be prosecuted by law, but also because of the fairness issue: copying software is like recording a friend's CDs on your blank audio tapes, or like photocopying a $150 engineering textbook for a twentieth that price. Why would anyone want to create new software, music or textbooks, if piracy undercuts the rewards for doing the work?

• There are very legal ways, though, for students to reduce their software costs. For one, when buying hardware, select a deal that includes your major software "bundled" with the package. Certain companies and dealers legally include with their computers almost all software most people really need, including major word processing, graphics and spreadsheet systems. The cost can be much less than if these items were bought separately.

• Many campus stores offer software to both students and teachers at educational discounts. Take advantage of these legitimate money savers. After all, companies want to hook you on their products while you are a student, so that when you are a professional you will buy their new upgrades forever.

• Even better, note that some campus computer labs are licensed to distribute certain software for free, as in the case of computer virus protection programs mentioned earlier. Go with your blank diskette and take advantage. As for "shareware," though—programs distributed at no cost or an extremely low cost, but which then ask you to contribute more if you find them useful—these do not include any major software that will answer your word processing or spreadsheet or design needs.

• Finally, note that it is legal to buy used software. If your budget is scraping bottom, consider, for example, finding someone who has switched from one major word processing system to another, and then pay a tiny price for the old one. The seller should keep in mind that this is not legal in the case of mere upgrades, and that other copies on his or her hard drive or on floppies must be deleted so that the deal does not become a form of piracy.

So can you afford to compute at home? All these principles, along with some current prices from dealers, should help you decide. If you do go for it, remember that some colleges and universities offer leasing through major companies. After you have paid a monthly fee for a year or two, as you would with a leased car, you may opt to buy the machine at a price lowered because of depreciation. Also note that some banks make special loans to students who need a computer. In our present hard times, though, with governments chopping budgets right and left, it may be that none of these alternatives will work for you. Well, then, how about sharing with a brother or sister, roommate or friend, and splitting the cost? If even that will not do, then go right back and make the best of your school's computer lab. The price is right.

First spell check and the electronic thesaurus, then *Grammatik*...where will it all end? By now dozens of software programs are out there to help the writer invent and organize essays, to check the style, and to provide drills on editing points. But the question is, do they work??? The answers are mixed.

Grammatik, for example, is now widely used, since it comes bundled with other software. Some businesses even make employees run every document through it to check usage and style. The actual experience of students, though, reveals that no more than half the advice it gives makes sense, while the other half ranges from irrelevant to totally off. It may find some sentence fragments and other editing errors, but it may also do things like advise using less negative language—even if the topic happens to be funerals or World War III! Sure, use it if you wish, but then use your own common sense to evaluate everything it tells you.

EDIT! and *Editor* are two more style checkers. The first is very basic; the second is at a more sophisticated level. Both share some of the same limitations as *Grammatik*, and both include detailed manuals, in case you decide to try them.

Writer's Prologue is typical of software meant to help writers invent and plan essays. It offers fairly imaginative questions and prompts, to guide the student through planning and writing different kinds of assignments. Its advice on stimulating narration, for example, is "Think about times when—You felt yourself in danger; you were exhilarated by a new sensation; you had to keep a secret or a secret was revealed; your heart pounded and the rush of adrenalin left you light-headed."

Still other software gives instruction and drill in editing skills. *Verbcon*, for example, is oversimplified but quite user-friendly, giving practice in verb use both for native speakers of English and ESL students. *PerfectCopy* is a much larger system, well-liked at many community colleges. Probably the best of the drill programs, it is less oversimplified and covers many areas (including abbreviations, beginning and ending punctuation, apostrophes, capitals, commas, irregular verbs, pronouns, subject-verb agreement, and other punctuation). It is extremely easy to use with mouse support.

But let's face it: apart from spell check, the thesaurus, and word-processing programs, themselves, all this software for the writer is at an early stage of development—like the Model T Ford in the history of cars. Most of it is just starting to be useful. Stay tuned.

Part Three

Paragraphs

Imagine a book, or even a magazine article, without white space. You, the reader, are staring at a solid mass of grey print, with no breaks, no breathing spots, no room to give encouragement or show where one part ends and the next begins. You begin to sweat. It is hard to breathe. You have thoughts of climbers labouring up the cliffs of Mount Everest. Does anyone think you will actually read the thing? What is missing, obviously, is the user-friendly device of *paragraphing*.

Everyone knows what paragraphs are: units of thought several sentences long, set off from each other by an indented first line (the first word begins several spaces in from the margin). And most people have some natural feeling for how to paragraph: without even thinking about it, they pause at the end of a passage. They close off that part, mentally take a breath, then indent the next line to signal a plunge into the next phase of the topic.

Our first chapter, "Process in the Short Essay," suggests this approach for discovery drafts. If you concentrate on too many things at once—thinking about paragraphing while trying to fill up that monitor screen or blank page—you might not have enough attention left to generate your argument. But once your thoughts are safely out in the open, you can look over what you've done and tinker with it. As you examine the spontaneous paragraphing in your discovery draft, see whether it makes sense. Have you fallen into one of these traps?

1. *Ignoring paragraphs totally.* Some inexperienced writers will crank out a whole paper with no paragraph breaks at all. In effect, their one "paragraph" might be five pages long. After their breathless first draft they must now go back to find the natural breaks in their thought—and signal them by indenting. If they do not, the reader is standing at the foot of Mount Everest.

2. *Making paragraphs too short and too numerous.* Far more common is this weakness. A whole essay of mini-paragraphs only one or two sentences long may at first appear reasonable, especially if you are not computing; after all, if your handwriting is large and you are double-spacing, even a tiny paragraph can *look* big. Besides, paragraphs as short as one sentence or even one word sometimes do serve to give special emphasis. But a series of mini-paragraphs will almost always identify an essay that is seriously underdeveloped— that lacks enough examples to be interesting or even clear.

People who fall into this trap may be thinking of newspaper style. A good news article, though, is not underdeveloped; it is simply indented after every sentence or two because of the newspaper's single-column format. An eight-sentence paragraph in a single column would look so long that it could scare off readers (especially of newspapers that devote themselves to UFOs, axe murders and sightings of Elvis). But in the full-page format of your own word-processed essay, as in the full-page format of a printed book, a longer paragraph looks fine. Where you need eight sentences to round out a good point, anything less is too little.

3. *Using "block" form in an essay.* Most people write more letters than essays. And since many business letters are written in the "block" style, which separates paragraphs with an extra line of space instead of an indentation, these people may forget to indent. Just remember that in essays, unlike letters or business reports, paragraphs are always indented—and therefore they do not need a whole line of space to separate them from each other.

KINDS OF PARAGRAPHS

The way many teachers and textbooks used to explain paragraphing, you would have thought these chunks of writing were cars rolling off the assembly line. The head designer had found the right formula, the workers made sure each nut and bolt was in place, and then someone at quality control checked to make sure each unit was alike. The only problem with this logical view is that it did not correspond to real life.

Picture the students of an English class: after making sure each paragraph of their essay had a beginning, a middle, and an end, all in exactly five sentences, the students would go home, pick up some magazine, and see paragraphs missing most or all of these features. So why were published writers getting away with things that English teachers said were wrong? It was because *there are many kinds of paragraphs that serve many different purposes*—a fact that we see much more clearly today.

Now let's look at each of these major kinds of paragraph.

The Introductory Paragraph

Let's begin with this, since it begins the essay. A short paper might have only one paragraph of introduction, while a longer one might have several. Therefore an introductory paragraph may do its work all alone, or there may be two or more working together. Whatever the case, an introduction has two main functions: to *interest* and to *prepare* the reader.

Rather than putting your potential reader to sleep with a flat statement of intent, tease your reader's curiosity. Note the difference in effect between these potential introductions to the same paper:

A. This essay will be about governmental spending cutbacks and the ways in which they affect the lives of students. It will attempt to show some of the difficulties the average postsecondary student has when expenses go up in response to these cutbacks. Finally, it will endeavour to suggest solutions to this growing problem in today's society.

B. A Toronto community college student, Paul, used to think he could have it all. With a summer job and part-time work on weekends he could pay tuition, buy textbooks, go to clubs, and even keep driving the car he had in high school. What Paul did not foresee, though, was the cuts to education that the Ontario government would soon make, in its attempt to fight the public debt. When tuition fees rose out of sight, when parking fees tripled and lab fees skyrocketed, Paul got his dose of the new reality. "It was bad enough when I couldn't keep up the payments on my car," he said over a meal of french fries and gravy at the school cafeteria. "I began working so many hours that my grades went down, but I lost the car anyway. Now if things get much worse I'll lose my

computer, too. Did I tell you," he added with a grim smile, "that I'm a computer major?"

Thousands of students, like Paul, are now tightening their belts, doing with less, and even dropping out of school. In a time of severe governmental cutbacks, what can these future workers and leaders of society do to keep their future on track?

How do these two potential introductions compare? Let's face it, version A is a bore. It does announce its subject, but in a clumsy and official manner. By contrast, version B seduces us with a story (and who doesn't like stories???). It *shows* an actual example of the problem, the plight of one student who represents the many. It even "shows" what he is eating: an unhealthy but cheap meal of french fries and gravy. Now, having attracted our concern for Paul, this introduction moves into its second paragraph with the user-friendly device of a question, which will then lead to the main point of the paper: the approach these victims of educational cutbacks can take to keep their future alive.

Note that version "A" has only one paragraph, a sign that this introduction may be underdeveloped. Instead of "showing" us anything at all, it drones along with generalizations and stuffy phrases such as "This essay will be about...."; "It will attempt to show...."; and "it will endeavour to suggest...." By contrast, version B has two paragraphs, because it does "show" us Paul, as well as generalizing on the subject. Its energy level is higher too: it attracts our interest with dynamic and concrete phrases such as "rose out of sight," "skyrocketed" and "got his dose of the new reality."

The first introduction tries for a *thesis statement* as a base for the argument that will follow, but merely gives a vague idea that solutions will be offered. In contrast, "B" moves towards its point more surely: in times like these, when citizens cannot depend much on their governments, what can students, themselves, do to ensure their future? Now the road has been paved for a thesis statement (yet to come) that will begin to answer the question.

On page 8 we have already seen how the thesis statement introduces, focuses and then guides the essay. Now let's examine more closely the other function of an introduction: to *interest* the reader. Try these widespread techniques in your introductory paragraphs:

• *Fill in some background information.* If your topic is unusual or difficult, help your audience relate to it by sketching in the context: give a bit of historical, social or technical background.

• *Tell an anecdote.* Everyone likes a story. As in the account of Paul and his financial troubles, tell a short incident—unusual, perhaps funny or tragic—that leads to your topic. This favourite technique of public speakers works equally well on paper.

• *Give a quotation.* Use the index of *Colombo's Canadian Quotations* or *Bartlett's Familiar Quotations* to find a good opening. Whether your subject is war, sex, taxes or sport, find out what Shakespeare or Albert Einstein or Margaret Atwood said about it. Then lead from this to your own thesis.

• *Give statistics* to introduce your topic. Use the newspapers or consult such collections as the *World Almanac and Book of Facts* or the *Canadian Almanac and Directory.* The statistics with most impact are those that alarm or even scare the reader.

• *Make an unusual or puzzling statement* that draws readers into your topic. Do not exaggerate or falsify, but do search for an unusual angle that will tease your reader's curiosity.

The "Main" Paragraph

Between the introduction and conclusion of an essay comes the main part, the "body," which is made up mostly of what we could call "main" paragraphs. Here is where the "main" work of illustrating, explaining, arguing and convincing takes place. Since they do similar work, these "main" paragraphs tend to be alike in at least two ways:

1. Many or most have a "topic sentence" that announces the point to be developed in the paragraph.

2. Everything else in the paragraph develops that point.

Let's look more closely at these two features.

The Topic Sentence

Researchers in the field of composition have debunked the old idea that every paragraph must have a *topic sentence.* In fact on the average, fewer than half of all paragraphs in published writing have one, especially when we consider that many paragraphs have specific uses: introducing, narrating, bridging major sections, and concluding.

But a great many of the workhorse paragraphs that do the illustrating, explaining, arguing and convincing in the body of an essay do have a topic sentence and develop it throughout their other sentences. In this sense a "main" paragraph is like a miniature essay: the topic sentence (like a thesis statement) sets out the point that all the rest will support. Let's see how Annie Dillard uses this pattern in a paragraph from her book *Pilgrim at Tinker Creek*:

Parasitic two-winged insects, such as flies and mosquitoes, abound. It is these that cause hippos to live in the mud and frenzied caribou to trample their young. Twenty thousand head of domestic livestock died in Europe from a host of black flies that swarmed from the banks of the Danube in 1923. Some parasitic flies live in the stomachs of horses, zebras, and elephants; others live in the nostrils and eyes of frogs. Some feed on earthworms, snails, and slugs; others attack and successfully pierce mosquitoes already engorged on stolen blood. Still others live on such delicate fare as the brains of ants, the blood of nestling songbirds, or the fluid in the wings of lacewings and butterflies.

After reading this paragraph, can you reasonably doubt that "parasitic two-winged insects, such as flies and mosquitoes, abound"? Every sentence, by use of example, furthers our understanding of the main point and our belief in its validity. Not one given fact is irrelevant to the topic sentence.

How does a topic sentence work? It normally fulfils these three expectations:

• *A topic sentence limits the scope of its paragraph.* It cuts off a chunk of thought that is neither too large nor too small for treatment in the several sentences of a paragraph. Some subjects are so minuscule or so obvious that to state them in one sentence is enough. A statement such as "I have two legs" is hardly worth building a paragraph around, for it is self-evident.

The opposite case is by far the more common problem: a statement that is too large in scope for development in the small space of a paragraph. Pity the person who begins a paragraph with the words "Many countries are interesting to visit." How many countries does this writer hope to cram into five or eight sentences, and in what ways are they all "interesting"? In fact, what does "interesting" mean? One reader may expect an account of historical and cultural sites, another an account of bars and nightclubs, and another an account of the characters this traveller met while hitchhiking.

The fact that entire books are written about one country sheds some light on our writer's problem: the topic is far too broad. Let's narrow it down drastically to "Spaniards are the friendliest people I have ever met" or "Camping on the beach in Mexico was the most dangerous thing I have ever done" or "It is easy to get lost in the Paris subway." Now a few good examples will bring these topic sentences alive.

• *A topic sentence, like a thesis statement, often makes a generalization.* We could simply state a fact, such as "Fifty thousand Canadian lakes have died from acid rain," but if we can also give this information a direction (present it as an opinion), it will make for a stronger paragraph: "The fifty thousand Canadian lakes that have died from acid rain are proof that our industrial society is in trouble."

Of course the way you cast your topic sentence depends on the flow of your argument: what you wrote in paragraphs that came before and what you will write in those that come after. For example, you may often need a paragraph of pure fact to develop a preceding part of the argument. But where possible, begin a "main" paragraph with an idea worth supporting, not just a fact alone.

• *A topic sentence usually occurs at or near the beginning of its paragraph.* Thus the reader sees what is coming and is better prepared to deal with it. Annie Dillard's passage about insects is a typical example of this most common of all paragraph forms. It is easy to understand, because a kind of summary in advance tells us what to look for as we pass through the sentences that follow.

If you don't feel like playing it safe, though, this order can be reversed. By putting the details first, and waiting till the end to make the point, you can introduce a suspense that greatly increases the drama of the argument. This approach requires some polish, though. It is best reserved for an occasional special effect.

Unity in "Main" Paragraphs

When a topic sentence is used in a paragraph, it should dominate. **Every single sentence of the paragraph should in some way support the main idea in the topic sentence.** Where does the following paragraph go wrong?

> Three memorable rides have cured me forever of my desire to hitchhike. The first was a speedy trip in an Alfa-Romeo that met its fate on a cliffside road in Spain. We sideswiped a long truck, were whirled right around and came to rest with one wheel over the cliff. I looked down at the Bay of Biscay as the driver cried over his twisted car. The next was a ride with a wild young Kentuckian who had the most decrepit Chevy I've ever seen. Every time he swerved to make a pedestrian jump into the ditch, my door swung open and I grabbed for the seat to stay aboard. One of the best rides I've ever had, though, was with a family going to Montreal. They let me drive their new Oldsmobile and even bought me lunch at the rest stop. All in all, I've found hitchhiking to be exciting—too exciting for me.

It doesn't take long to see that this writer has given two examples which strongly support the topic sentence, but a third which contradicts it. The result is a weak argument: we're not sure what this person does think of hitchhiking. Let's replace that third example with one that does support the point. Here's the revised paragraph (with the new part in italics):

> Three memorable rides have cured me forever of my desire to hitchhike. The first was a speedy trip in an Alfa-Romeo that met its fate on a cliffside road in Spain. We sideswiped a long truck, were whirled right around and came to rest with one wheel over the cliff. I looked down at the Bay of Biscay as the driver cried over his twisted car. The next was a ride with a wild young Kentuckian who had the most decrepit Chevy I've ever seen. Every time he swerved to make a pedestrian jump into the ditch, my door swung open and I grabbed for the seat to stay aboard. *The third ride was an early morning trip on glare ice. My driver seemed to think his Trans-Am could go twice as fast as anything else on the road. It did: we soon passed all the traffic while sliding backwards, on our way to the shoulder where we snapped off two guard posts and sank into the ditch.* All in all, I've found hitchhiking to be exciting—too exciting for me.

The Paragraph of Narration

Since people love stories, *narration* is a natural and attractive way to communicate. In our "Introductory Paragraph" section (pages 40–41), we saw how the anecdote about Paul's financial problems could lead into an analysis of Ontario's cutbacks to postsecondary education, and to the effects on students. Narrative can also serve other parts of an essay: the *body* and the *closing*.

Often several paragraphs of narration will occur in a row, to tell a story illustrating a point. In such a case it is clear that individual paragraphs will not have the common "main" paragraph structure of topic sentence and development, but will merely tell a chunk of the story in time order. Furthermore, if people in the story are speaking, we indent each time the speaker changes, to help the reader know who says what. Such a paragraph can be tiny or large, but in either case will be different from the "main paragraph"—because its function is different.

Now let's look at a series of narrative paragraphs that might appear in our essay about cutbacks to education:

The new cutbacks take a toll not only in student finances but also time. Paul now spends an hour and a half taking two buses, the subway and another bus to school from his parents' home in Mississauga. "If I still had my car," he said in the corridor between classes, "I'd be there in half an hour. Or if I could afford my own room, I'd be there in ten minutes."

Looking at his watch, he added, "By the time I got here this morning all the computers were taken in the lab, so now I have to spend noon hour working on spreadsheets instead of eating lunch. It'll save $2.98 anyway."

"Hey Paul," said a friend passing by, "Coming to the party tonight?"

"No, I'm working."

"Thought you just worked weekends."

"Well that was last year."

Note how short these narrative paragraphs are, and how none but the first contains anything resembling a topic sentence. Also note that although these paragraphs are not standardized and do not argue a point in logical fashion, their overall effect is to provide a strong example that illustrates the main point of the essay: student hardships in a time of cutbacks to education.

Note: In academic writing such as research papers, narration is rarely used. In personal, less formal writing, though, you may use paragraphs of narration now and then when they work well to support your ideas. Remember, though, that a composition made up entirely of narrative will not be an essay at all; it might be fiction, news, history or autobiography.

The "Bridge" Paragraph

Bridges help to unify geographical regions: they permit us to cross from one part to another. They do the same for an essay. In short papers a "bridge" is just a word or two of transition: "then" or "first" or "next" or "finally" or "in conclusion." Longer essays use not only these, but also longer "bridge paragraphs" that move us from one main section to another. Let's examine one:

Despite his economic problems this year, Paul is one of the lucky ones. His parents give him free room and board, and he has part-time jobs that more or less pay his bills. But what about

the less lucky students? How about those whose parents cannot help them because they, themselves, may have been laid off and lost their homes? How about those who cannot find part-time or summer jobs? How about single parents who do not have time to raise their own children, work to support them, and also go to school?

The opening reference to Paul recalls earlier parts of the essay that focus on his individual example. The next sentence then sets up a contrast between Paul, whose troubles are at least still manageable, and those who have even more serious problems. Finally, the series of questions moves us forward, setting the stage for the next section about the students hardest hit by cutbacks.

Perhaps a later bridge paragraph will link this next section to a concluding part, which will fulfil the promise of the introduction: showing ways in which Paul and the other students can try to overcome the problems posed by cutbacks. Like our "bridge" above, it will probably be short, and will look in two directions—backward at what has just been said, and forward at what is coming next.

Bridge paragraphs, then, differ from "main" paragraphs. Their opening may resemble a topic sentence, as in our example. But unlike "main" paragraphs, bridge paragraphs do not develop such a statement throughout, for part of the way through comes the shift that moves us on to the next topic. Paragraphs are certainly not all alike. As in architecture, form follows function.

The Closing Paragraph

Like an introductory paragraph, a closing paragraph is special because of its location. You have probably seen how productions as different as a speech, a sermon, a play or a film close on a high point, or climax. From symphonies to rock and roll, music ends literally on a "high note," while TV police dramas close with the excitement of a tire-screeching car chase or a shootout. (This approach is not new; have you ever counted the bodies lying onstage in the last scene of *Hamlet*?)

Most essays follow this pattern of ending in excitement. What could be worse than a closing paragraph that trails off into minor details? Suppose that our essay on student cutbacks ended like this:

> In conclusion, the cutbacks to education that have been implemented by the governments of Ontario and most other provinces have placed undue burdens on postsecondary students. Only through real motivation and a good plan of action can these victims of government policy stay in school and finish their education. Things will

probably get better, though, in the future. Ten years from now, when they are mowing grass at their houses in the suburbs, these people will probably have forgotten all about their former financial troubles, not to mention the other minor problems that students have from day to day.

This paragraph ignores a major principle: the ending occupies the most prominent position in an essay. Its potential either for impact or for boredom is even greater than that of the introduction. If our closing paragraph or paragraphs do not leave the reader convinced or inspired, we have wrecked the rest of the essay as well, no matter how good it was. Let's look now at an alternative model:

> In conclusion, today's students can no longer rely on their governments to help them through school. As legislators continue their fascination with the "bottom line," the state of the deficit will seem more important than the future of the citizens. At a time when lawmakers are turning their backs on postsecondary students, the victims must heighten their motivation and carefully construct a plan of action that enables them to stay in school. Only in this self-reliant way can they achieve the education that their parents' generation took for granted. If they fail in this task, then the students of today will become the unemployed of tomorrow.

See how instead of trailing off, this closing paragraph rises to its peak of significance in the last words. As it does so, it also moves upward in time from the present to the future. Both these movements merge in the final ominous phrase, "the unemployed of tomorrow," which impresses upon readers the importance of the whole essay.

Though closing paragraphs come in many kinds, most good ones follow the upward pattern of our example, like the grand finale of a symphony. Often the best closings end deliberately on a key word. (In fact, keep this technique in mind for all paragraphs: play around with the last sentence until you can place the most important word at the very end, where it will do the most good.)

Here are the most widespread techniques used for the closing paragraph or paragraphs of an essay:

• *Refer back to the thesis statement* to give a sense of completion.

• *Ask a question* that either makes your reader think or that has an answer obvious from the content of your essay. Either method will encourage involvement, through your reader's participation in the closing.

• *Give a quotation* that seals your argument with the opinion of an authority, or that puts your view in more vivid or memorable terms than you could devise, yourself. As with introductory quotations, consult the index of *Colombo's Canadian Quotations* or *Bartlett's Familiar Quotations*.

• *Use transition signals.* In combination with other closing techniques, use expressions such as "finally," "last," "in summary" or "in conclusion" to prepare the reader for your final words.

• *Reveal the significance* of your argument, as in our sample closing, which points to unemployment as the long-term result of cutbacks. Showing the importance of your point will help to involve the reader personally.

• *Give a summary*, but only at the closing of essays so long or complex that your reader may have forgotten key points. Avoid boring repetition; keep any summary *short*.

• *Draw a conclusion*. A "conclusion" is not just an ending, but a diagnosis or verdict on the subject of your essay: taxes should be raised or lowered, euthanasia outlawed or permitted, nuclear weapons maintained or scrapped, the voting age raised or lowered. Feel free to make any judgment that is rooted clearly in the logic of your argument.

• *Make a prediction*. What could be more appropriate than closing a discussion of a subject's past or present with a look at its probable future? (Remember the financially burdened students of today who may become the unemployed of tomorrow.) This approach is a good way to "reveal the significance."

LENGTH OF PARAGRAPHS

Since there are different kinds of paragraphs, with different jobs to do, they will of course have different lengths. "Special" paragraphs that introduce, narrate, bridge or close an essay can be as short as one sentence, for special effect, or can be several sentences long. Most tend to be short, though, in the range of two to five sentences, because major explanations tend to occur in the "body."

"Main" paragraphs of the body can also vary in length—from one sentence, for special effect, to as many as ten or more sentences in a complex explanation. Keep this natural range in mind: if you do not vary the lengths of your "main" paragraphs, your style may be flat or even boring. Aim for an up-and-down effect, like that of waves in the ocean.

On the average, though, "main" paragraphs are substantial: from about three to eight sentences. Of course sentences, too, vary in length, and this in turn affects the length of paragraphs. A tense passage of ten short sentences may result in a fairly small paragraph, while a single very long and involved sentence may create its own long paragraph. (If you have read Victorian novels, you have seen more than a few of these.)

Whatever the lengths of their sentences, if your "main" paragraphs are too short, you cripple your impact as a writer. We have already discussed this common flaw of "making paragraphs too short and too numerous" (page 41).

Find an essay you have written in the past and actually count the number of sentences in each paragraph. You could be surprised to find that most of your paragraphs are only two or three sentences long, especially if you wrote by hand, which makes everything look bigger than it is. Using the graph on page 46, compare your numbers to the number of sentences in the paragraphs from the revised draft of our sample short essay "The Better Way" (pages 22–26).

Though variety is achieved by paragraphs as short as four, three or even two sentences, the overall average for "The Better Way" is almost six sentences per paragraph.

Are your own paragraphs big enough? Do they have the depth of detail that allows for clear thought? Do they sparkle with examples, with images, with facts? Or are they "thin"? Do they just limp along half-developed, only half doing their job? Your own sentence count should help you decide. If they are "thin," you should take very seriously the worksheet on page 55: "Improving 'Thin' Paragraphs." Do it, review it, remember it, and in your own essays apply it.

Finally, remember that we save these concerns mostly for the editing process. Do try to generate details as you write your "discovery draft," but at that point avoid the tactical error of stopping to rework a paragraph: by the time you get it right, the next ten things you were going to say may have slipped from your mind. It is later, in the second or even third draft, that we practise carefully the art of paragraphing.

**Paragraph Lengths
in the Short Essay "The Better Way"
(second draft, pages 22–26)**

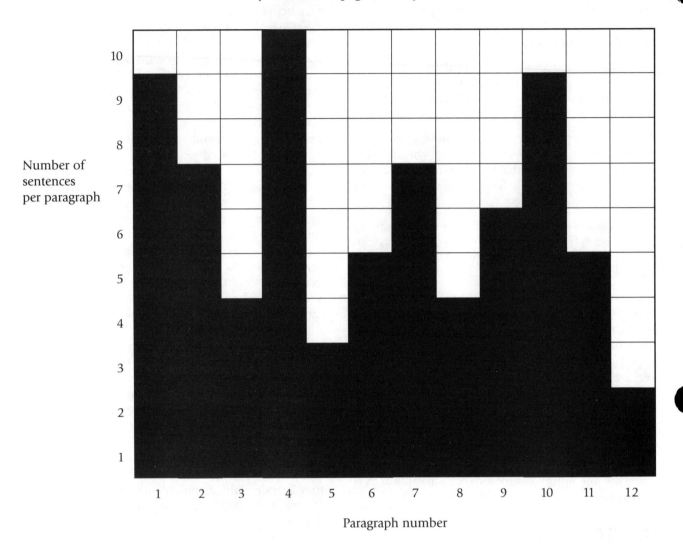

Number of
sentences
per paragraph

Paragraph number

NAME _____

The "Main" Paragraph: Worksheet

*Good topic sentences often give an opinion. See how each one below does. Support that opinion with at least four examples. (If you disagree with the opinion given, change it and then support your own.) In either case, as you fill out **a.** through **d.**, avoid any material that does not support its topic sentence.*

1. Cars cause many problems in the city.

    a.

    b.

    c.

    d.

2. Today, most unemployment is caused by technology.

    a.

    b.

    c.

    d.

3. Quebec is truly a "distinct society."

    a.

    b.

    c.

    d.

4. Unfortunately, the main educator of today's children is television.

    a.

    b.

    c.

    d.

5. Sports are excellent training for life.

    a.

    b.

    c.

    d.

Think of a good topic sentence to unite each of the following groups of material.

1. _____

   _____

   _____

   a. French fries contain large amounts of oil and salt.
   b. Most milkshakes contain artificial colour and flavour, as well as large amounts of sugar.
   c. Hamburgers are made of fatty beef and served on buns made of white flour.
   d. Soft drinks are basically water, sugar and artificial flavours and dyes.

2. _____

   _____

   a. Bars of metal and even pieces of salt were once used as money.
   b. For thousands of years metal coins were the main source of exchange.
   c. Paper money permitted large amounts of value to be concentrated in easily portable form.
   d. Chequing accounts and then credit cards permitted greater versatility in exchange.
   e. Now "smart cards" and purchases by credit on the Internet permit instant financial transactions with little or no paperwork.

3. _____

   _____

   _____

   a. Car exhaust is a major source of acid rain.
   b. Vast amounts of farmland in North America have been paved over in the construction of streets, highways and parking lots.
   c. Gasoline has produced high concentrations of chemicals in the air and soil along major traffic routes.
   d. Carbon dioxide from the internal combustion engine is a major cause of the "greenhouse effect," which has already triggered disastrous changes of climate.

4. _____

   _____

   _____

   a. Single-glazed windows are a major source of heat loss.
   b. Heated air leaks rapidly through cracks around doors and windows.
   c. Many houses are insulated poorly or not at all.
   d. Furnaces that need adjustment, cleaning or a new filter can waste a great deal of energy.

5. _____

_____

_____

   a. Clearcutting, in such places as Vancouver Island, turns old-growth forest into expanses of stumps and trimmed branches.

   b. Heavy rains in British Columbia wash away the soil from clearcut hills and mountains, polluting trout and salmon streams.

   c. Several species of wildlife have become endangered because of clearcutting in British Columbia.

   d. The dried brush left after clearcutting is a major fire hazard.

NAME _____

Topic Sentences: Worksheet

Underline the statement you think would make the best topic sentence of a paragraph. Remember that a point of view or opinion is preferable; a statement of pure fact may not be enough.

1. a. Chainsaws make a great deal of noise.
    b. The chainsaw is the most dangerous tool that can be operated without a permit.
    c. All chainsaws now have a chain brake to reduce bucking.

2. a. In Toronto the lineups for movies are often a block long.
    b. I go to the movies almost every weekend.
    c. The convenience of watching videos will never replace the thrill of going to the movies.

3. a. We used to shoot off firecrackers every Victoria Day.
    b. A cousin of mine lost the last joint of his index finger by holding onto a "TNT bomb" too long.
    c. Fireworks are still a hazard to children.

4. a. My sister spends hours a day on the Internet.
    b. The "Information Highway" is growing every year.
    c. Most of what I read on the Internet bulletin boards is garbage.

5. a. Scuba diving can be a safe sport if you know what you are doing.
    b. A scuba diver I know almost drowned when he caught his foot on some old wire at the bottom of a river.
    c. The word "scuba" stands for "self-contained underwater breathing apparatus."

6. a. Ice cream is a popular food.
    b. I often eat ice cream as a snack.
    c. Ice cream contains more chemical additives than almost any other food we eat.

7. a. You see pickup trucks everywhere these days.
    b. City people drive pickup trucks for the same reasons they wear blue jeans and cowboy boots.
    c. Most pickup trucks get worse gas mileage than cars.

8. a. I saw wolf tracks one morning outside our cabin.
    b. The wolf is a large mammal of the northern forest.
    c. It is our prejudice against wolves that leads to their destruction.

9. a. I love hockey.
    b. Hockey is an extremely popular sport in Canada.
    c. Wayne Gretzky is the greatest player in the history of hockey.

10. a. Medical drugs can be just as dangerous as street drugs.
    b. I often take two aspirins when I'm getting a cold.
    c. Drugs sometimes have a negative effect on the human body.

11. a. Some people lose their shirts on the stock market.
    b. My uncle made $80,000 in one year on gold stocks.
    c. Only by diversifying into several economic sectors can the average investor reduce the risk of playing the stock market.

12. a. The bicycle is the most energy-efficient form of transportation ever invented.
    b. Someone stole my mountain bike by cutting the chain.
    c. My cousin rides her bicycle all year round except January and February.

13. a. I love the smell of pine needles in the early morning.
    b. Pine trees, like other conifers, keep their needles all year long.
    c. The Austrian pine has become a favourite of landscapers because it resists urban pollution.

14. a. Some novels are a bore.
    b. The more concise a novel is, the more interesting it tends to be.
    c. *Wuthering Heights* is the first novel we studied in Introduction to Literature.

15. a. My mother likes a drink or two on a Saturday night.
    b. Alcohol is a major cause of heart disease.
    c. Wine is popular around the world.

16. a. Every morning my grandmother fixed pancakes and sausages on the wood stove.
    b. Not many people heat with wood these days.
    c. Heating with wood is cheap but time-consuming.

17. a. The geranium is a well-known house plant.
    b. There are several steps to propagating a geranium by cuttings.
    c. Geraniums have an unusual smell.

18. a. My family's lawnmower has a Briggs and Stratton four-cycle engine.
    b. Lawnmowers are machines often used by homeowners.
    c. A rotary-type power lawnmower can be dangerous both to the user and to bystanders.

19. a. Over the last five years, the cost of bread has risen considerably.
    b. Standard North American white bread is so devoid of nutrients that even mice won't eat it.
    c. White bread is more popular than brown bread.

20. a. Many people do crazy things these days.
    b. Sky diving has been popular for a number of years.
    c. Sky diving is one of the most dangerous sports ever invented.

NAME _____

Unity in "Main" Paragraphs: Worksheet

Revise the following paragraphs to achieve unity of purpose. First underline the topic sentence. Then delete or replace any material that does not support it. If the paragraph does not reflect the topic sentence at all, revise the topic sentence.

1. Many English teachers dress poorly. They wear blue jeans, corduroy jackets and sandals, as if they were still living in the sixties. Or they wear ragged pants and old baggy sweaters, as if they plan to dig in the garden after class. Or they wear shockingly mismatched colours—blue pants, brown jacket and purple tie—as if they were colourblind. However, I once had a math teacher who looked even worse: he wore a blue and red plaid jacket, green bow tie and grey and white pin-striped trousers.

2. Having to share a bedroom with my brother taught me how to get along with others. We each had to respect the other person's half of the room, for example, by not throwing our dirty clothes on each other's bed. We had to take turns cleaning and sweeping. We had to discuss what colour to paint the walls and which posters to put up. Most important of all, we had to be quiet when the other person was trying to study or sleep. As a result of this trying experience, I have learned that it is hard to get along with others. I'm glad that I have left home, because now all the fighting is over.

3. The Olympics have become a fraud in which innocent victims—the athletes and the general public—are manipulated by business and government. In a cynical bid for world prestige, totalitarian nations recruit and train their athletes almost like soldiers. These professional "amateurs" then walk off with the gold medals. In greedy schemes to attract tourists or to encourage construction and investment, cities lavish hundreds of millions on Olympic facilities—only to sink their own citizens in municipal debt for decades to come. And worst of all, in a spirit of crass hatred, terrorist groups hatch plans to murder the innocent and idealistic individuals who make the whole event possible: the athletes. Almost as bad is the illegal use of steroids by many of the contestants, both male and female.

4. The Volvo is an excellent automobile. It is true that the gas mileage is poor and replacement parts cost several times as much as those for a Ford or Chevy. But the average Volvo in Sweden lasts for around seventeen years. Of course, road salt is used much less there than in Canada. But the motor is excellent. For example, the crankshaft of the four-cylinder models has six bearings, which means such durability that many people salvage the engine from a wrecked or rusted-out Volvo and mount it in their boat as an inboard. Many Volvo odometers have gone around twice, and some even three times. One Volvo owner in Texas claims his car has gone a million miles. He has no doubt rebuilt it so often that little remains of the original car, but still, the Volvo fully deserves its fine reputation.

5. Many homeowners plant species of trees that cause problems later on. The Chinese elm that looks so attractive when it is ten feet high soon becomes a sickly monster dropping hundreds of little sticks onto the roof and lawn every time the wind blows. The silver maple that grows so conveniently fast soon becomes a rotten hulk ready to crush a roof or a parked car when a storm rips off its branches or even its trunk. (The sugar maple is much better, strong as well as attractive.) But the ailanthus, the so-called "tree of heaven" that is so delicately beautiful, clogs sewers with its greedy roots and every spring produces flowers that emit a sickening, rotten stench.

6. Jogging is an excellent means to physical fitness. Heavy persons should avoid it, though, to prevent a heart attack caused by the sudden overload of violent action. Women are advised to avoid jogging, too, because in some cases the movement can cause the uterus to loosen—a potentially serious medical problem. Bone spurs in the foot, tearing of the Achilles' tendon and deterioration of the knee joint are other common hazards of jogging. Some joggers have even been killed by traffic, because people with jobs often run at night when visibility is poor. But all in all, jogging has become one of our most popular forms of exercise.

7. Splitting wood is a very easy process. First you place a large piece of log on the ground, like a stump, for a chopping block. Then you put the sections of log onto it, which raises them to a convenient level. Whether you are using a splitting maul (a sort of sledge hammer with a blade) or wedges and a sledge hammer, the process is the same. First "trim" pieces off around the outside of the log, then split up the remaining centre. If you try to split a large log right across the middle, your maul or wedge will get stuck. In fact, it may get stuck even in the "trimming" process. When this happens, the best remedy is to use another wedge to get the first one out—but even the second one may get stuck, especially in an unsplittable wood such as elm. Many are the wood-splitters who have resorted to the most desperate remedy of all: the chainsaw.

8. Driving to work is greatly preferable to taking the bus or subway. First of all, being enclosed by the car affords a privacy impossible to achieve in public transit. Secondly, no matter how long your car is stuck in a traffic jam, you can relax by turning on the radio and having a cigarette. Need we mention the fact that no transit connections, involving lineups in the heat or cold, need to be made by the motorist? And finally, although it is true that driving costs about five times as much as taking the transit, some people can deduct this cost as a business expense.

9. Most cities do not have enough parkland. It is true that Vancouver has Stanley Park, while Toronto has its huge High Park and a network of exquisite ravine parks—an assembly of land so vast that it places an undue burden on the taxpayer. But a scarcity of green areas in major cities reduces the quality of life. In parks children can play on the swings or splash in a wading pool while their parents read a newspaper. Pensioners can sit on a bench in the shade and smoke. Homeless people can stretch out on the grass for a nap. And young lovers can stroll down the path to find the privacy so rare in everyday urban life. Yes, we can almost say that the worth of a city is summed up by the quality of its park system.

10. My favourite job was delivering pizza last summer. The restaurant I worked for made excellent pizza with homemade sausage and generous amounts of cheese. Every night I got a free pizza for supper, plus a soft drink. When five or six pizzas were ready in their boxes, I would roar around town in my old Pontiac, waving at my friends on the street and collecting big tips from the customers. I also collected ten or twelve traffic tickets, because although I usually drove at twice the speed limit, the boss called me "Speedy" because he thought I was so slow. And one night the clutch went out, costing me $325 in repairs. The boss lent me his van in the meantime, but charged an exorbitant rate for mileage. He was the worst skinflint I have ever seen.

NAME _____

Improving "Thin" Paragraphs: Worksheet

The most frequent weakness of paragraphs is "thinness." Add details to develop the following examples into vivid and convincing paragraphs. Write your new versions on a separate page, adding words, phrases or whole sentences of example, image or fact. Remember to follow, all the way through, the direction set by the topic sentence.

1. Having brothers or sisters is not easy. You have to tolerate each other's behaviour, and you must learn to share. But this effort is worthwhile, because it prepares you for your own family life in the future.

2. For many students, car ownership is not worth the expense. The car itself must be paid for, then maintained through costly visits to the garage. Gas and oil are increasingly expensive. Worst of all is the astronomical price of insurance.

3. Many parents dread rock concerts. They worry about the effect of the music on their children. They wonder what kind of people their children will meet. And they wonder whether their children will try new and forbidden experiences in the anonymity of the crowd.

4. American television drama has a heavy influence on our own. Many Canadians think CBC series are boring, and would rather turn to American sitcoms or police shows. Thus Canadian producers are tempted to win viewers by imitating the format and style of the American product.

5. This year's fashions for women are silly. Some of the clothes are unflattering. Others are uncomfortable. Why do we keep spending our hard-earned money on this trash?

6. School cafeteria food leaves something to be desired. It is heavy in starches, grease and sugar. It tends to be overcooked. Finally, it is often expensive.

7. Never before has music been so closely identified with the lives of its fans. People who dress in certain fashions and adopt a particular behaviour tend to favour one kind of music, or even a specific band. This music then becomes an expression of their lifestyle.

8. The Internet has taken over many people's social lives. They spend a great deal of time on it daily, communicating in new electronic ways with others on the Net. As a result, their contact with "R. L."—real life—has diminished.

9. A good holiday can shake us out of the old rut and show us new paths to follow. Going to other places stimulates the imagination. Meeting new people can teach us a great deal. Why stay at home all the time when there is so much to learn elsewhere?

10. Great numbers of people in other countries admire Canada and, if they had the chance, would move here. Canada is rich in natural resources. It is beautiful. It is relatively unpolluted. Its standard of living is among the highest in the world. Most importantly, it is a nation at peace.

Part Four

Editing: The Rest of the Process

Now that we have done the "big" things, we turn to the "little" things. Now that we have zeroed in on our topic, our thesis and our audience, now that we have unleashed our ideas in a first draft or two, we move on to the finer points of editing.

This phase covers a lot of ground. Each "little" thing contributes, for good or for bad, to the total effect of an essay. Now we tinker with words, replacing a weak one with a strong one, a vague one with a concrete one. We fix weird sentences. We change punctuation. We reach for the dictionary. And at the very end we give our good copy the final quality control of proofreading.

Frankly, the process doesn't always follow this plan. We did a bit of word-tinkering and happened to see a few errors even in the "discovery" draft. We didn't make an issue of it then, for we didn't want to lose our train of thought. But we took a moment here and there to change a comma to a period or replace "there" with "their."

And now that we're set to do all these tasks in the editing stage, the reverse may happen: a new idea may come rushing out of our mind. It may be perfect to round off a point we thought we had already finished. So we may interrupt the "little" things we are doing and for a while move back to the "big" things.

But apart from these exceptions, we now turn our attention to editing—to the material in the following sections. Different teachers will use the editing chapter in different ways. Some will select the parts they view as most important, to discuss and to practise in class with exercises. Others will choose sections and exercises as needed, according to what they see in essays from the class. Still others will assign a section only to individuals who need that particular skill. Whatever the approach of your teacher, though, keep four points in mind:

1. Not everyone needs everything in this chapter. If your punctuation is already good, turn your attention to other things, such as economy.

2. Almost everyone does need certain parts of this chapter that cover chronic problems. The two most often needed are probably "Pronoun Reference" and "Agreement."

3. Whatever material your teacher assigns, and in whatever order, remember that you can also use this chapter as a reference. If you feel unsure about commas, look them up. If your teacher has written "cliché" beside your favourite expression, find that section and study it. If your last paper was wordy, study "Editing for Economy." To find things, use the table of contents, the index, or simply the "Editing Guide" on the inside back cover.

   If you wish to do exercises on your own, note the answers given at the back of the book.

4. Above all, do not study all the editing sections *before* you write. If we tried to master the "little" before the "big," we'd never get to the first line of our first essay. Start writing, keep writing, and apply each new skill as you learn it.

EDITING FOR ECONOMY

One day you go shopping for shoes. The first store has a nice pair for $50. The second store has the identical shoes for $100, and a third has them for $150. *Need we ask which store gets your business???* Yet even though most students would spend the fewest possible dollars, when they use words they may spend like millionaires.

"Talk is cheap," the old saying tells us. Well, sometimes. People can jaw for hours in the cafeteria, not caring if others forget every word they say. But using words to pass the time is one thing; using them to make a point is another.

In essay writing, "talk" is not cheap at all. If we "spend" too much, our message suffocates under a mass of words. The reader yawns. The teacher reaches for the red pen. But if we spend words carefully like dollars, making each one contribute to the overall point, the power of our message grows and grows. What we say is easily read, quickly grasped, strongly felt.

Economy is central to other aspects of writing as well. For example, revising an early draft to make it more direct and concise automatically improves grammar, for streamlining our language gives errors fewer places to occur. Since time will be saved in other stages of revision, give this matter a high priority: edit for economy *before* you edit for the aspects of grammar discussed later in this chapter.

The two worst enemies of economical writing are *wordiness* and *repetition*.

Wordiness

Make every word count. Get rid of those that do not.

A. *Move swiftly to the main point of an essay* rather than padding the introduction. Avoid wordy beginnings like this one from an actual student essay:

> Well, the question I am going to write about raises a lot of problems, and can easily be debated with many people taking either side.

Any question worth writing an essay about "can easily be debated," and in a debate people usually take "either side." The author has wasted words telling us what we already know, but has failed to tell us the most important thing: the topic. (See page 40 for more discussion of introductions.)

B. *Stay on topic.* Give your reader all the explanation needed to understand your point, but do not waste time with information that does not explain it:

> Running promotes health. Excess weight that might someday cause a heart attack is burned off. After a few years, the heart becomes so strong that it may beat as few as 40 times per minute. The muscles become strong and flexible, which enables the runner to cope more easily with the tasks of everyday life. *And running is an inexpensive sport, costing only four or five cents per mile for shoes.*

Saving money has little to do with health. Even if the last sentence interests the reader, here it wastes time. Let's remove it, then, and someday put it into a different paragraph that does discuss the cost of running.

C. *Be plain rather than fancy.* Avoid trying to make your writing seem more important than it is:

> With a college education one looks forward to gaining sufficient knowledge whereby one can assist in the development of society. This education can assist in enlightening the masses of society or even in the utilization of knowledge gained to establish an institution to further scatter abroad information.

(This author would make a fine speech writer for a politician who must talk for hours while promising nothing.)

> The students who rioted were exterminated from school.

(This writer, pushing her vocabulary too hard, has had her subjects murdered instead of expelled.)

> The smells were sweet to his nasal palate.

(In other words, something smelled good to him. This writer should avoid decorating the message, and instead just deliver it.)

One of the surest ways to weaken your writing is to deliberately choose big words. Some people go through the first draft of an essay replacing small or plain words with long or fancy ones from the dictionary. "Think" becomes "ponder" or "cogitate"; "read" becomes "peruse"; "chew" becomes "masticate." In trying to seem bigger and better than it is, such writing is dishonest, flabby, and even ridiculous. Do use a big word when it is most appropriate, but in general choose the smallest one that exactly fits your meaning.

(For related material, see "Jargon," p. 83.)

D. *Manipulate sentence structure to avoid wordiness.* One student wrote this:

> The flavour of coffee tastes delicious to me. (8 words)

Did we not know coffee has a flavour? Let's omit the first three words, then, by using "coffee" rather than "flavour" as a subject:

> Coffee tastes delicious to me. (5 words)

So far, so good, but we could further concentrate the statement by using "I" as a subject:

> I love coffee. (3 words)

Another student wrote this sincere but wasteful message:

> The purpose of my composition is to give an explanation of why I do not drink strong beverages. The reason why I do not indulge in strong drink is based on my religious convictions. (34 words)

Note how the second sentence restates much of the first. Let's combine them:

This composition will explain how my religious convictions prevent me from indulging in strong drink. (15 words)

> Many people find it easier to cut waste from the computer screen than from the page. Learn how your system deletes text. There are simple commands that will instantly remove a letter, a word, a whole line, or a page. In major systems there are also commands that will bring these back in case you realize you made a mistake.
>
> Once such moves are automatic, words shift constantly, moving into gaps left by vanishing waste. Passages shrink in size as they expand in power.
>
> Your system no doubt has a thesaurus (see page 33). Use it. This tool is so fast that you can afford to check all the flabby words of your discovery draft and replace them with short and strong ones.
>
> If you suspect you are repeating a certain word too often, try your system's "search" function to find each occurrence quickly and then see whether it could be changed (see page 133). This technique might waste time in short papers, but will probably save time in long ones.
>
> Count words electronically. Most word-processing software allows you to do so quickly, either through the speller or through a separate menu. Consult your manual for the commands. Count often, to track your gains in economy.
>
> Is a passage hopeless? Move it down the screen with your "Enter" key, put the cursor in the empty space, and do a quick new version not looking at the old one. If it comes out shorter and better, delete the original.
>
> *In summary, word processing frees you up to do the experimenting that is at the heart not only of economy, but of our whole "process" approach to writing.*

So far we have fewer than half the original words, but the sentence is still inflated. Why mention "this composition" if we already realize this is the author's own composition? Why mention "convictions" if they can be assumed from the idea of religion? And why use "indulging in strong drink" instead of the single word "drinking," which in this context clearly refers to alcohol? Let's try a new sentence, "spending" as little as possible:

My religion keeps me from drinking. (6 words)

E. *Avoid the passive voice, which is wordy and weak; use the active voice, which is concise and strong.*

PASSIVE

The contest was won by me. (6 words)

ACTIVE

I won the contest. (4 words)

PASSIVE

The crash was witnessed by five people. (7 words)

ACTIVE

Five people witnessed the crash. (5 words)

Repetition

Saying something more than once is by far the most common way of wasting words. To improve your efficiency and your style, avoid repetition of fact and of vocabulary.

A. *Avoid stating a fact more than once.*

Computer viruses are a danger *and a hazard* to our future.

How much difference is there between a "danger" and a "hazard"? If not much, then in this statement one of them is a waste.

B. *Avoid stating a fact easily assumed from another fact already given.*

The chair was green *in colour.*

Did the author think we do not know green is a colour? Or did she just neglect to edit? Let's help her by chopping out the last two words. Here is another example:

Knowledge is crucial to the survival of the *investor's* investment.

Did this writer think we do not know investors invest? Are we going in circles? Then let's chop out the word "investor's."

Radio and television personalities use repetitious language so often that certain expressions will pop into your mind as you write. *Avoid these self-repeaters and any like them:*

absolutely perfect
at this point in time
completely surrounded
consensus of opinion
contributing factor
crisis situation
deeply profound
an emergency situation
end result

equally as good
final conclusion
for the purpose of
future generations to come
in actual fact
many different kinds
mutual agreement
mutual co-operation
my personal opinion
no other alternative
repeat again
return back
solid fact
sufficient enough reason
truly remarkable

C. *Avoid trying to strengthen a word that is already strong. Intensifiers such as "very," "highly" and "extremely" add nothing to words such as these:*

crucial	miserable
definite	obese
fascinating	perfect
horrible	tragic
impossible	unique
intriguing	wonderful

One person wrote this:

Training a cat to do tricks is *very* impossible.

How can something be more impossible than "impossible"? Let's remove "very" and remember that it is one of the most overused words in our language.

D. *If you avoid repeating words, especially long ones,* your message will be more efficient and your style will be more pleasing.

A sign in a church parking lot proclaimed this:

Parking *permitted* by *permission* only. (5 words)

Naturally, "permission" implies that something is "permitted." Let's omit the word:

Parking by *permission* only. (4 words)

The student who wrote this one may have been desperate to meet a required essay length:

The author's *imagination* is very *imaginative.* (6 words)

Not only is the sentence wasteful, but it irritates the reader, who is being led in circles. An obvious revision is to remove one of the repetitious words:

The author is very *imaginative.* (5 words)

The word "imaginative," though, is strong enough that we can also omit "very":

The author is *imaginative.* (4 words)

Better still, we could use "imagination" as the subject of a sentence that gets on to the next point:

The author's *imagination* is evident in the fresh imagery of the poem.

Finally, we must recognize that not all repetition is bad. Would the following passage be as effective if the main word occurred only once?

We drive *American* cars, read *American* books, listen to *American* music and go to *American* movies. If our habits do not change, we may someday even become *American*.

This repetition of "American" is deliberate, not accidental. Far from wasting words, it strengthens and emphasizes the message. Feel free to use repetition this way as a device of style—as long as you realize what you are doing.

A dictionary of synonyms, such as *Roget's Thesaurus*, will help you find replacements for a word repeated too often. It will also help you choose the word that most exactly fits your meaning, a process that tends to make your writing more concise. Buy one of these useful books, available in paperback, and keep it where you write. (Or use the electronic thesaurus of your word processor, as suggested in the earlier text box.)

E. ***Repetition even of similar sounds can irritate, and in such cases should be avoided.*** Read drafts aloud to detect clunkers like this:

Population *density* of great *intensity* creates social chaos.

Let's revise to avoid the accidental rhyme:

High population *density* creates social chaos.

NAME _____

Economy: Diagnostic

Put an "X" beside each passage that clearly contains wordiness or undesirable repetition.

1. Crying happens in both sexes, men and women. _____

2. In terms of the climate of Somalia, it is very hot and dry. _____

3. Society considers pit bulls to be killers because a few of these dogs have killed or fatally injured someone or another animal. _____

4. What can I say about culture in Vancouver? Well, first it is a multi-cultural culture. _____

5. Today in industrialized nations, 80 percent of the people live in urban areas, while 20 percent live in rural areas. _____

6. I closed my eyes to relive the incredible experience again. _____

7. The front of the building faces north while the back faces south. _____

8. Choosing a life partner is not easy. _____

9. It's very fascinating to see Yonge Street at night. _____

10. The best job I have ever had was at the London Public Library. It was the best job because it was interesting. There were a number of facts that made the job interesting. One of the major facts that made the job interesting was the people who worked at the library. _____

11. It was New Year's Eve night. _____

12. The average wattage of a car sound system ranges between 100 and 300 watts. _____

13. Having possession of an automobile is something many people would want. _____

14. Even though the novel *Erewhon* came under some criticism, the overall opinion was that of a positive one. _____

15. Our neighbour was at the door and she was worried because of all the commotion that was happening. _____

16. My full-time job was two hours away. _____

17. Language links people together by communication. _____

18. My grandmother once broke her leg. As a result, she limps quite a bit when she is walking. _____

19. The piston is connected to a connecting rod, which in turn is connected to the crankshaft. The crankshaft is connected to a large metal disk called the flywheel. _____

20. Relationships are brief and short-lived. _____

21. After ten minutes in the cold, I could hardly feel the existence of my limbs. _____

22. We find that some teachers are negligent of criteria essential to the students' comprehension of a subject. _____

23. Government spending stimulates the economy by pumping money into the economy. _____

24. It is hard to get a job. _____

25. In the opinion of my dad, he says that the quality of workmanship in luxury cars is what sets them apart from economy cars. _____

26. Swimmers who vary their pace will get very exhausted. _____

27. With a tax increase, it can create a black market or an underground economy.   _____

28. Why do teenagers marry? There are many reasons why teenagers marry.   _____

29. In my opinion, I would advise anyone to choose a front-wheel-drive car.   _____

30. Taking a trip to Mexico would be the trip of a lifetime for us.   _____

31. Walking is the safest exercise.   _____

32. Nowadays, teenagers prefer driving a motorcycle to driving a car, due to the fact that driving a motorcycle is more exciting than driving a car.   _____

33. Smoking is a major risk in women's pregnancies.   _____

34. Winter is very unique.   _____

35. I have to pay an annual insurance premium of three thousand, five hundred and seventy-eight dollars and twenty-three cents per year.   _____

36. A family is something you will always have forever.   _____

37. The difference between a room with plants in it and one with no plants is extremely obvious.   _____

38. The only seasons Indonesia has are the wet season and the dry season.   _____

39. Politicians know that if they want to be re-elected, they must lower taxes.   _____

40. There is a Chinese saying that says, "A family that has an elderly person has a treasure."   _____

NAME _____

Economy: Worksheet, Level 1

To chop waste from your draft, examine each word. Does one repeat another? Does one even imply the meaning of another? If so, cross one out. Practise this strategy on the following expressions that were found in actual student essays.

1. truly astounded

2. in the future ahead

3. products produced by industries

4. the final result

5. good advantages

6. emotional feelings

7. cheap in cost

8. very fascinating

9. a true fact

10. at that moment in time

11. very unique

12. share together

13. 8:00 a.m. in the morning

14. in the coming future

15. our surrounding environment

16. very crucial

17. fatal deaths

18. self-confidence in myself

19. and etc.

20. $150 dollars

21. quite obvious

22. very fascinating

23. extremely miserable

24. positive self-esteem

25. reappear again

26. wet moisture

27. very obvious

28. 600 hundred students

29. very chaotic

30. so crucial

31. rectangular in shape

32. a light green colour

33. quite impossible

34. in the month of June

35. in the year 1998

36. light brown in colour

37. rather unique

38. no other alternative

39. competitive competition

40. in my own personal opinion

NAME _____

Economy: Worksheet, Level 2

Heighten the economy and style of these passages by crossing out wordiness and repetition, or where necessary by revising more fully in the space provided. If no revision is needed, write "Concise" in the space.

Example: England offered me fascinating scenery ~~to see~~.

1. Living away from home is a very unique experience.

   _____

2. I have noticed a change in my mental attitude.

   _____

3. My room is square in shape.

   _____

4. From a worldwide perspective, Canada has been rated as one of the top countries in the world in which to live.

   _____

   _____

5. In my opinion, I think Canada should increase its level of immigration, because the increase of immigration will boost up Canada's economy.

   _____

   _____

6. Gravelbourg, Saskatchewan, is a French community of 1800 hundred persons.

   _____

7. Many teenagers' lives have been snuffed out by fatal car accidents.

   _____

8. Gangs are, essentially, groups of youths who share a common bond to each other.

   _____

9. With a word processor you can delete any paragraph you don't like and write another.

   _____

   _____

10. I could, at this point, carry on and stretch this paper to maybe ten pages, but I'm sure you could easily recognize the padding.

    _____

    _____

11. It was interesting to hear the British accent when people spoke.

    _____

12. Another useful item is the grape crusher, which crushes the grapes.

13. The time was 9:30 p.m. at night.

14. My boss was very obese.

15. Nicotine gum contains nicotine, which will help smokers to avoid a sudden drop of nicotine in their blood when they quit smoking.

16. One disadvantage of the assembly line is that the worker on the line is dehumanized and not treated as a living person. Manufacturers and business executives are turning blue-collar workers into things.

17. The oil machines have openings which, when opened, allow the oil to flow into a filtering machine, which filters the oil.

18. There are different credit cards for every type of purchase. Some examples of credit cards are major credit cards, store credit cards and even gasoline credit cards.

19. There should be no hesitation to use chemical food additives in our food, since they provide safety, freshness and many other protections to our food which we as consumers should have.

20. The subway must be the worst way to travel around town. Several times I've been literally pulled out of a subway car. On one occasion when I was pulled out of the subway car, at Yonge and Bloor, the man who pulled me out of the subway car ripped my shirt. When the doors began to close, I retaliated and gave him a punch in the face.

NAME _____

Economy: Worksheet, Level 3

Heighten the economy and style of these passages by crossing out wordiness and repetition, or where necessary by revising more fully in the space provided.

1. The sea was calm as I skimmed swiftly and silently over the water's surface on my sailboard, along the scenic coast of an enormously incredible panorama. On one side of me there was an enormously wide and long gold-coloured sandy beach, with huge mountains in the background. On the other side of me was nothing but clear water that seemed never to end.

    _____

    _____

    _____

    _____

    _____

2. The heavy lifting was fine with me, but what I really hated was the dirt on the clutches. It was unbelievable to see so much dirt on the clutches. I was always working with the dirt, having only a laboratory coat protecting me from the dirt. My pants were black all the time from working with the dirt.

    _____

    _____

    _____

    _____

3. For my English assignment, I am supposed to describe the best or worst job I have ever had. The topic of the essay has made me think. What is a best or worst job? What has been my best or worst job? I have pondered on the topic for a while, and have come to the conclusion that there is no best or worst job. Any job can be either enjoyed or hated, because all jobs possess both good and bad points. In other words, a job is what you make it.

    _____

    _____

    _____

    _____

    _____

4. When a fluorescent light is first turned on, the light seems to slowly float through the room. The light from a fluorescent bulb travels at the same speed as the light from an incandescent bulb, but it does not seem to be as responsive. The light from a fluorescent tube is produced by the emission of radiation from the tube. The light that is produced seems to be a pale, dull-blue light. There is very little heat generated from the tube, but a slight humming can be heard from within the tube. The life of a fluorescent tube is much longer than that of an incandescent bulb. The average bulb would last six to twelve months, but most tubes last three to five years.

    _____

    _____

    _____

    _____

    _____

    _____

    _____

    _____

5. We all know healthy food is essential to our health. Dieticians and nutritionists always talk about the importance of healthy food. Yet most of the people in North America don't always eat healthy food. Instead they eat junk food. Many fast food businesses spend lots of money on advertising junk food through television or newspapers. In other words, junk food is popular, well promoted and widespread. Every day, large numbers of food stores or restaurants sell greasy hamburgers, hot dogs and french fries. As a result, many people who eat junk food suffer short term and long term health problems.

    _____

    _____

    _____

    _____

    _____

    _____

    _____

    _____

EDITING OUT LANGUAGE ABUSE

Good writing is honest. Just as people have many reasons to speak, people have many reasons to write. Some want to reveal facts, while others want to hide them. Some want to make an issue clear, while others want to cloud it over. Most writers do want to convince us of something, which is a normal human desire. But while some argue fairly, through appeals to our reason, others bypass this process to distort the truth and sometimes to attack our emotions. These language abusers actually hope we will *not* think.

Such attempts to avoid logical communication, to avoid real thought, may seem almost normal in our world of advertising campaigns, corporate hype and political propaganda. Our exposure to this abuse has been immense. Yet as you will see in the examples that follow, dishonesty of different kinds can produce not only self-serving and antisocial writing, but sometimes lazy, weak and boring writing as well.

As you study the clichés, euphemisms, bias words and jargon that follow, you will note how categories overlap: euphemisms and bias words tend to be clichés, and jargon tends to be euphemism. The reason for this may be the very fact that, in different ways, they are all dishonest. *Edit them out of your writing.*

Clichés

A large part of writing honestly is being original. We all know that handing in another's essay as our own

"You're right. It *was* a herd of elephants up here."

From The Second Ben Wicks Treasury, *by Ben Wicks. Methuen, Toronto, 1987. Reprinted by permission of Ben Wicks.*

is a serious offence, and that someone who copies another person's book for publication will end up in court like any other thief. Yet many of us cheerfully repeat other people's expressions every time we write. These worn-out sayings are termed *clichés*, after the French word for a printing plate that makes many copies of one original.

Every time we write "sadder but wiser," "few and far between," "a sight for sore eyes" and "hit the nail on the head," we are lazily avoiding the work of being original. Like parrots, we are letting our language slip into pre-established channels, a process that discourages real thought and therefore bores the reader.

It must have taken real imagination for the first person to say for the first time, "I've got butterflies in my stomach." The first listener was probably dazzled by this new image that so clearly described nervousness. But today, when we hear those words for the thousandth time, we don't even think about butterflies. We may not think about anything at all, because repetition has deadened us.

Other clichés describe situations that no longer exist. A sailor once had to "know the ropes," but do we? If not, why do we write it to describe our job driving a taxi or programming computers? People still say "Hold your horses," though for decades we have driven cars. The bubonic plague once killed a third of Europe; with today's antibiotics we no longer fear the disease, yet still avoid things "like the plague."

When we no longer "see" what a cliché means, we will unknowingly stick it into ridiculous situations. One student wrote, "Right off the bat, nine seconds into the hockey game, a goal was scored by the guest team." We might be so numbed by the cliché that we do not "see" its image. But if we do, we might wonder what a bat is doing in a hockey game. This example, like the others above, shows the harm that clichés can do: *they keep us from thinking.* For that reason, *avoid them all.*

Are clichés automatic? See for yourself. How many of the following expressions can you complete without even thinking about them?

1. *birds of a* _____
2. *blind as a* _____
3. *by hook or by* _____
4. *cool as a* _____
5. *a diamond in the* _____
6. *hook, line and* _____
7. *in the nick of* _____
8. *last but not* _____
9. *make a mountain out of a* _____
10. *raining cats and* _____

NAME _____

Clichés: Worksheet

Here are some tired old clichés found in student writing. First identify each, then substitute fresher words to fit the meaning. If you see a passage that contains no cliché, write "Correct" in the space.

Example: The first day at work I was ~~bright eyed and bushy tailed.~~ *enthusiastic*

1. I grabbed the front of the toboggan, holding on for dear life.

   _____

   _____

2. There was never a dull moment at work. I was on my toes day in and day out.

   _____

   _____

3. The next year I played defence on the soccer team.

   _____

4. When June rolled around, Standard Tube hired me and I was ready to put my shoulder to the wheel.

   _____

   _____

5. The government tried to battle inflation, but the unemployment crisis was bursting at its seams like a swollen dam.

   _____

   _____

   _____

6. Calculus was the last straw. I was bored stiff.

   _____

   _____

7. Two of my bosom buddies and I found a neat little apartment overlooking English Bay.

   _____

   _____

8. In this day and age, family members need to touch base each and every day.

   _____

   _____

9. Rush hour in Toronto is not my cup of tea. The buses and subway cars are jammed like sardines.

_____

_____

_____

10. My new interest in fitness is mind-boggling, because in the past I avoided exercise like the plague.

_____

_____

11. The hustle and bustle of the city takes its toll, and the individual can only grin and bear it.

_____

_____

12. My three weeks in the woods made me realize that life is not a bowl of cherries.

_____

_____

13. I passed my ordeal with flying colours. It was a breeze.

_____

_____

14. The bottom line is that parents should be on their toes whenever their children are glued to the tube.

_____

_____

15. Marsha's schools, clothes and even friends were chosen by her parents.

_____

_____

16. Our country is going down the tubes. The feds are pulling the wool over our eyes, and the public is on the short end of the stick.

_____

_____

_____

17. Many stores decided to bite the bullet and open on Sunday.

_____

_____

18. A great book shows the whole world and its problems in a nutshell.

_____

_____

19. I was spending money left, right and centre for my entertainment.

20. With spring just around the corner, I'm thinking about a summer job.

21. Going to the cafeteria and paying an arm and a leg for two Dad's oatmeal cookies really gets my goat.

22. At age three I was ready, willing and able to take on the trials and tribulations of nursery school.

23. It's in my blood to get up and go.

24. I get sick and tired of working the bugs out of the system each and every time.

25. Canada is really and truly at a standstill. It's time to get the lead out and jump-start the economy.

26. If the big cheeses get away with murder on their tax returns, why should the rest of us toe the line?

27. It was just my luck to have roommates who smoked like chimneys.

28. Many pets are spoiled rotten.

29. Each and every night I burn the midnight oil.

   _____

   _____

30. Canada has become a mere clone of the United States. It is about time for Canadians to stand on their own two feet and start making waves.

   _____

   _____

   _____

Euphemisms

When we use one word instead of another, we choose not only between meanings but also between feelings. Why do we call one person "slim" but another "skinny"? Is it because we like the "slim" one better? The philosopher Bertrand Russell poked fun at our habit of selecting terms to promote our attitudes, when he said "I am firm; you are stubborn; he is pigheaded."

Some people view language as an objective system, a kind of Morse code of words that will reveal truth clearly and fairly. But of course language is as vulnerable and human as we are, reflecting all our feelings and prejudices. The experienced essayist knows that the same set of "facts" can be made to sound good or bad, cheerful or gloomy, plain or fancy, approving or condemning, all depending on what words she or he dresses them in.

Consider the terms people choose to describe their professional roles. Since we all want to feel worthwhile, a janitor is now a "maintenance engineer," a garbage worker is a "sanitary engineer," and a barber is a "hair stylist." An undertaker, who at the time of Shakespeare was called a "grave digger," rose in status to become a mortician (rhymes with "physician"), and in some cases now, as a "funeral director," has even joined the ranks of executives. Terms like these, which make things seem better than they were, are called *euphemisms*.

Companies naturally hope that we, the consumers, will feel good about their products and services. Again, euphemisms do the job. When ground beef becomes "Salisbury steak," when lawn mowing becomes "vegetation management," when dangerous pesticides are now only "crop protection materials," when ink is "writing fluid," when glasses are "eyewear," when used cars are only "pre-owned" and when hairdressing becomes "hair sculpture"—we spend and companies profit.

Since organizations want us to like them, they choose carefully the words that describe their actions. In our era of cutbacks and layoffs, companies no longer fire people or give them the sack or throw them in the street; now companies only "dehire" us, "terminate" us or "select us out." In fact, some employers no longer even do these kind acts themselves, but hire a "career transition company" to supply "outplacement consultants" who will properly "downsize" the "human resources" that are "redundant," so that "nonretention" can take place. If the employer is feeling generous enough, we might even receive, for going out the door, a "termination gratuity."

If none of this enhances the company's "productivity" and it is still losing money, we will read in the business section that the company is merely undergoing "negative economic growth" or even earning "negative profits." Of course the government will never raise the company's taxes, either, but will only require more "revenue enhancement measures."

Speaking of governments, in our polite new times their armies never "attack" or "kill," but only "control," "manage" or even "pacify" (literally "make peaceful") the enemy. And now countries making war no longer indulge in propaganda or lies, but only in "disinformation."

For years this desire of individuals and organizations to improve their image through euphemisms has grown. In our decade, though, a new and controversial twist has appeared. We all know that words naming groups of people can be loaded, and that reasonable persons have never used the bad words for those of other races, cultures or gender. But now word choice has become a political struggle. Groups that have felt marginalized, shut out of economic or social or political power, are now using and demanding language that is "*politically correct.*"

A whole new code of terms has now emerged. People who were once "disabled" are now "differently abled." The formerly "deaf" are now "hearing impaired" and the formerly "blind" are now "visually impaired." Those who were once rape or incest "victims" are now rape or incest "survivors." Those once said to be "dying" of AIDS are now "persons living with AIDS."

In our cosmopolitan nation, even names of racial and cultural groups are changing. For example those once called "Indians," then later called "native peoples," are now increasingly called "first nations people"—to remind others that they were here first.

Persons of good will have always respected the wishes of minority groups by using the suggested terminology. After all, such words are meant to convey kindness and respect, in a society in which everyone belongs to a minority.

Lately, though, some people have grown uneasy about the whole trend, sensing extremism and even totalitarianism in language. The idea of saying "herstory" for "history" or "animal companion" for "pet" reminds them of George Orwell's nightmare novel *1984*, in which a police state literally rewrites the dictionary so that words like "liberty" and "democracy," which once made rebellion thinkable, are now forgotten. Those who object to the new "political correctness" in our own society accuse its proponents of now using censorship to tyrannize over others.

So who is right? No one can tell you. As an essayist, you can feel good about writing some euphemisms out of kindness to others. Your grandparents may not be "old" but merely "senior citizens." However, there may come a time when you sense you are not writing the truth but stretching it almost to the breaking point. When that happens, you must make your own decision—one that is at the same time linguistic and political.

NAME _____

Euphemisms: Worksheet

All the following terms are euphemisms. Circle those you would feel comfortable using in an essay, and in the space explain why. Cross out those you would not use in an essay, and in the space explain why. (Of course there is no set of "correct" answers; this exercise is meant to encourage your own awareness and free choice.)

1. informal housing (for "slums" or "shacks")

2. animal companion (for "pet")

3. between jobs (for "unemployed")

4. big (for "fat")

5. sex worker (for "prostitute")

6. correction (for a "drop" in the stock market)

7. developing nations (for "poor" nations)

8. expectorate (for "spit")

9. eye fashions (for "glasses")

10. frank exchange of views (for "argument")

11. golden agers (for "old people")

12. hearing impaired (for "deaf")

13. downsizing (for "firing")

14. low-income neighbourhood (for "slum")

15. negative assets (for "debt")

16. pass away (for "die")

17. perspire (for "sweat")

18. selected out (for "fired")

19. senior citizens (for "old people")

20. visually impaired (for "blind")

21. special child (for "mentally handicapped" child)

22. starter home (for "small house")

23. terminate (for "fire" or for "kill")

24. upscale (for "expensive")

25. sleeping together (for "having sex")

NAME_____

Euphemisms and Their Opposite: Words Biased Pro or Con: Worksheet

If euphemisms distort truth by making things look better than they are, negative bias words distort truth by making things look worse than they are. In this exercise practise identifying both extremes, so you can more easily detect and avoid bias in your own writing.

Here are 25 words that can be used for "underweight." Write each in the column where you think it belongs. Use the dictionary if necessary.

bony, cadaverous, delicate, emaciated, fleshless, gangling, gaunt, haggard, lanky, lean, raw-boned, scrawny, skeletal, skinny, slender, slight, slim, spare, spindly, svelte, thin, underfed, undernourished, underweight, wizened.

VERY NEGATIVE	NEGATIVE	NEUTRAL	POSITIVE	VERY POSITIVE

Here are 25 words that can be used for "overweight." Write each in the column where you think it belongs. As above, use the dictionary if necessary.

beefy, big, bulky, burly, chubby, chunky, corpulent, elephantine, fat, fleshy, heavy-set, obese, overweight, paunchy, plump, ponderous, portly, pudgy, rotund, stocky, stout, thick-set, tubby, well-fed, well-padded

VERY NEGATIVE	NEGATIVE	NEUTRAL	POSITIVE	VERY POSITIVE

Jargon

Our society adores technology. Now that we humans have walked on the moon, explored the ocean floor, zoomed through cyberspace and cooked dinner in three minutes with electronic rays, we find ourselves speaking and writing like the scientists and technicians we admire.

Even in nonscientific areas like the arts, many of us borrow technical or showy words to dress up the message. Those who prefer the direct approach describe such talk as "bafflegab," "technobabble" or "gobbledygook." Its more common name is *jargon*.

Of course technical words have their place. Computer engineers could hardly discuss their work without referring to "megabytes," "motherboards," "macros" and "merge codes." But now the rest of us cannot hold a meeting without "interfacing" through "input" and "output," without "accessing" data falling within our "parameters," and without "feedback" on how all this will "impact" our "outcomes." A visitor from Mars, hearing us talk, might think that humans, themselves, were the machines.

At its extreme, jargon takes on the impenetrable and ugly quality of this example which the linguist Mario Pei found at "a great university":

> The functional methodology shall be based on an inter-disciplinary process model, which employs a lateral feed-back syndrome across a sanction-constituency interface, coupled with a circular-spiral recapitulatory function for variable-flux accommodation and policy modification.*

Do you know what the passage means? Perhaps you were not supposed to. One Toronto executive admits to writing short and plain reports when he has something to say, but long and fancy ones when he does not. On those occasions he seeks not only technical terms but any other intimidating and unclear language, such as "cognizant" for "aware," "impact negatively upon" for "harm," and "in the foreseeable future" for "soon."

Jargon can make a subject appear so important or difficult that the average person will leave it to the experts. In this way institutions such as business and government can hide their true objectives, and professionals such as lawyers and tax accountants can force us to buy their services because, on our own, we cannot understand official documents.

Jargon has invaded even our personal lives, as terms from fields such as sociology spread into everyday conversation. We no longer go on a date with our girlfriend or boyfriend, but with our "significant other." We no longer have mothers and fathers, but "caregivers," and no longer have sisters and brothers, but "siblings." Then when we, ourselves, join with our significant other to form a "nuclear family," we will no longer raise children but attempt a thing called "parenting," which, if well done, involves a great deal of "dialoguing." At the end of it all, we no longer aim for "happiness" but for a thing called "self-actualization." We might well ask, now that everyday life has become technologized like everything else, whether it is better.

Self-important language like these examples may be creeping into our speech, but as essay writers we can reject it. When we actually *need* technical words, let's use them (making sure to define any term the audience may not know). But in nontechnical applications, jargon leads to wordiness, clichés and euphemisms. It is not clear or even honest. *Avoid it.*

(See p. 13 for the related topic of *audience*, and see p. 57 for another related topic, *economy*.)

---

* Mario Pei, *Double Speak in America* (Hawthorn Books, Inc.), ©1973 Hawthorn. All rights reserved.

NAME _____

Jargon: Worksheet

Here is some widespread jargon. Translate each example into plain, honest English, using the dictionary or thesaurus where necessary.

Example: due to the fact that   *because* _____

1. to access   _____

2. on the back burner   _____

3. significant other   _____

4. the bottom line   _____

5. decision-making process   _____

6. dialoguing   _____

7. discussant   _____

8. feedback   _____

9. guesstimate   _____

10. sibling   _____

11. to impact   _____

12. input, output   _____

13. insightful   _____

14. to interface   _____

15. limited time factor   _____

16. low profile, high profile   _____

17. maximize, finalize, utilize   _____

18. a must   _____

19. parameters   _____

20. parenting   _____

21. at this point in time   _____

22. the principal thrust   _____

23. profit-wise (and most other "-wise" words)   _____

24. shortfall   _____

25. outcomes   _____

EDITING FOR APPROPRIATE LANGUAGE

As we will see in the next section, "Editing for Complete Sentences," people tend to write as they speak. If you grew up hearing people say "can't hardly" or "real good," you probably use these expressions yourself—and if you say them, you may also write them.

The problem is not that "can't hardly" or "real good" are morally or intellectually inferior, but just that they are not found in the work of experienced writers. Since we do not see these expressions in carefully produced books, magazines and newspapers (except in dialogue to represent people talking), they seem inappropriate for serious writing tasks.

Though such expressions will always work in conversation with people who are used to hearing them, we also need to **write in language appropriate for our readers**. This means that in essays, reports and business letters, we use the same "standard" English that other writers use.

Appropriate language in writing also means avoiding the slang that seems so natural when you speak. Napoleon's invasion of Russia may have been a failure, but in your history essay he did not make a "boo boo," get "put down" or get "trashed."

Though no linguist would call standard English "better" than nonstandard, everyone knows how important a tool it is for success of the individual in society. The main thing is to be practical. Look over the material that follows, to be sure you are using the standard and appropriate language that communicates best when you write.

Better yet for the long term, cultivate the reading habit, to avoid the trap of writing the way you speak. The more "standard English" you run through your head in the form of other peoples' writing, the more easily and surely you produce your own. (See page 209 for suggested reading matter.)

Finally, as with other editing, revise for appropriate language *after* you have the content of your essay safely down on paper.

Standard and Nonstandard English

"Standard" English is what you usually read in a book or magazine, and what well-read persons normally say in conversation. Though "nonstandard" expressions such as "hadn't ought" or "I seen" may be accepted or even expected by some people in conversation, depending on their background, almost all readers—and above all, teachers—view such usages in an essay, report or formal letter simply as errors.

Common sense tells us that, although nonstandard English may be as appropriate in some situations as standard English is in others, if we wish our writing to succeed, we must use the standard code of expressions that readers expect. In the list that follows, identify any nonstandard expressions you use in writing, and instead use the "standard" equivalents:

NONSTANDARD	STANDARD
ain't	*is not, am not*, etc.
alot	*a lot*
anyways, anywheres, somewheres	*anyway, anywhere, somewhere*
can't hardly	*can hardly*
could of, might of, must of, should of, would of	*could have, might have, must have, should have, would have*
different than	*different from*
disinterested (meaning "not interested")	*uninterested* ("disinterested" means fair or impartial)
enormity (meaning "hugeness")	*enormousness* (an "enormity" is a terrible wrongdoing)
enthused	*enthusiastic*
hadn't ought	*should not, ought not*
in regards to	*in regard to*
irregardless	*regardless*
_____ *is when*	_____ *is*
a long ways	*a long way*
me and the gang	*the gang and I*
most all	*most, almost all*
the reason is because	*the reason is that*
real good	*very good*
I seen, they seen	*I saw, they saw*
this here	*this*
try and	*try to*
where you are at	*where you are*
youse	*you, all of you*

Slang and Colloquialisms

Slang, with its colourful expressions, is fun. So are the somewhat less racy words and expressions called colloquialisms—that is, very conversational language. These ways of speaking make us feel like part of the group, giving us the sensation of being with it and cool. Slang and colloquialisms may even be more concise and therefore stronger than other language. Why, then, do teachers say not to use them in your essays? Are they just trying to stop your fun? Well, see how you enjoy reading the following paragraph full of slang:

> Well, I was so stiff I nearly turkeyed off from the line, but I decided to wait. I pulled out from the line at 4 a.m. and hailed a limber on the road. Fritz landed a daisycutter and the transport driver done his block and took his hook. He absolutely dropped his bundle, and, to make matters worse, I had started off with a duck's breakfast, but I saw a cookhouse and decided to give it a pop for a binder.*

Having trouble? The problem may be the fact that you are not from New Zealand, and that you never fought in World War I—because this passage is written in the slang mode used by New Zealanders who did fight that war. Living now and in Canada, how could you be expected to know these terms? You have just seen three problems with slang: it is often restricted to a certain time, a certain place and a certain group.

Your slang will be equally remote to people of a different age, geographical area or group. The conclusion is obvious: avoid slang when writing for the general reader. This means, for example, your essays.

Another problem with slang is that it is often vague. For example, what, exactly, does the seventies' term "far out" mean? Do we even know if it signifies good or bad?

Other slang terms, such as "goon" and "pig," are so emotionally loaded that they convey a bias unfit for serious writing, which should be fairly objective. Just as bad, many slang terms are clichés that replace original thought by rushing automatically to mind.

Colloquial language is not quite as vivid as slang, and not as restrictive, but is too chatty for essays, reports and business letters. It is the breezy language of conversation, of sports reporting, of disk jockeys and of the lovelorn columns ("If hubby doesn't toe the line for a sweetie like you, he's the dumbest jerk around"). You hardly want to sound like this, or like someone telling jokes in a bar, when you are writing the analysis of a poem by Margaret Atwood, or assessing the future of Canada without Quebec. Instead, *choose language appropriate to the situation.*

Finally, putting quotation marks around slang and colloquial expressions does not so much tame them for serious writing as merely call attention to them. Avoid examples like this:

I believe that our police force is not just a "dinky" one.

A few of the slang and colloquial terms that follow have stayed current for many years; others are long out of date but still used by people who have not changed since learning them; still others will become dated by the time you see them here. Therefore, consider the lists as only a demonstration of what extremely informal language is like, so that you can detect other examples when you write them. The division between slang and colloquialisms is, of course, arbitrary, because even dictionaries disagree as to the status of expressions.

SLANG	COLLOQUIALISMS
bad (amazing)	blab
bummer	brainer
cheesy	chill out
couch potato	cool
ego trip	cop
geek	to eyeball
hardhead	hangup
head honcho	heavy
humongous	hick
nerd	kind of, sort of
pig (police officer)	loser
psyched	nitty gritty
rad	not!
to rip off	O.K. or okay
stoked	pal
to trash	slob
turkey (person)	snow job
wasted	street smart
wicked (amazing)	surf the web
wimp	take a spaz
wired	thug
Xer	veg out

---

* A. E. Strong of Auckland, New Zealand, quoted by Eric Partridge, *Slang To-day and Yesterday*, 4th ed. (London: Routledge and Kegan Paul Ltd., 1970), p. 287.

NAME _____

Slang and Colloquialisms: Worksheet

Cross out the slang and colloquial language in the passages that follow, and replace it with more objective terms appropriate to an essay, report or business letter. If a passage is already free of slang or colloquialisms, write "Appropriate" after it.

Example: My friends thought stealing was ~~okay~~. *fine*

1. In English class there's this one guy that has a mouth like a hippo, but he's an okay person.

2. When a computer makes a boo boo it's usually a biggie.

3. People were eating up the grunge trend, big time. That goes to show that as long as a popular musician sports something new, people will die for it. Whether it be good looking or ugly doesn't matter. It is the new trend on the block and that is all that matters. If you're not down with the latest trend, you're simply not hip.

4. Yesterday in history we yakked for a whole hour about Hitler and his hangups.

5. Pressure drives students bananas.

6. Stopping at the traffic light, I noticed a black and white pig machine beside me.

7. I used to get tons of jobs babysitting around the neighbourhood.

8. I am a diehard Leaf fan, even when my team is shellacked to the tune of 10–1.

9. To verify your account, you must go to the computer lab at W73 in Kerr Hall. There a computer dude will make sure you actually have an account and that it functions properly.

10. Max Beerbohm is not a serious writer.

11. Some people think gambling is an alright thing to do, but it turns me right off.

12. Saccharin, which was the most widely used artificial sweetener, was shot to pieces after a study showed toxicity in rats.

13. I'm really into the outdoors.

14. When I was in grade school, having the most friends and belonging to the coolest group was where I was at.

15. Mr. Ebert is a really neat old man to talk to if you're into stuff like war stories.

16. Sending a document by express mail costs at least twenty bucks.

17. At a party, I feel separated from other people because they begin to feel "high" while I am still "straight."

18. Don't gripe and beef, just get with it.

19. In a game between Toronto and Philadelphia a few years ago, a Leaf player was sent to the penalty box for fighting. The fans at Philadelphia went "nuts." They tried to get at the Leaf player while he was in the "cooler." They threw beer cans, shoes and eggs at him. They even tried to break the protective glass around the "cooler" so they could get hold of the poor Leaf player. Finally the cops were called to escort the helpless guy to his dressing room and safety from the mild-mannered hockey fans.

20. For students new to the e-mail scene, there are a couple of things to follow so you can surf the net.

21. Usually when one of my friends calls to shoot the breeze, I'm up to my eyeballs in homework.

22. Nuclear plants scare the hell out of me.

23. Almost anyone can get married.

24. Well, I took care of the first guy that hassled me, but the other two I couldn't handle.

25. My friends are now hooked on the booze, and blame it all on their parents.

26. My grandma is just shy of 70, and every morning she treks on out to work.

27. To change your image, you must be willing to trash part of your existing wardrobe.

28. Had Darcy not hurt Elizabeth's pride, they could have got it on a lot sooner, but then Jane Austen wouldn't have had anything to write about.

29. By 7 a.m. I was busting my butt down the dirty rows of the tobacco field.

30. Many people who play electronic games don't know what's going on. How many times have you watched people playing a game shout "All right!" when really they got blown away?

Words are only one part — maybe the smallest part — of communication face to face.

Photo courtesy of Suzanne Conrad.

EDITING FOR COMPLETE SENTENCES

Sometimes people talk like this:

"Hi. How's goin'?"

"Good. You?"

"*Killer* math test. What a week!"

"Yeah. Goin' out tomorrow?"

"Maybe the Flamingo. Or El Rancho."

"Cool."

"Or the Phoenix. Or Sabor Latino."

"With Elly?"

"Yeah, and Luis and Sandra, maybe Reza. Wanna come?"

"Yeah. What time?"

"Don't know. Gimme a ring."

"No problem."

Seeing a conversation like this on the page, we recognize its fragmentary nature: a great many words are *left out*. But is there any doubt that our two speakers understand each other?

Their words are only one part—maybe the smallest part—of their real communication. As any actor learning a script will know, those words are heightened by raisings and lowerings of the voice, by posture, gesture and other body language, and by facial expressions so obvious that a small child could "read" them. And if either person does fail to catch something, a quick "What?" will clear things up. The reason, of course, is that *the speakers are in the same place.*

When they go home to write their essay for English or history or economics, though, they will encounter a totally different situation. If they write as they speak, they may produce "sentences" like these found in student essays:

A love affair that was doomed.

New highways leading to smaller cities.

Although his children encouraged him to retire.

Medicine and law, two rewarding fields.

The reader of these partial statements will hear no voice, see no gesture, ask no question. All he or she will have are these symbols on the page—and in their incomplete form these symbols are not enough to make the message clear.

No wonder, then, that readers expect complete sentences. This tradition is so strong—at least in serious explanatory writing such as essays, reports and formal letters—that an incomplete sentence (or **sentence fragment**) is usually perceived as a serious error. Here and there we may accept a *fragment* that is deliberately placed for emphasis. But probably the most important step in editing errors out of a manuscript is to revise all accidental fragments into complete sentences.

A word about technical terms: Although overuse of technical terms can be an abuse of language, some terms really are needed. Just as electricians need to say "diode" or "capacitor" to talk about their subject, we will need a few terms to talk about ours. You know the most important ones already. Learn the rest as you study this section, because you'll need them in later sections.

The essential parts of a complete sentence are one SUBJECT and one VERB. The subject is what the sentence is about, and the verb tells us what the subject does or is.

SUBJECT	VERB
Cars	*pollute.*
Snow	*fell.*
Roger	*sleeps.*
Jane	*studies.*
They	*danced.*
We	*won.*
Honesty	*pays.*
Time	*flies.*

The Subject

The SUBJECT is a noun or pronoun. A NOUN is a person, place or thing, while a PRONOUN is a word such as "she" or "they" that substitutes for the noun. A sentence with a pronoun as the subject can be "complete" even if we don't know what the pronoun refers to:

They danced.

Of course if nearby sentences do not show us what is going on by revealing who "they" are, then another error is made: faulty pronoun reference (see pages 145 to 146).

Some subjects, such as "honesty" and "time" in our examples, do not have a physical form. Yet these abstract nouns are "things," because they do exist and we can state what they do:

Honesty pays.

Time flies.

The Verb

The VERB is usually described as an action word, such as "danced" and "flies" in our list of examples. But even in our other sentence "Roger sleeps," where there is no obvious action, the verb still tells what the subject *does*. **Other verbs, such as "is," "am" and "are," tell not what the subject *does* but what it *is*:**

> Canada *is* the second-largest country in the world.
>
> I *am* a Nova Scotian.
>
> Women and men *are* equal in law.

In statements like these, words of explanation are added to the verb. The verb plus all the words that complete its meaning are together called the **PREDICATE**. We could enlarge our definition of the sentence, then, by saying that **a complete sentence has a subject and a predicate.** Yet that predicate means nothing without its key part, the verb:

> Canada the second-largest country in the world.
>
> I a Nova Scotian.
>
> Women and men equal in law.

Some verbs are made of more than one word. Instead of saying "We *won*," we could say "We *have* won." Or we could substitute any of the following and many more:

had won	*may win*
had been winning	*might win*
were winning	*might have won*
could win	*might be winning*
could have won	*might have been winning*
did win	*would win*
have been winning	*shall win*
are winning	*will win*
do win	*will have won*
can win	*will have been winning*

Each of these, like a one-word verb, can be called a complete verb, and in the sentence each functions like a one-word verb.

Directions and *commands* are exceptions to the normal sentence pattern, since often they have only a verb. The unwritten subject is "understood":
Stop! (*You* stop!)
Begin. (*You* begin.)
Drive carefully. (*You* drive carefully.)

NAME _____

Completing Sentences: Worksheet

Try this short exercise, designed to show how natural and easy it is to provide the noun and verb. In this first part, add a noun or pronoun to form a subject and thus complete the sentence. Circle the verb.

1. A hungry _____ ate my lunch.

2. A large _____ ran down our street.

3. My _____ always chases cars.

4. Seven _____ escaped from the penitentiary.

5. _____ are really gross.

6. An old _____ slept on the park bench.

7. _____ hopes to be the next prime minister.

8. A _____ attacked the swimmer.

9. _____ keeps me awake at night.

10. A large _____ climbed the tree.

In this second part, add a verb to complete the sentence. Circle the subject.

1. I usually _____ on weekends.

2. The team always _____ before the game.

3. The crowd _____ the band.

4. His dog always _____ on the chair.

5. My uncle and aunt _____ their money in Las Vegas.

6. The dog _____ the cat.

7. After the film we _____ at a restaurant.

8. The riot police _____ the demonstrators.

9. I _____ all night before the final exam.

10. After the game the fans _____ the referee.

Variations on the Sentence
Reverse Sentence Order

The subject usually comes before the verb, an arrangement that helps us to identify both. Do not be confused, though, by the occasional sentence that puts the verb before the subject:

> V   S
> At last *came spring*.

> V   S
> In the car *were* five *gangsters*.

Just remember that the *subject* is what the sentence is about, while the *verb* tells what the subject does or is. Think of the sentence in normal word order, to make sure it has both a subject and verb:

> S   V
> *Spring came* at last.

> S   V
> Five *gangsters were* in the car.

Compound Subjects and Verbs

A sentence may have two or more subjects:

> S   S
> *Summer* and *fall* are Quebec's best seasons.

A sentence may also have two or more verbs:

> V   V
> Spring *comes* late and *is* short.

A sentence may have two or more subjects and two or more verbs:

> S   S V   V
> *May* and *June are* beautiful but *go* too fast.

Do not make fragments by separating the parts of a compound subject or verb:

SENTENCE	FRAGMENT
May and June are beautiful.	But go too fast.

Longer Sentences

To discuss sentences longer than our example so far, we need more concepts:

A. A **PHRASE** is a word group that does not contain both a subject and a complete verb. Alone, it is a fragment:

> waiting for spring
> night and day
> after the robbery

To make sense, these must be added to a complete sentence:

> S   V
> *Waiting for spring*, Jane studied *night and day*.

> S   V
> The gangsters escaped *after the robbery*.

These phrases now do a job, giving more detail to explain the core sentence.

B. A **CLAUSE** is a word group that has both a complete verb and its subject:

• An **independent clause** can stand alone as a sentence:

> Spring arrived.
> Jane studied.
> The gangsters escaped.

• A **dependent clause** cannot stand alone as a sentence. By itself it is a **fragment**:

> though spring arrived
> while Jane studied
> when gangsters escape

(See pages 99 to 101 for a fuller explanation of dependent clauses.)

C. Longer sentences, then, can be made of several combinations:

• A **compound sentence** has two or more independent clauses, usually joined by words such as "and" or "but":

> S V   S   V
> Spring arrived and summer followed.

> S V   S   V
> Jane studied but Roger slept.

```
      S         V        S         V
The police came but the gangsters escaped.
```

• A **complex sentence** has at least one independent clause and at least one dependent clause:

INDEPENDENT CLAUSE	DEPENDENT CLAUSE
Canadians rejoice	when spring arrives.

DEPENDENT CLAUSE	INDEPENDENT CLAUSE
Since she is determined,	Jane studies.

• A **compound-complex** sentence has two or more independent clauses and at least one dependent clause:

INDEPENDENT CLAUSE	DEPENDENT CLAUSE
The gangsters escaped	after they robbed the bank, but

INDEPENDENT CLAUSE	DEPENDENT CLAUSE
the police caught them	when they were at the next bank.

In any combination of clauses, *phrases* such as "at noon" or "in the car" may be added to help explain the clauses.

In summary, it is mainly these patterns that give sentences length, variety and versatility. Remember, though, that any combination of word groups, to be a complete sentence, must have at least one independent clause. As we said at the beginning, it will have *a subject and a verb*.

Causes of Sentence Fragments

Now that we have examined the basic parts of the sentence, let's look at the most common ways in which those parts are omitted or are prevented from doing their work.

A. Fragments can lack a subject or verb, or both, because of plain old *carelessness*:

Am a Blue Jays fan. (no subject)
I a Blue Jays fan. (no verb)

Such errors are usually caused by hurry or by fatigue, and can be caught more easily later as you edit. If you make fragments this way, be especially careful in your editing and in your proofreading. When you are checking, *don't let your eyes glide along the lines. Make them stop at every word*, because when you read fast your mind will supply words that your eyes do not see. *Try isolating sentences from each other by checking the final sentence first, then the second-to-last, and so on from back to front. Try reading aloud, so your ears can help your eyes.*

The correction for careless fragments, then, is of course to supply the missing word(s):

```
S V
I am a Blue Jays fan.
```

B. Fragments can occur *when writing is confused with speech*. As we saw in the little dialogue that opens this section, fragments may be fine in speech but serious errors in writing. If you listen too much to that inner voice in your head, you will end up writing as you speak. The result will be fragments like these:

Maybe.
One more point.
No way.

Do not rely on speech, then, as your model for writing. Instead, take other peoples' writing as your model. This means turning the TV off and reaching often for a newspaper, magazine or book. (See p. 211 for a suggested list of novels.)

C. Other fragments result from a deeper cause: *unfamiliarity* with sentence structure. Most people with this problem have not read enough to have control of their own writing. Again, the solution is reading. Over the long term, one of the best investments you can make in your future is to read regularly—an hour or two a day outside of studies. However, if you are only now beginning the reading habit, then the short-term solution is to study and apply the points that follow.

Fragments: More Causes and Remedies
Participles, Gerunds and Infinitives

Some words *look* like verbs but are not. Used as verbs, they produce fragments. **A present PARTICIPLE is a verb form ending in -*ing*:**

Roger *sleeping.*

This fragment does not state anything clearly because it lacks a real verb. (Though "sleeping" is a kind of verb, note how it does not tell us *when* the action occurs. In English, all complete verbs specify a tense—that is, a time period—whether past, present or future.) Now let's try some verbs that do this:

Roger *is* sleeping.
Roger *was* sleeping.
Roger *has been* sleeping.
Roger *could have been* sleeping.

Do not confuse present participles with gerunds. **A GERUND looks like a present participle but is used as a noun.** It can be the subject of a sentence:

S   V
Sleeping is Roger's hobby.

An INFINITIVE is the word "to" plus a verb:

Roger *to sleep.*

This confusing little statement is a fragment, because the subject, Roger, lacks a real verb. Let's try some:

Roger *wants* to sleep.
Roger *has* to sleep.
Roger *decided* to sleep.

Now the infinitive *to sleep* is part of a complete verb (*wants to sleep*) that completes its sentence.

Fragments caused by infinitives occur most often in lists like this one:

This essay has three purposes. To describe the computer in its earliest forms. To explain the functions of a modern computer. And to show how mass production has lowered the price of this extraordinary machine.

Let's punctuate the list as one sentence so that the subject and verb, *essay has*, make all that follows complete:

This *essay has* three purposes: to describe the computer in its earliest forms, to explain the functions of a modern computer, and to show how mass production has lowered the price of this extraordinary machine.

Note that although an infinitive cannot be a complete verb, it can be the subject of a sentence:

S   V
To sleep is Roger's wish.

Relative Pronouns

Relative pronouns (*who, whose, whom, which, that*) can be a problem. As the name suggests, **a RELATIVE PRONOUN *relates* word groups to each other:**

INDEPENDENT CLAUSE	DEPENDENT CLAUSE
Some teachers work too much,	*which* tires them out.

Make sure, then, that you do not break the *relationship* by putting a period before the relative pronoun:

INDEPENDENT CLAUSE	FRAGMENT
Some teachers work too much.	Which tires them out.

The resulting fragment is corrected, of course, by removing the period and restoring the comma. Like this one, most fragments involving a relative pronoun are corrected by being joined to the previous sentence.

Sometimes, though, a relative pronoun does not belong in its sentence at all:

FRAGMENT

Surprisingly, with education becoming so popular *that* a university degree is no longer enough to guarantee a job.

Getting a good night's sleep is the best way to avoid errors like this. If you discover such a fragment, remove the relative pronoun:

SENTENCE

Surprisingly, with education becoming so popular, a university

S   V
degree is no longer enough to guarantee a job.

Subordinators

Certain words can change a sentence to a fragment. **Put before a subject and verb, these words will *subordinate*, or make less important, what follows. We can, therefore, call these words *subordinators*.** They produce the *dependent clauses* which, as we said on page 97, cannot stand alone as sentences. There are several kinds of subordinators:

- *Words of time relationship*: as, after, as long as, before, till, until, when, whenever, while

- *Words of logical relationship*: although, as if, as though, because, even though, except that, if, in order that, since, so that, though, unless, whereas, whether, why

- *The words "where" and "wherever"*

The examples in the following table show how these words can instantly subordinate sentences into fragments.

SENTENCE	FRAGMENT
The sun rose.	*While* the sun rose
We ate breakfast.	*As* we ate breakfast
We packed the canoe.	*After* we packed the canoe
We pushed off from shore.	*When* we pushed off from shore
The river was high.	*Even though* the river was high
We entered the rapids.	*When* we entered the rapids
The canoe hit a rock.	*Where* the canoe hit a rock
The canoe tipped over.	*So that* the canoe tipped over
We swam.	*After* we swam
We could grab a log.	*Until* we could grab a log
It was fastened to the shore.	*Because* it was fastened to the shore
We dried out.	*As* we dried out
We discussed next summer's mountain climbing trip.	*While* we discussed next summer's mountain climbing trip

The sentences on the left make sense, because they are self-contained. The fragments on the right do not make sense, though, because their subordinators tell us to expect more. (Read the fragments aloud to feel their lack of meaning.) What should we do, then, to correct the fragments? Let's look at two basic alternatives:

- *Remove the subordinator.* This simple method gives us what we began with, the complete sentences on the left. Our fragments are now corrected. But have you noticed how short these sentences are, and how choppy they would sound together? Read them aloud: the story will make you think of your grade one reader.

Removing a subordinator, then, can correct a fragment here and there, but usually there is a better way:

- *Combine fragments with sentences.* You've no doubt noticed how some of the examples belong together logically: one explains another or follows another in time. Subordinators are *signals* that point out these relationships. As you proofread a paper, realize that *a fragment beginning with a subordinator will almost always belong to either the sentence before or after it.* Join the two, in most cases just by changing a period to a comma and the following capital to a small letter. This gives us a *complex sentence*, whose pattern we discussed on page 98: an independent clause with a dependent clause. Let's try the pattern, taking a sentence and a dependent clause (fragment) from our list:

DEPENDENT
CLAUSE

S   V   _____

The sun rose *as* we ate breakfast.

DEPENDENT
CLAUSE

S   V   _____

We ate breakfast *as* the sun rose.

DEPENDENT
CLAUSE

_____   S   V

As the sun rose, we ate breakfast.

DEPENDENT CLAUSE

_____   S   V

As we ate breakfast, the sun rose.

Finally, here is a point that confuses some people: are these last two examples fragments because the subordinator comes before everything else? They sound complete. And they are, because a subordinator affects only the words to which its meaning applies:

SUBORDINATED

_____   S   V

As the sun rose, we ate breakfast.

SUBORDINATED

_____   S   V

As we ate breakfast, the sun rose.

Note that the subordination usually ends at a comma, after which a subject and verb complete the sentence.

> Since we can usually correct a fragment by joining it to a neighbouring sentence, *we could describe most fragments as punctuation errors: periods in the wrong places*. Don't take this idea to extremes, though, by simply avoiding periods for fear of making fragments. (The next section will show the bad effects of using *too few* periods.)

Now let's look at a new version of the whole list:

We ate breakfast *while* the sun rose. *After* we packed the canoe, we pushed off from shore. The river was high. *When* we entered the rapids, the canoe hit a rock and tipped over. We swam *until* we could grab a log fastened to the shore. *As* we dried out, we discussed next summer's mountain-climbing trip.

The story is now correct and reasonably clear. It might do for a diary or postcard, but we can hardly call it a work of art. To become a developed piece of writing it needs all the expansion, focus and purpose discussed in the opening parts of this book. And if it is to please us with its style, it will then need the kind of extensive editing discussed in the rest of this section.

"Correctness" alone is certainly not enough. Our readers do require it, but if the larger purposes of writing are not met, no degree of correctness will convey our message. Eliminating error is essential, but is only one part of the writing process.

NAME _____

Complete Sentences: Diagnostic

Write "F" in the blank beside each passage that contains a fragment. In sentences already complete, underline the subject and circle the verb.

1. Running up the escalator to save those extra seconds, so I could catch the next train. _____

2. Who are the homeless? They are people just like you and me. All with similar needs and desires. _____

3. Though not all television programs are suitable for children. _____

4. Ignoring my injured leg, I continued to practice. _____

5. For example, blood cancer. _____

6. After changing into work clothes, which consist of longjohns, two pairs of work socks, a heavy sweater, overalls, a safety belt, a hard hat and safety boots. _____

7. Think about how terrible pollution is getting. No more swimming in the river. No more swimming in the lake. _____

8. Spider webs on the ceiling, ripped wallpaper, dirty ashtrays and old carpets that spew dust when a person steps on them. _____

9. I really believe that some dreams have an effect on us, either good or bad. _____

10. By owning a computer gives you an edge in the world. _____

11. Crowds of people everywhere in the streets, in the subway and restaurants. The frenzy of people rushing around racing to get to their destination. _____

12. Just imagine: every summer thousands of tourists pouring into Toronto. Hotel and restaurant businesses booming, vendors everywhere, gift shops on every corner, little cafés on the beaches. _____

13. When bringing groceries from a car into a house is a very easy task. _____

14. Winter is a time when the trees are bare and people wear heavy coats to keep warm. _____

15. City people always seem to be late for something. Always trying to get where they're going as fast as possible. Never stopping to see what is around them. Never thinking for one instant how great it is to be alive. _____

16. Anorexia nervosa, a term for a disease that results in self-starvation. _____

17. Although I cannot imagine my life without my family. _____

18. Some families send their children to weekend heritage classes. In part, to stimulate appreciation for their own culture or as a supplement to what the children learn at home. _____

19. If war is the last resort, and if the cause is just, then Canada would probably get involved. _____

20. If teenagers don't have strong guidance from their parents, they will follow their peers to seek life on the street. A life full of excitement and danger. _____

21. By not depending on a man for my financial welfare meant that I had to decide how I was going to look after myself. _____

22. Classification in the movie industry can be both good and bad. Good because it helps us to decide what type of movie we want to see. Bad because it doesn't leave room for individual or creative movies that cannot fit into the five main rating categories. _____

23. I knew that at some moment I would have to confront my doctor about the swelling and the pain in the lower left side of my back. _____

24. No little brothers or sisters running around driving you up the wall, and no older ones to boss you around. _____

25. Christmas Eve the worst time to go shopping. _____

26. AIDS is essentially a disease of the immune system. Because it destroys the very mechanisms that we rely on for protection. _____

27. The basic sports fan who sits in front of the television set, with eyes glued to the tube, moving only when necessary to grab a can of beer. _____

28. To avoid robbery, it is wise not to wear too many valuables such as jewelry. Especially when you are in New York City. _____

29. Educating new drivers is more important than fining them, because after an accident everything is too late. _____

30. Petroleum refineries produce two major things that we need to survive. Fuel and plastics. _____

31. In this present age, teenagers have to overcome the peer pressures around them. The pressures to smoke, to join gangs and to fight. _____

32. Everyone has his or her choice in music. Ranging from opera to blues, from reggae to hard rock, and from jazz to country. _____

33. Have you been to the Hub lately? Located on the first floor of Jorgenson Hall, a cafeteria that serves most of the off campus students. _____

34. Ever since I can remember I have had a sweet tooth. From fruit flavoured gum drops, to milk chocolate candy bars. I loved it all! _____

35. As I focus the picture in my mind, imagining myself behind a huge office desk, at the helm of a huge company, slouched into a lazyboy office chair, looking out the window from the fifty-first floor of my newly acquired company office tower. _____

NAME _____

Complete Sentences: Worksheet, Level 1

Underline the complete sentences. Correct all the fragments, adding or changing words or punctuation where necessary.

Example: ~~Garbage~~ in the streets. *I saw garbage*

1. Tourism being the number one employer in Canada and the world.

2. My mother, a 51-year-old woman who looks 35.

3. In the rain forest many species of mammals, reptiles, insects, birds and fish.

4. A federal election is divided into four stages. Enumeration, revision, advance voting and election day.

5. Looking out my window, up at the bright twinkling stars.

6. My cousin, who is in her thirties and doesn't want to get married.

7. I heard screams of fear as the roller coaster unleashed its power.

8. Because the stores open on Sunday.

9. When people are drunk they do things that normally they would not. For instance, race cars.

10. My father, a professional worrier.

11. Women or men who are qualified to work at a certain job.

12. Cars constantly moving every which way, horns honking and people yelling out of their windows.

13. Vancouver is experiencing an employment crisis. Which leaves many people on the streets. Lining up at food banks.

14. Joseph, a problem teenager who ran away from home after a big quarrel with his parents.

15. When the sun begins to set. The sky changes its colour.

16. Sports fans, a group of people screaming and yelling when a goal is scored or a penalty is called.

17. To work your way to the top and feel satisfied once you are there.

18. "Murder-Ball," a fighting game that I will never in my life forget.

19. Deep black smoke poured from the house across the street.

20. People pushing each other to get by.

21. It was challenging to sit in the upper level of a double decker bus. When sometimes it felt like the bus was going to tip over during a sharp turn.

22. If you peeped in Carol's bedroom you would be shocked. Clothes everywhere, shoes, books, papers everywhere, an unmade bed, a terrible sight.

23. Many teens flee their homes to escape a number of problems. For example abusive parents, cruelty from family members, or alcoholism.

24. Since many physicians have concluded that high-fibre foods can protect people against many diseases such as cancer and cardiovascular disease.

25. When you first walk into the Olive Garden you are greeted by a very warm and homely smile. The kind that you receive only from your dearest friends and family.

NAME _____

Complete Sentences: Worksheet, Level 2

Underline all the complete sentences. Correct all the fragments, adding or changing words or punctuation where necessary.

1. Ah, cruising down the Don Valley Parkway in a 1996 Suzuki Jeep.

2. The pushing and shoving of people trying to get on the subway, packing one another into a boxcar like a herd of cattle going into the city.

3. I cannot speak of Toronto without mentioning Yonge Street. The longest street in the world. Much action goes on there at night. Especially between Bloor and College. Street kids, prostitutes, drunks, people shopping, others working. A very typical scene on Yonge Street.

4. Every kind of person was downtown that night: punkers with pink and green Mohawk haircuts, leather fanatics, and men singing songs about dreams that would never come true.

5. When I think of Montreal, I always picture St.-Denis Street. Especially between Ste.-Catherine and Ontario. That was my favourite place. A very French district of Montreal. Where you can smell the odour of strong coffee and the famous Gitanes cigarettes.

6. Although most Canadians outside Quebec do not speak French, and are not very aware of Quebec's role in Canada. Most Quebeckers can speak both English and French, and are not ignorant of the rest of Canada.

7. As I walked down the street peering in the windows at electronic equipment and fashionable clothing, thinking how nice everything looked, wishing I could have it all.

8. The day you start wailing in the hospital signifies the beginning of your life. A life that can lead to rocky patches, unexpected turns, and constant stops and starts.

9. Trips with your family create memories. That you can look back on and cherish. Even if you went to see your aunt in Sudbury or drove on the Cabot Trail. It was or can be a time to spend and get to know each other all over again. All in an automobile.

10. Wives and husbands, parents and children, all laughing, chatting and having fun browsing in the stores, looking at exciting new merchandise and making their purchase decisions together.

11. On April 27, 1995 seemed to start like any other day.

12. Hearing the sound of jet fighter engines in the sky, looking up and seeing the fighters diving to bombard you. A few seconds later when the smoke and dust settle down, nothing but blood and dead bodies everywhere.

13. Hazardous materials are items we take for granted and use daily in our household chores. Items such as bleaches, glass, oven and toilet cleaners, varsol and paint removers, etc.

14. When the doctors finished with my back, they took me to the x-ray department. There they threw me on the table like a sack of potatoes.

15. For people who have never been in an abusive situation, it is not a pleasant experience to scream in silence. A silence so deafening, so all consuming, that the victims continue to be battered because they are certain their cries for help will never be heard.

16. People all around splashing in the water, tanning their bodies on the beach, and couples walking hand in hand along the shore.

17. Arguments cannot be avoided, because everyone in this world has a different background and education.

18. Oh, yes, the plate of cookies and glass of milk that the children leave out for Santa Claus when he comes on Christmas Eve to bring goodies to fill the stockings and give the presents that he's read about in the letters.

19. Canada without Quebec would become more Americanized. With Canadians already under the influence of American television, cars, politics, and even the American economy.

20. Coyote chasing after the Road Runner; Coyote falling off the cliff or being squashed by a boulder. Sylvester trying to eat Tweety Bird and always failing, with Sylvester falling out of the building or being run over by a car.

NAME _____

Complete Sentences: Worksheet, Level 3

Underline all complete sentences below. Then correct all the fragments, adding or changing words or punctuation where necessary.

1. A friend of mine who was eating at the school cafeteria for one year, and in that time he gained 50 pounds.

2. The famous electric can opener with "reliable rotating engine, high speed cutting heads, easy to clean lever, and high quality galvanized steel frame," all guaranteed never to fall apart.

3. Irate clients wanting their cheques cashed, unsatisfied customers requesting closure of their accounts, couriers picking up banking statements for companies. Just another uneventful day at the bank.

4. How strange it is to see a lake without life. Its crystal clear waters unable to sustain even the simplest life forms.

5. If technology could invent a hologram of the places we would want to visit, or if we could rent a video that gave a tour of the place. Would people stay home instead of travelling?

6. We often hear of parents who leave teenagers home alone to go on holiday. Only to return home and find that some disaster has occurred in their absence.

7. Sooner or later almost everybody buys a car. A choice that is difficult to make. An investment that loses money, because the value of the car decreases day by day. A decision that leads to environmental tragedy as well.

8. In the First World children have the right to leave home and become independent as soon as they reach age 16. After which, some would rarely return home to visit their parents. Why, then, would parents want to have any children?

9. Before us was a 15-foot hydraulic rapid waiting to consume our raft. Everyone paddled wildly, then, pow, we hit, and hundreds of gallons of water rushed over my body. Crushing my chest against the front of the raft, my head bouncing around as if it were in a washing machine.

10. In conclusion, through the great sufferings of the Haitian people, a goal of peace, democracy and a hope for the country to rise out of its state of poverty.

11. Acid rain, thousands of dead or dying lakes, pollution in the atmosphere, water and food contamination, disease, birth defects, land and wildlife devastation, the deteriorating economy, war as well as hunger in Third World countries, the Middle East crisis and the possibility of nuclear war.

12. Over the next few days I took numerous tours of the island. The sugar cane fields full of people cutting the canes down by hand to make sugar and sell to the local islanders. All of the banana trees full of ripe bananas ready to be picked, and fields of pineapples growing on the ground in clumps. Driving by on the bus and seeing the cattle along the side of the road, with no fences or restrictions on where they wandered and grazed.

13. The stages of life are divided into several parts. The child, so helpless and yet so giving. The young teenager, so ardent and so full of optimism. The worker struggling to make a name, so as to be respected in a world where money and power are the true motivations. The spouse and parent, who are true confidants. And then, that final door that we fear, death.

14. The long, frustrating hours at work, coming home smelling like the special of the day and the filthy plates I took off the tables, at times doesn't seem worth it. Especially when I come home to a messy room and a desk piled up with a collection of notes to organize from three days of classes. While another list is on top of a large pile of binders and textbooks that has essays and drawings which have to be done as soon as possible.

15. As you walk down Princess Avenue, the main street of downtown Kingston, you discover the street is full of specialty shops. Army surplus, mountain equipment, art galleries, athletic stores, computer shops all packed onto one long street that flows down to the harbour.

EDITING OUT THE COMMA SPLICE AND FUSED SENTENCE

To "splice" a rope is to fasten two or more parts into one. To "fuse" pieces of steel is to melt them to each other, as in welding. Such procedures are good in manufacture and repair, but not in writing the sentence. **Joining independent clauses (or, roughly speaking, "sentences") with nothing but a comma produces a *comma splice*. Jamming the sentences together with no punctuation or connecting word at all creates a *fused sentence*.**

Why do most readers perceive these as serious errors? Because by omitting the right punctuation or clear joining words, *we fail to show the relationship between thoughts*. The result is confusion. How would you like to read an essay made of sentences like this?

> Cuba is my favourite holiday spot before I went to Barbados.

In this double sentence melted together, we can hardly tell whether the writer went first to Cuba or to Barbados. Signalling the logic with punctuation makes all the difference:

> Cuba is my favourite holiday spot. Before, I went to Barbados.

It is true that some readers no longer object to the comma splice in informal writing. Sometimes a novelist, such as Margaret Atwood, will even use it on purpose for special effects. But most experienced writers of essays will be sure to edit the *comma splice*, and its cousin the *fused sentence*, out of their drafts.

Though these two defects are widespread, you can avoid them if you learned in the previous section to identify independent and dependent clauses (review if necessary). *This section now examines four main ways to edit a comma splice or fused sentence out of your writing.*

COMMA SPLICES

1. Spanish is easy, German is hard.
2. I applied early, I got the job.
3. Income tax favours the poor, sales tax favours the rich.

FUSED SENTENCES

1. Spanish is easy German is hard.
2. I applied early I got the job.
3. Income tax favours the poor sales tax favours the rich.

Apart from rewriting the whole thing, there are four easy ways to correct a comma splice or fused sentence:

A. **Put a *period* between the independent clauses:**

1. Spanish is easy. German is hard.
2. I applied early. I got the job.
3. Income tax favours the poor. Sales tax favours the rich.

This method may be easiest but is not always best. Rather than joining the independent clauses, it separates them, which in many cases can hide the logic of their relationship to each other. Besides, having many short sentences produces a choppy style.

B. **Join the independent clauses with a *coordinator* (*and, but, for, or, so, yet*):**

1. Spanish is easy, *but* German is hard.
2. I applied early, *so* I got the job.
3. Income tax favours the poor, *but* sales tax favours the rich.

Your writing improves when you choose the joining word that best displays your meaning. Do not always reach for "and"; it may be easy to use but is so vague that it can mean almost nothing. Instead, choose "but" to show contrast, "or" to show an alternative, "so" to show cause and effect, etc.

(See above how the comma goes *before* the coordinator, not *after*. If the "sentence" before the connecting word is short enough, the comma can be left out. For example this might be done in numbers 1 and 2, but probably not 3.)

C. **Reduce one of the independent clauses to a dependent clause by putting a *subordinator* before it:**

1. *Although* Spanish is easy, German is hard.
2. *Since* I applied early, I got the job.
3. Income tax favours the poor, *while* sales tax favours the rich.

(Note that a comma usually joins the dependent and independent clauses, though it may be left out when the first word group is short.)

Choose the subordinator that most exactly shows your logic. Here are more, with some of the most useful in bold print:

after	*so that*
although	***though***
as	*till*
as long as	***unless***
because	*until*
before	*when*
even though	*where*
except that	*whereas*
if	*whether*
since	***while***

(For more on using subordinators, review pages 99 to 101.)

D. **When two independent clauses are closely related in meaning, and especially when they are also balanced in form, join them with a *semicolon*:**

1. Spanish is easy; German is hard.
2. Income tax favours the poor; sales tax favours the rich.

For most people the hardest comma splices and fused sentences to avoid are those followed by certain joining words called *conjunctive adverbs*:

also	*instead*
anyway	*likewise*
besides	*nevertheless*
consequently	*otherwise*
furthermore	*similarly*
however	*still*
indeed	***therefore***
in fact	*thus*

(The three worst offenders, which together cause up to half of all comma splices, are boldfaced.) The words in this list do not *subordinate* what follows them, so there is no problem when they begin a sentence. But be careful when they *join* sentences: if you punctuate them like sub-ordinators, with a comma before, you will make comma splices. If you put no punctuation at all before, you will make fused sentences. Instead, the more accurate punctuation is a semicolon *before* and a comma *after*:

1. Spanish is easy; *however*, German is hard.
2. I applied early; *therefore*, I got the job.
3. Income tax favours the poor; *however*, sales tax favours the rich.

Though these conjunctive adverbs signal your sentence logic clearly, use them sparingly to avoid a slow and heavy style that puts readers to sleep. Would you want to read an essay with a "conse-quently," "furthermore" or "nevertheless" on every line? Use the semicolon sparingly, too, for it is also heavy and slow. (See page 127 for more dis-cussion of these words and of semicolons.)

Finally, in identifying comma splices and fused sentences in the exercises that follow, concentrate on the independent clauses and their proper join-ing or separation. Do *not* be distracted by phrases or dependent clauses that may occur before, between or after the independent clauses. These expanded versions of example 1 still contain in-dependent clauses improperly joined:

COMMA SPLICE

Spanish is easy, *because the grammar is uncom-plicated*, German is hard.

ONE POSSIBLE CORRECTION

Spanish is easy, *because the grammar is uncom-plicated*; German is hard.

FUSED SENTENCE

Spanish is easy German is hard, *because its gram-mar is complex*.

ONE POSSIBLE CORRECTION

Spanish is easy, but German is hard, *because its grammar is complex*.

Remember: If you change a comma splice by just removing the comma, you create a fused sentence. If you change a fused sentence by just adding a comma, you create a comma splice.

A Special Case: Punctuation and Quotations

Many people whose punctuation is otherwise good may suddenly "lose it" when writing research essays. They think that somehow, when they add quoted words to their own sentences, the principles of punc-tuation are suspended.

Nothing could be further from the truth. Except for adding the required quotation marks, when you join a quotation to your own sentence *you should in most cases punctuate as if all the words were yours*.

A TYPICAL CASE from an actual essay:

Raoul Cedras gave a challenge to the Americans "We are ready for combat."

It is not hard to identify two independent clauses (or "sentences") here, jammed together at the first quotation marks. But the fact that the right half was said by someone else, a Haitian general, makes no difference: the lack of punctuation is still an error, a *fused sentence*. Could we put in a comma?

Raoul Cedras gave a challenge to the Americans, "We are ready for combat."

Despite still having the quotation marks, it is clear that now we have only traded one error for another: the same two "sentences" are now joined by nothing but a comma (*comma splice*).

When choosing punctuation to use with a quotation, do not take as your model the "speech tags" found in dialogue. Though in fiction a comma does often introduce a quotation ("Then she said, 'Drop dead'"), this is a special case used mainly to identify the speaker.

And though we know a period can go between independent clauses, surely something different is needed here, to signal how the writer's words *introduce* the general's words. Try a colon:

> Raoul Cedras gave a challenge to the Americans: "We are ready for combat."

Here is another typical example, from a literary paper:

> On page 121 Shields sums up the whole novel, "The real troubles in this world tend to settle on the misalignment between men and women...."

Again the problem occurs where the essay writer's words meet those of the quoted person, in this case the narrator. Quotation marks do not hide the fact that two "sentences" are just jammed together with a comma. Again, it is a colon that makes most sense, whether or not there are quotation marks:

> On page 121 Shields sums up the whole novel: "The real troubles in this world tend to settle on the misalignment between men and women...."

NAME _____

Comma Splice and Fused Sentence: Diagnostic

Write "CS" in the blank beside each comma splice and "FS" in the blank beside each fused sentence. Some examples are correct.

1. Indonesia is very large, it consists of more than 13 600 islands. _____

2. Trendy clothing is something you can buy in the stores, however, style is something you are born with. _____

3. Jennifer and Tony were high school students they quit school and got married. _____

4. In the past, the computer could not do as many things as it can today. _____

5. The lake was frozen over, some boys had cleared a spot of ice and were playing hockey. _____

6. Many people do not know how to cook, therefore they end up eating junk food. _____

7. I was the eldest of three brought up in an affluent family, my father was a colonel in the Shah's army and my mother was a doctor. _____

8. I opened the mailbox to my surprise it was full. _____

9. The clock was ticking away with two minutes left in the game we were on our own five-yard line. _____

10. Sickle cell anemia is passed genetically therefore it is not contagious. _____

11. Anorexics and bulimics alike are people with a serious problem that must be dealt with in a serious manner, otherwise their lives are in danger. _____

12. The scene was horrible and unbelievable, people screamed and were helpless. _____

13. The black belt has nine levels, each level is called a dan. _____

14. Date rape is a serious crime in our society, however, it can be prevented through education. _____

15. There are some good things about living in a big city, but they don't outweigh the bad things. _____

16. On April 27 of each year since the accident, I have held a party to celebrate being alive. _____

17. Hail is nothing to be afraid of however, caution is always a good thing. _____

18. Canada is a free and multi-cultural democratic country therefore many people hope to come here and stay the rest of their lives. _____

19. Finally we arrived at the hospital we checked into the birthing area. _____

20. In high school I had no respect for books, I wrote in them and ripped pages out for reference. _____

21. I never inherit money from a rich uncle it is always the person next door who has all the _____ luck.

22. Children with permissive parents seem to be wild and crazy. _____

23. Abusive men become angry when they lose control, "violent men often try to track down _____ their wives and threaten them, or their children, if they don't come home." (Gibbs 39)

24. Driving a car makes people lazy, they no longer walk anywhere. _____

25. In law class we study about people's rights, the richer the people are the more rights they _____ have.

26. An old woman fell as she crossed the street, but the New Yorkers near her kept walking; it _____ was only when I offered a hand that she got back on her feet.

27. Education is essential in every society, it's the tool that builds a country's future economic _____ growth.

28. The basement was dark, a mouldy smell filled the air. _____

29. As we age, our metabolism slows down however, many women and men keep on eating as _____ much food as when they were young.

30. Philip Bentley had always wanted to be an artist, therefore throughout the novel, he doo- _____ dled, drew and painted.

31. The day my cousin began high school, she came home and told her parents she needed a _____ computer.

32. Dealing with the public can be a very rewarding experience, it can also be trying. _____

33. Let's imagine you are working for a strict and stingy boss, would you work diligently for this _____ person?

34. Our cedar hedge had been flattened there were tire marks across our lawn. _____

35. I swung around to catch a guy charging at me I grabbed him and threw him to the ground. _____

36. Careers are unpredictable, we never know what will be awaiting us just around the corner. _____

37. The night before my driver's test I couldn't eat or sleep, I was in a stupor. _____

38. When I think about life I envision an individual with many opportunities for happiness, _____ success, education, the list seems endless.

39. During rush hour the streets of Canton are full of bicycles, the buses travel slowly to avoid _____ hitting them.

40. Chris and I released ourselves from the seat belts, making sure we didn't have any broken _____ bones, we sighed with relief as we both seemed all right.

NAME_____

Comma Splice and Fused Sentence: Worksheet, Level 1

Correct the comma splices and fused sentences below. If an item contains no error, write "Correct" after it.

1. I looked at my fingers they were covered with blood.

2. Lies have a snowball effect, they get larger and larger.

3. The night was silent, time stood still, I had no thought of the events going on around me.

4. It was five in the morning the street was filled with broken glass.

5. I ran toward the back of the house to see what had happened.

6. Winter came, the wind was howling outside.

7. Dr. Robinson was an unpleasant man he smiled seldom.

8. Some hockey clubs have three or four goon players however, this strategy may not win games.

9. Some people view abortion as an act of murder, others view it as a solution to a problem they do not want to face.

10. Now Prince Edward Island is my favourite vacation spot before it was just another place on the map.

11. I wasn't sure of myself, I thought she would laugh at me.

12. Even with government help, student finances are tight.

13. I was shocked I didn't know what to do.

14. In a few minutes the dentist came in she put on a mask and a pair of gloves.

15. I knew I was caught. The cops came over to where I was hiding, they were very large and very angry.

16. I was stressed out, I needed to slow down and be in control again.

17. Children are impressionable, they believe everything they hear.

18. My summer job pays for my tuition and books, working Sundays provides me with pocket money for the week.

19. In the past, bicycles were made to last a lifetime.

20. It was a beautiful July day in Edmonton there was no sign of rain and not a cloud in the sky.

21. I couldn't stop crying during the movie, I was a little embarrassed.

22. Night people simply like to accomplish their tasks at night therefore they need more sleep in the morning.

23. In winter the Northern Hemisphere is tilted away from the sun, spreading the rays over a greater distance; therefore, the temperature falls.

24. The town is in a valley, there are snow-covered mountains on both sides.

25. In our society there is an ever increasing amount of crime the police cannot be everywhere at once.

26. I really hope we start to recognize Canadian singers, there are many of them and they are just as good as the Americans.

27. Rush hour was busy, this made the trains very crowded, we must have waited for three trains till we got on one of them.

28. New York City was just a mess, there were people living in broken-down houses and run-down apartments, there were potholes in the street and there was garbage all over the sidewalks.

29. We were a quarter of a mile away when we heard 10 or 15 shots we turned around to see a wave of human beings heading in our direction. We heard more shots and the wave built, there were women screaming and men shouting as a cloud of dust rose behind them.

30. Many business people choose to wear glasses to give them a more professional look, some wear them even if the glasses are non-prescription.

NAME _____

Comma Splice and Fused Sentence: Worksheet, Level 2

Correct the comma splices and fused sentences below. Don't bother to recopy the passages if you can just change punctuation or add the right joining word above the line. If an item contains no error, write "Correct" after it.

1. Some people drive like maniacs, they do not stop at red lights, they speed as if to win an award.

2. I loved the scent of the double cheese spewing from the sides of the pizza box, and the grease dripping from my fingers was enough to drive me into a frenzy.

3. For a thrill, a laugh, a lesson or a reason for a date, go to the movies.

4. Credit allows you to buy now and pay later, once you sign, that stereo, shirt or whatever it is you want, is yours to take home immediately.

5. Cash offers worry-free payment, there are no interest charges or end of month horrors, once the payment is made it can be forgotten.

6. It does not matter how successful you are if your luck turns bad you may be the next homeless person.

7. Trees are the anchors of the earth when they are cut down the soil is washed away.

8. I could not put pressure on my foot, therefore, I could not walk, run or dance.

9. In Somalia our home was close to the beach I knew quite well how to swim the raging waves, the technique I used was not to struggle with the waves, I just followed them.

10. We took the F train to downtown Manhattan, when we got off I was almost run over by a police officer he told me to get out of his way the next time.

11. Cats snuggle up to the owner for only one thing, food; otherwise, they just play around or get into mischief.

12. I was sitting in the front of the stalled van when I saw the train, with my heart pounding I shouted to the others to get out.

13. Solitude scares the narrator and leaves her feeling shallow inside, "The river slips past, unperturbed by our coming and going."

14. Mrs. Bentley uses the word "seized" again "he seized the pipe, slammed out of the kitchen with it, and threw it in the fire."

15. When I saw 12 members of the Hells Angels stop, I was scared to death, they asked what had happened and helped to fix the bike. Then I rode with them to the next town and offered them a couple of drinks, the only problem was that their couple of drinks ran my bill up to a hundred dollars.

16. You can't hide; as long as there is wind, acid rain can reach you.

17. Every mountain rose out of the valley, yet each was distinct; some had faces where avalanches had wiped out all the trees, others were bold bare windblown slopes.

18. I was talking to another student about the protest when two explosions sent clouds of tear gas into a scattering crowd. This was the little spark that ignited the fury of the people they charged the army with bottles, stones and any piece of metal they could put their hands on.

19. Some critics felt the novel lacked sustained power, it had inconsistent ideas, some went so far as to say it was a dull book.

20. Banff is a postcard paradise, it is an incredible place to see, but don't just take my word for it ask the seven million people who visit each year.

21. AIDS is a real killer disease, it shrinks the work force, apartment occupancy and church attendance, it separates friends, destroys families and paralyzes the medical system.

22. The great feeling of freedom we get when we travel makes us receptive to the surrounding culture and country, we can touch and smell different objects, we can explore new places, we have the freedom of decision.

23. My mother arranged for me to escape from Iran, she paid an enormous amount of money to a smuggler to get me past the border and on my way to Canada.

24. We drove as far as we could, the smuggler said it would be safer to spend the day in Tabriz and leave for the border at night.

25. Finally we reached the border, from that point we could no longer drive the journey was now by foot. The howling of the winds answered the cries of the wolves that roamed the mountains. Many hours later we reached a village in Turkey, we were to endure yet another night before we reached our next destination, Istanbul.

EDITING FOR PUNCTUATION

The tiny dots and squiggles of punctuation on your page may look insignificant. They may seem like minor details. In fact some people view them as mere decorations, ornaments to be strewn here and there ("Let's throw in a comma because the last sentence didn't have one"). But how would you like to read an essay made of statements like this one found in a student paper?

> I don't smoke myself because I've tried it and don't get anything out of it.

While it may be true that few people enjoy smoking themselves, what the author had in mind was probably something more like this:

> I don't smoke, myself, because I've tried it and don't get anything out of it.

The small change in punctuation signifies a great change in meaning. And this is what punctuation is all about: the period, comma, semicolon, colon, question mark and exclamation point are above all *logic signals*: like road signs by the highway, they show us where we are going.

One problem arising from the tiny size of punctuation marks is that, if you write by hand, they may or may not end up looking like what you meant them to be. For example if you form a period by jabbing at the paper, as people in a hurry do, it might come out so long that your reader will see it as a comma. Always proofread closely for punctuation, but especially if you write by hand.

In reviewing the following summary of the main uses for punctuation, keep in mind that these small marks powerfully influence your writing for better or worse. If you select among them to highlight your logic, you are taking one of the most important steps on your writing journey.

Period (.)

A. Use a period to end a *statement* or *command*:

STATEMENT

> There is no status quo.
>
> —Diane Francis

COMMAND

> Just do it.

B. Use a period after most *abbreviations*:

> At 3 p.m. Dr. Rubright removed Mr. Gagnon's appendix.

(See also "Abbreviations," pages 207 to 208.)

Apostrophe (')

(See "Apostrophes," pages 198 to 199.)

Comma (,)

The period and comma are both heavily used. The period, though, is easy to manage, while the comma takes some real thought: it can serve in many more situations and mean many different things. The old folklore that a comma is a "breath" is to some extent true, but is a risky guide for the writer (is a period not a "breath" as well?).

Another complication: some commas are optional. One person will stuff every possible comma into a paragraph, while another will use as few as possible. Though the first preference is more traditional and the second is more modern, both are correct—which means that in using commas you will develop your own style.

As you begin this section on commas, start by reviewing pages 111 to 113 on the "**comma splice**," the most important matter of all: If you place a comma where a period should go, your reader cannot sense where one statement ends and another begins.

A. Use a comma to separate items in a *series*:

> The most productive vegetables for a small garden are beets, carrots, lettuce, onions, beans and tomatoes.

> A gardener's rewards are the glow of outdoor exercise, the pleasure of fresh air, the satisfaction of honest work, and the freshest vegetables in town.

(Most people now omit the optional comma between the last two items of a series, especially if the items are short. In the second example, though, see how the final comma contributes by separating larger word groups that might otherwise run together.)

B. If an *introductory word group* is long, use a comma to separate it from what follows. If it is short leave it unpunctuated. (Examine the preceding two sentences as examples of the rules they state.)

C. Place a comma before the *coordinator* of a *compound sentence*, unless the first independent clause is short:

The Laplanders have retained the most traditional culture of any European society, *but* modern Scandinavia has now begun to assimilate them.

A canoe is fast *but* a kayak is faster.

(Note how the comma occurs *before*, not *after*, the "but" or other coordinating word.)

D. Modifiers (to review briefly) are word groups that elaborate on a more important part of the sentence. Not everyone understands their relationship to commas. First of all, a modifier is said to be "restrictive" if it is crucial to the basic meaning of a sentence, and "nonrestrictive" if it is not. *Set off a nonrestrictive modifier with commas* to show its limited relationship to the sentence, but *leave a restrictive modifier unpunctuated* to show how its importance integrates it into the sentence.

RESTRICTIVE

Some people *infected with the HIV virus* live more than ten years.

We sense that "infected with the HIV virus" is a restrictive modifier, because without it the whole point of the statement is lost:

Some people live more than ten years.

This modifier, then, is so important that we do not want commas to distance it from the rest of the statement.

NONRESTRICTIVE

The HIV virus, *unknown a generation ago*, is changing the nature of our relationships.

Although the words "unknown a generation ago" do add information to the idea, taking them out does not drastically change the statement:

The HIV virus is changing the nature of our relationships.

Thus we do need commas at each end of this modifier (like parentheses) to signal its more distant relationship to the main idea.

E. Put a comma after the *salutation of an informal letter*:

Dear Brandon,
Dear Mom,

Use a colon, not a comma, if the letter is more formal:

Dear Ms. Jessamy:
Dear Sirs:

F. Put a comma between the date and year. A comma is optional between the month and year:

July 19, 1941
July, 1941
July 1941

G. Use a comma wherever necessary to *avoid a misreading or other ambiguity*:

AMBIGUOUS

After drinking the three men played cards. (Did the three men drink or did something drink them? We are distracted for a moment, losing time and attention, while deciding what the statement means.)

CLEAR

After drinking, the three men played cards.

AMBIGUOUS

What I really dislike is the size of the city and the people. (Are the people the wrong size?)

CLEAR

What I really dislike is the size of the city, and the people.

AMBIGUOUS

Alcohol in my eyes only adds to people's troubles. (Where is the alcohol?)

CLEAR

Alcohol, in my eyes, only adds to people's troubles.

Of course feel free to revise more thoroughly, when this produces an even clearer and more graceful version:

What I really dislike is the size of the city and the rudeness of its people.

I think alcohol only adds to people's troubles.

H. Normally, *do not place a comma between a subject and its verb.* Many student writers suffering from a condition that could be called "comma-itis" put commas in places such as this:

The ever so popular Madonna, is known for her sense of style.

Note the effect of this extra comma: it actually separates the two parts of the sentence that should be most closely connected: the subject "Madonna" and the verb "is..." which goes on to tell what we want to know about the subject. Another example:

COMMA-ITIS

S V
Our neighbour's *dog, ran* away.

REVISED

Our neighbour's *dog ran* away.

On the other hand, if expressions such as a nonrestrictive modifier (review item "D") interrupt between subject and verb, of course use a comma at both ends of the interruption (like parentheses) to separate it from the core sentence:

CORRECT

S   V
Vultures, the scavengers of death, *circle* their prey before moving in.

NAME _____

Commas: Worksheet

The passages below all appeared in actual student essays. Where you see a comma that does not belong, cross it out; where you see that a comma is needed, add it. If a passage already uses commas well, write "Correct" after it.

Example: Patients must be fed when they are too weak to eat, themselves.
                                                                    ∧

1. As I put my coat on the dentist and receptionist had a brief discussion.

2. Sharon flirted outrageously with Michael and Kenny and Jason flirted with her.

3. My brother grandfather and I had been going to the races since before I could remember.

4. North Americans, believe in eye contact.

5. The fastest sports are soccer, hockey football, rugby and basketball.

6. People in Istanbul, seem to think that hamburgers and fries are not worth eating.

7. O.J. Simpson the famous athlete, a hero to many was an abusive husband.

8. Once, I placed, a couple of lines on the paper, some thoughts, began to appear.

9. Players who fight during a game, should be suspended for the whole season.

10. Our media especially television are to blame for sexism in society.

11. If you can use cash or make your payments promptly.

12. While Dad was putting the lights on my brothers and I started to place the star on the Christmas tree.

13. Adoption, is an event that dramatically changes a child's life.

14. Children, who were victims of their parents' violent outbursts, may undergo mental illness or personality disorder when they grow up.

15. Our diet should contain dairy products rich in protein and vegetables.

16. I am amused by how fast Hollywood stars fall in love, get married, have affairs, get divorced, fall in love again, get married again and so on.

17. Shopping malls, such as the Bay and Eaton Centre attract tourists.

18. Marriage, is a big commitment.

19. If you write a word without being completely sure of how to spell it you may be making a mistake.

20. For hundreds of years English Canada, had social and political control over Quebec.

21. Although stubborn Hagar is one of Margaret Laurence's most admirable characters.

22. As I mentioned before Ontario has a low level of education.

23. When planning your holiday visit or phone the tourist information centre in your city.

24. It's no secret that a life of freedom, especially in small and less powerful countries, is a rare commodity.

25. Photo radar fails as a true safety device on our roads because the real problem, the driver who is weaving in and out of traffic cutting people off and causing accidents is not being stopped.

26. Once the needle is in the plunger is retracted to check for blood.

27. One thing that really bothers me, is the idea of a large dog being kept in the city.

28. I love to play hockey but, studies come first.

29. Alcohol has become a problem for our schools and teachers are deeply concerned.

30. The truth is that many alcoholics never seek help resulting in their own destruction.

31. As society becomes more and more prosperous, and small cities become big cities, the crime rate also increases.

32. Ham radio, has become my obsession.

33. Our friendship lasted for years, within which time we sinned, lied, cried, laughed, argued, shared and grew together.

34. Harsh lighting, produces harsh photographs.

35. My problems in math started the day I began school.

36. One of my math teachers, helped me learn, to achieve my goal, in the subject, by spending a great deal of time working with me.

37. When rivers lose their velocity suspended particles of clay and silt are deposited creating fertile soils in river deltas.

38. Brian McDonald, a youth worker in Vancouver says one of the major reasons for school violence is the "slow response of a clogged court system."

39. The last step is to record the time drug and dosage on the patient's chart.

40. I love to cook myself and eat at home.

Semicolon (;)

It is possible to live your whole life never using a semicolon. Many people do. After all, the uses of this punctuation mark are not as easy or clear as those of commas or periods. Further, some people who do use the semicolon abuse it, sprinkling five or ten of these very heavy items on each page, creating a style that feels like a herd of elephants marching through the forest. Clearly it is better not to use this punctuation mark at all than to misuse it.

On the other hand, in the right places it is eloquent and powerful. If you wish to use the semicolon, study the examples that follow:

A. Use a semicolon between independent clauses (or, roughly speaking, *between closely related "sentences"*), when there is no joining word:

Keenly, for the first time, I felt that I was a stranger in a strange land; my heart yearned intensely for my absent home.

—Susanna Moodie, *Roughing It in the Bush*

Note how the semicolon, in the middle, seems to pull the two parts together, emphasizing their close relationship. The effect is even stronger and more eloquent when the two "sentences" are not only related, but mirror each other in form:

Becoming independent is the easy part of a revolution; staying independent is the hard part.

Americans make money; Canadians count money.

B. Use a semicolon between independent clauses (that is, between "sentences") that are joined by one of these *conjunctive adverbs*. (The ones you probably use most often are boldfaced):

anyway	*instead*
besides	*likewise*
consequently	**nevertheless**
furthermore	*otherwise*
however	*similarly*
indeed	*still*
in fact	**therefore**

The most heavily exposed parts of the negative receive the thickest deposit of silver; *therefore*, these areas appear darkest.

See how the semicolon comes *before* the joining word and the comma *after*. **Remember that** putting a comma *in front of* one of these conjunctive adverbs creates a serious error: the comma splice (if necessary, review pages 111 to 113 now).

C. Use a semicolon between *items in a series* if these items have internal punctuation:

If you borrow a garment of any kind, be sure that you will tear it; a watch, that you will break it; a jewel, that you will lose it; a book, that it will be stolen from you.

—Susanna Moodie, *Roughing It in the Bush*

D. Incorrect semicolons will harm your writing more than correct semicolons will help it. Remember that apart from separating internally punctuated items in a series, *the only normal function of a semicolon is to join independent clauses*. Avoid other uses:

• Except for the case of item C above, *do not use a semicolon as a comma*:

WRONG

As the guitar and the drums began to roar; the crowd began to scream.

BETTER

As the guitar and the drums began to roar, the crowd began to scream.

WRONG

Only two problems; the cost and the danger, limit skiing as a sport.

BETTER

Only two problems, the cost and the danger, limit skiing as a sport.

• *Do not use a semicolon as a colon*:

WRONG

There are two groups of unemployed; the undereducated and the overeducated.

BETTER

There are two groups of unemployed: the undereducated and the overeducated.

Colon (:)

The colon is a lively punctuation mark that strongly pushes the reader's attention ahead. Most student writers could exploit it more fully, adding force to their writing. Use it more often than the slower semicolon.

A. *Use the colon to formally introduce a statement,* whether your own or a quotation:

This is the main point: censorship is dangerous.

The main question is this: do taxes increase inflation?

Goethe's most famous words are his last: "Light—more light!"

This is Talleyrand's recipe for coffee:

> Black as the devil,
> Hot as hell,
> Pure as an angel,
> Sweet as love.

Of course quotations, especially short ones worked into your own sentence, may also be introduced by the comma:

On his deathbed Goethe said, "Light—more light!"

B. For *emphasis,* use a colon to introduce even a single word:

Scrooge loved only one thing: money.

C. Use a colon *when a second statement explains a first:*

The climate is changing: by the year 2050 our winters will be noticeably warmer.

D. Probably the best-known use of the colon is to *formally introduce a series:*

The cylinders of a V-8 engine fire in this order: 1, 8, 4, 3, 6, 5, 7, 2.

Here is one point of style commonly ignored, but usually followed by careful writers: in introducing a series, do not place a colon right after the verbs *is, are, was* or *were,* or after the words *of* or *to,* because this separates closely related parts of the sentence.

WEAK

The causes of inflation *are*: low productivity, high wages, depletion of resources, and government debt.

BETTER

The causes of inflation *are* low productivity, high wages, depletion of resources, and government debt.

BETTER

These *are* the causes of inflation: low productivity, high wages, depletion of resources, and government debt.

BETTER

The causes of inflation *are* as follows: low productivity, high wages, depletion of resources, and government debt.

E. Put a colon *after the salutation of a formal letter:*

Dear Ms. Vargas:	Dear Concha,
	BUT
Dear Sir:	Dear Grandpa,

Question Mark (?)

The question mark may seem easy to use, but actually it causes many little errors. Be sure to put it where it belongs, and guard against putting it where it does not belong. *Place a question mark after a direct question but not after an indirect question.*

DIRECT QUESTIONS

What time is it?

I asked myself, "Would I help a person being attacked on the street?"

INDIRECT QUESTIONS

I wonder what time it is.

I asked myself whether I would help a person being attacked on the street.

Notice how the direct questions are the *exact words of a question,* while the indirect ones merely *report* a question. If you would not ask "What time it is?" or "Whether I would help?" then you know they are indirect, and therefore do not require question marks.

WRONG

When I reached home I asked my mother what was happening? (Omit the question mark after this indirect question, *or* make the question direct.)

BETTER

When I reached home I asked my mother, "What is happening?"

WRONG

Why is car insurance so high. (The person who wrote this may have sensed it was a direct question, but just forgot the question mark. Many little errors are made like this: proofread to catch them.)

BETTER

Why is car insurance so high?

Exclamation Point (!)

In the comics, even the most ordinary statement by Bugs Bunny or Superman or the latest alien or monster will end with an exclamation point—or even a whole row of them. At first this tactic may heighten the readers' attention (!!!!!), but soon these punctuation marks become so common, so cheap, that they mean nothing at all. It is better to save this strongest of all punctuation for the strongest expressions of feeling. To end an ordinary statement with an exclamation point is to swat a fly with a sledge hammer.

A. Use an exclamation point to express *strong emotion* such as fear, anger or sorrow:

"Save me!" he cried, "I'm drowning!"

Ruin seize thee, ruthless King!
—Thomas Gray, "The Bard"

Alas! alas! that ever love was sin!
—Chaucer, "The Wife of Bath's Prologue"

B. Do *not* try to make an ordinary statement exciting by adding an exclamation point. Avoid excesses such as this:

When the fair is about a month away, farmers begin to clean their livestock. First the cows are hosed down with warm water and soap in order to get their hair as clean as possible! After the hair is rinsed, a blow dryer is used, along with a comb, to get the hair as fluffy as possible! In some places, styling is needed to make the hair go the right way!

NAME_____

Semicolon, Colon, Question Mark and Exclamation Point: Worksheet

These examples were found in actual student essays. Wherever a semicolon, colon, question mark or exclamation point is wrong, or wherever it is needed but missing, fix it. (Sometimes there is more than one item per sentence to change.) If a passage is already well punctuated, write "correct" after it.

1. At Yonge and Bloor there are many Chinese, Italian, Jamaican and Japanese fast food restaurants!

2. Since I had arrived early and knew the area well; I went to a nearby doughnut shop for a cup of coffee.

3. A person cannot get AIDS from: telephones, toilet seats, swimming pools, whirlpools, hugging, sharing glasses or dishes, buses and subways, kissing, or mosquitoes.

4. How can a teenager resist wanting to look as great and as happy as the models in magazines.

5. The computer will ask if you are ready to send your message?

6. There are two parties involved in an option contract; the writer, who sells the contract, and the holder, who buys the contract.

7. Traits of violent children include: low self-esteem, impulsive aggression, short attention span, and, in many cases, high intelligence.

8. Living with four people I learned two things compromise and respect for others.

9. Permissive parents always say "yes"; strict parents always say "no."

10. Seven is the most popular lucky number, while 13 is considered extremely unlucky!

11. Banning guns from the public does not necessarily mean that a person who really wants a gun won't get one, however; it does prevent crimes of passion.

12. University students have many responsibilities that take a great deal of time: major research papers; employment; and family matters.

13. In Toronto two of the largest buildings are: the Eaton Centre and Commerce Court!

14. Try to analyze what kind of car you need? Is it for city driving? Are you going to use the car in your work? Do you mind the gas money, or is convenience all you care about?

15. I wonder how bus drivers put up with the rush-hour crowd every day.

16. The main advantage of working while being a student is: learning effective time management!

17. Although I was swamped with projects, essays and homework; I now know that the workload could have been worse.

18. There are five major types of energy. Mechanical, chemical, electrical, atomic and solar.

19. As soon as I saw my brother; I knew that something was wrong.

20. Wife abuse crosses geographic and income lines; can be found in both rural and urban households, and spans the diverse cultures of any given society.

21. The girls' uniform consisted of five pieces; white shirt, a tie, a green vest, a plaid skirt and a pair of green socks with the school logo embroidered on them.

22. Nowadays the thought of a couple happily married after 50 years is incomprehensible to many people; however, my Grandma and Grandpa Wilcox are living proof of a happily married couple after 50 years of togetherness.

23. "Hey buddy, got any change," is the most frequent question asked today in Halifax.

24. Bank robberies are meticulously planned to the finest detail to include: the time of the operation; the getaway route; disguises; choice of bank; and a look at police surveillance in the area.

25. On page 71 Dickens describes Stephen "He was a good power-loom weaver, and a man of perfect integrity."

26. In prison we could play: volleyball, soccer and table tennis.

27. Depending on the size of the tree; the roots may be thin or thick!

28. Even little children who can hardly skate are seen trying to copy the methods and techniques of their favourite hockey player; which usually involves some form of violence.

29. At a wedding you see bright happy colours such as: red, white, purple, green and pink. At a funeral you see dark depressing colours such as: blue, brown and black.

30. As speeders roar past, we wonder what they will hit or whose life they will take today?

31. How we all love to eat!

32. I wonder how families can afford more than one car?

33. Why is it that Canadians go south for the winter, instead of looking for something in their own backyards.

34. If I don't stop eating chocolate bars, I will soon have to be rolled around from place to place; just like a big ball.

35. Many people buy lottery tickets every week; and gamble at the race track every day; because they want to win a lot of money.

36. A hundred years ago a person looking for entertainment could not: turn on the TV, go to a movie, play a couple of hours of racquetball, or lie back and listen to the stereo.

37. In Canada we encounter four different seasons spring, summer, fall and winter.

38. Before you even start looking for a car, decide exactly how much money you are able to spend?

39. I crave the night life of the city; the bright lights, concerts, movies, cafés, shows and nightclubs.

40. The younger students walk down the long school halls with open ears, hearing what decisions the graduating students have made; dreaming that someday they will be doing the same thing.

Dash (—)

The dash, like the exclamation point, is dramatic—and, like the exclamation point, often abused. Since the dash can fit almost anywhere, some writers use it as an escape from the bother of choosing more exact punctuation. ("Let's see, do we put a colon or a semi-colon here?—oh well, let's just throw in a dash.") Some people routinely scrawl dashes between phrases, between sentences, anywhere, because this punctuation is lively, fast—and, above all, easy. Such a strategy may be fine for very informal writing such as personal letters. In essays, though, strewing dashes right and left makes the logic harder to grasp, giving a breathless and even scatterbrained impression.

On the other hand, there are times when the dash achieves an effect better than any other punctuation can. These are probably its best uses:

A. A dash can set off *parenthetical material* (extra explanation that is not crucial to the sentence) more dramatically than commas or parentheses can:

> And then—was it hours or minutes after I arrived?—he opened his eyes.
>
> —Margaret Laurence, *The Stone Angel*

B. A dash can set off and thus emphasize *a key word or phrase at the end of a sentence*:

> Only one investment will endure forever, cannot be taken from where it is, and over time will almost always increase in value—land.

Parentheses and Square Brackets ( ), [ ]

Like dashes, parentheses are almost too convenient. Some writers rely on them as substitutes for more specific punctuation, while others use them to legitimize irrelevant matter that should be cut from their writing. For these reasons, and because the clutter of parentheses can slow down your reader, this device should be used sparingly.

Note that, although square brackets appear on computer keyboards, they are limited to certain specialized situations. It is the rounded parentheses that are used in the traditional manner:

A. Use parentheses to *enclose matter that does not fit into the grammatical structure of a sentence*:

> Caligula (A.D. 12–41) was the most corrupt and tyrannical of all Roman emperors.

B. Use square brackets *in quoted material* as you would use parentheses in unquoted material:

> "Angling [fishing with line and hook] may be said to be so like the mathematics that it can never be fully learnt."
>
> —Isaak Walton, *The Compleat Angler*

Since "fishing with line and hook" is an editor's explanation, it is placed in square brackets so we will not think Isaak Walton wrote these words.

EDITING TO AVOID THE RUN-ON SENTENCE

When a sentence is a monster in length, it is a run-on. Even if it is short, but has word groups too casually stuck together with loose connections such as "and," it is a run-on.

Some people also label as run-ons the "comma splice" and "fused sentence" which we discussed on pages 111 to 113; while there is some overlap, in the present section we focus more on sheer length and on flabby connecting words.

While not as serious as its opposite error, the sentence fragment, the run-on is not good: its logic may be hidden, and in extreme cases its length will totally confuse the audience.

A. Change monster sentences by *breaking them into parts*, by *avoiding overuse of coordinators (but, for, or, so, yet, and especially and)* and *by cutting out deadwood*.

> How would you like to read a whole essay made of sentences like this?

> A hundred years ago people were not as busy as they are today, *and* they could sit down *and* write letters *and* send them to their friends *and* their business associates, *but* in our modern times people are really busy, *and* they find that writing is too much work, *so* they just pick up the telephone *and* make a call to someone else. (63 words)

Joining many thoughts loosely in one statement is something we do in speech, for we often talk faster than we think. When we write, though, our opportunity to revise leaves no reason for unorganized and wasteful language.

In our example above, not only does the repeated word **"and"** sometimes fail to make logical connections between parts, but the confusion has also allowed **deadwood** to come in. First let's look at a revision that improves only the connections:

A hundred years ago people were not as busy as they are today: they could sit down and write letters to send to their friends and their business associates. But in our modern times people are really busy. They find that writing is too much work, so they just pick up the telephone and make a call to someone else.

So far, so good. We have cut the monster sentence into three manageable parts. We have also replaced some of the "ands" with more precise connections such as good punctuation or more exact connecting words. But now let's look at a more radical revision that also cuts out the deadwood that smothers the meaning:

A hundred years ago people had time to write letters, but today we are so busy that we just pick up the telephone. (23 words)

Now we have one sentence of medium length whose parts are so tightly joined that the vague word "and" never occurs at all. In addition, the message has been shortened and concentrated by removing self-evident facts. For example when we "pick up the telephone" it is obvious that we are going to "make a call to someone else" (have you ever called yourself???). So why write it if your audience already knows it?

In revising monster sentences, do whatever you have to: adding periods or substituting better connecting words may be enough sometimes, while other times only a full rewriting will do the job. (See "Editing for Economy" on pages 57 to 61 for more on cutting deadwood.)

B. *Join the parts of even short sentences accurately.* In particular, avoid **"and"** whenever a more specific connection can be made. Our first example had

Almost all word processing software contains a strong tool for detecting overuse of "and"—or of any other term.

Learn to use the "search" function of your system, entering "and" as the word to find. (Your software may work better if you enter a space both before and after the term, so that larger words such as "sand," which contain "and" within them, will not also be identified.)

As the cursor comes to rest at each occurrence of the word, ask yourself whether this particular "and" signals a logical joining of two items (like "bacon and eggs") or whether it was applied like Crazy Glue just to hold stuff together. If the latter, now replace the "and" with a more logical word or with appropriate punctuation.

63 words. This one from a student essay has only 18 but is still a run-on:

The goalie has only one job to do *and* that is to keep the opposing players from scoring.

Here the word "and" is illogical: it implies that keeping the opposition from scoring is *in addition to* the goalie's job, when actually it *is* the job. A better connection than "and" would be a colon, since the beginning word group introduces the rest of the sentence:

The goalie has only one job to do: keep the opposing players from scoring.

> . . .AND. . .AND. . .AND. . .AND. . .AND. . .
>
> "And" is the most overused word in English. Avoid it except to show that one thing is genuinely *in addition to* another.

NAME _____

Run-on Sentence: Diagnostic

Which of the following are run-on sentences? Write "ROS" in the blank beside them. Remember that not all run-ons are long; many are short, caused by loose connections such as the often vaguely used "and."

1. In one day I went through two interviews and I was hired and asked to start the next day at six in the morning. _____

2. Our car slid into an embankment and the shock threw us forward as if we were rag dolls in the seats and fortunately for us we had our seatbelts on. _____

3. I had my first date when I was 15. _____

4. There is only one sign of my grandfather's aging, and that is a hearing problem. _____

5. I called the lab advisor over and she took a careful look at the situation and apologetically informed me that the printer was now out of order. _____

6. A dog knows when you're happy and it shows it's happy too and it knows when you're sad or hurt and it tries to show that it understands. _____

7. My niece is in grade two and all they do in school is drawing, playing outside and twice or three times a week they have spelling and math for one hour. _____

8. The purpose of e-mail in business is to improve communication and make management more efficient and it can release the manager from the boundaries of traditional office time. _____

9. How is it that we spend one-third of our lives in sleep, yet we still know so little about it? _____

10. I am somewhat clumsy and tend to miss the pass and the ball goes off the field and out of bounds. _____

11. In New York City people cannot walk the streets after 9:00 at night, because they might get mugged. _____

12. One day I decided to try and get a job and about three weeks later I was doing dishes. _____

13. Steroids are used for strength and this is seen in football and wrestling, where it is important for the athletes to be strong and have hand to hand combat with the other players. _____

14. There was only one problem with my teachers, and that was that they did not know how to teach. _____

15. When farming was the way of life, a family would have six or seven children. _____

16. The youngest of my roommates is called Sue and is still in her teens, and keeps confessing that this is her first time on her own, away from home. _____

17. Cats are much smaller than dogs and belong more in a home and they're not vicious little things like dogs. _____

18. I ordered a Hawaiian pizza and I found only four pieces of pineapple and the cheese covered only the middle of the pizza, leaving the edges with nothing but sauce.   _____

19. When inspecting your home for places where burglars may break in, check the basement windows carefully.   _____

20. I strongly believe that, to have a better world, men must make up their minds to learn to share ideas, household duties and child-care duties, and let women become more active in social and political life and accept women as their equal partners.   _____

21. I work in a store and some people come in and charge for items under one dollar.   _____

22. I know of an employee who had worked faithfully for a number of years for the company and a pay raise had never been granted.   _____

23. In the police stories we watch on television, a crime is committed and the police have a car chase and a shootout and capture the criminal.   _____

24. He threw a punch at me trying to catch me off-guard, and seeing it coming I ducked and gave him a shot to the ribs, and feeling him buckle under the punch I knew I had won the fight.   _____

25. A breakfast of bacon and eggs is filled with cholesterol.   _____

26. I saw one thing in Thailand that still gives me the shivers, and that was lizards.   _____

27. I passed the first semester of chemistry, but failed the second semester.   _____

28. Take the time to learn about the place you want to travel to and try scheduling an itinerary (leave room for surprises) and you'll find that the trip will be rewarding.   _____

29. At age 14 I decided I was ready to become part of the real world. I felt I was maturing and ready for a part-time job, and so I got one.   _____

30. The brakes failed, and suddenly the driver knew his only chance to try and save us from going over the cliff was to steer the van towards the side of the mountain.   _____

NAME _____

Run-on Sentence: Worksheet, Level 1

Inaccurate use of the word "and" is one of the main causes of run-on sentences. Below, cross out all the "ands" you can. Replace them with more exact **coordinators** *(review pages 133 and 134), with well-chosen* **subordinators** *(review pages 99–101), or with appropriate* **punctuation***. Where necessary, rewrite in the space.*

Example: I flicked the switch several times A̶N̶D̶ *but* no light came on.

1. Each day a great miracle occurs AND a newborn child enters the world.

_____

_____

2. People in the city do not try AND make contact with others.

_____

3. I have learned an important lesson in my life, AND that is, there is no need to impress anyone.

_____

_____

4. I tried with difficulty to tell the cab driver where to go, AND the cab driver did not understand me.

_____

_____

5. Love is true AND lust is false.

_____

6. The audience simply adores action AND excitement AND hockey has it in every game.

_____

_____

7. Sometimes in the middle of the night Granny can cough for an hour AND the next day she will be walking around the house with a cigarette hanging from the corner of her mouth again.

_____

_____

_____

8. My car is eight years old, AND it still looks AND drives like new.

_____

_____

9. Mom doesn't like it when I talk back AND she gets upset AND I know I have it coming.

_____

_____

10. I went up AND down all the halls, AND I still couldn't find the room.

_____

_____

11. I know one thing AND that is to fight.

_____

12. Unfortunately the bank never forgets about you, AND at the end of each month you get your statement.

_____

_____

13. In the social work program more than 1000 people applied, AND fewer than 300 were accepted.

_____

_____

14. Good coaches motivate their athletes AND reinforce their good behaviour AND punish their bad behaviour.

_____

_____

15. The old man tried to cross the street at a crosswalk AND the cars did not even stop.

_____

_____

16. One officer pulled his gun AND said not to move AND hearing this AND having a gun pulled on me I didn't even want to breathe for fear of my life.

_____

_____

_____

17. Now it is evening AND the sun is setting in the west AND the sky is changing to a clear bright blue.

_____

_____

18. Handguns have the power to work for you, AND at the same time against you.

_____

19. As a male driver I would have to pay $4500 for insurance AND my sister would have to pay approximately one-fifth as much.

_____

_____

20. Soon after the accident, a woman who was driving by stopped AND asked if she could help AND my neighbour put me in the car AND the woman took me the rest of the way home, AND my neighbour brought my dog home.

21. If you feel you are hungry enough to eat a horse AND do not want to gain any weight, a Chinese restaurant would be best.

22. On the bus we started to talk AND he asked about my daily routine AND what I was doing tonight AND what I liked to do during the weekends.

23. The problem of garbage has existed since the beginning of time, AND only now has it become much worse.

24. One myth is that women aren't committed to their work AND they will leave when they get married AND have children.

25. If you want to double your money at the races, fold it in half AND put it in your pocket AND just watch.

NAME _____

Run-on Sentence: Worksheet, Level 2

*Revise these run-on sentences by substituting more accurate **connecting words** or **punctuation**, by crossing out all **deadwood**, or, if necessary, by completely rewriting in the space.*

1. In five minutes a slow song came on and I walked across the dance floor and asked her to dance and she said, "sure."

   _____

   _____

2. It rained that afternoon, and planning to get a suntan on the beach was out of the question.

   _____

   _____

3. My sister went through a lying phase, and it got to the point where she could not find any more excuses and so she moved out.

   _____

   _____

4. I started to panic because I knew that the stop sign was too close for me to make a safe stop, and I did what any inexperienced driver would do in my situation and that was to slam on the brakes.

   _____

   _____

   _____

5. We left my house around eleven, because it's just before midnight when the strip really becomes crowded, because that's when the theatres close, or if there's a concert on at the Gardens, it usually ends around midnight, and few people go home right away, because they go for a walk on the strip and meet all the lunatics they can find.

   _____

   _____

   _____

   _____

6. The topic of rape is not a pleasant one, and the majority of individuals would rather not think about it, or if they do, they usually envision a stranger with a knife hiding in the bushes or in a dark alley waiting for unsuspecting prey to come along, but statistics tell us that 80 percent of all rapes are carried out by people the victim knows.

   _____

   _____

   _____

7. Let's look at the Philadelphia Flyers, a hockey team that plays a very aggressive game whether winning or losing, and when they're losing they maintain their aggressiveness and you notice signs of hatred and revenge in their game, such as the cheap shots and especially the stick coming down on their opponents.

_____

_____

_____

_____

_____

8. When I started a computer business two years ago with my brother, I entered a world full of long hours of working and dealing with every little problem in the job and also worrying about it all the time, which does not happen with regular hours with a series of known responsibilities at a job with the government or a private company.

_____

_____

_____

_____

_____

9. When I looked to see the other driver, he was still in his car. A group of people ran over to this car and tried to talk to him, but they couldn't figure out if he was all right or not, and they tried the door and it wouldn't open. So they kept on trying till the door opened and the driver came out and he had only minor bruises and he was in a state of shock. Oh, I forgot to mention that when the accident happened one of the women waiting outside with me went and phoned the police and they didn't show up till everyone seemed to be fine.

_____

_____

_____

_____

_____

10. Up ahead my favourite high speed bend was coming, so I clicked her into fifth and opened the throttle and without warning my bike was all over the place. My back wheel had become loose and before I could stop, it fell off and I went flying over my handlebars and right over the cliff, and I landed in the water next to a big sharp rock, so I feel lucky to be alive today, because when you come that close to death it really makes you think how easily you can be killed through no fault of your own.

_____

_____

_____

_____

_____

11. The story is told in a narrative way with Frederick Henry narrating for us, and giving us a good literary description of the surroundings and happenings at the present time period of World War I by speaking of common occurrences during the war, such as shell-marked iron of different structures which were hit by enemy artillery during the war, which, in part, is being described generally and fluently by our narrator, who is an ambulance driver for the Italian army, who is also an American who, as mentioned earlier, donated or sold his skills and techniques to the Italian Army during this time of hardship for the Italians and other warring peoples who are taking part in the war which is spoken of in the story.

12. Many well-known companies have undergone extensive economic hardship as a result of unions demanding higher incomes, superior benefit packages, overtime and shift premiums and incentives that give employees a false sense of being indispensable, for example, employees tend to slow down their work, take advantage of overtime and sick leave and when supervisors try to discipline the employees, the union will step in and take control of the situation, usually not to the benefit of the employer.

EDITING FOR PRONOUN REFERENCE

Pronouns are handy. In substituting for nouns, they save time and spare us clumsy repetition. But like shortcuts on a journey, pronouns can also cost us time or even stop us from reaching our destination. So use these shortcuts wisely: **make a pronoun refer clearly to the word for which it substitutes.**

A. **Most pronouns need an *antecedent*** (that is, a *noun or other pronoun to which the pronoun refers*). Otherwise, isolated pronouns such as "she," "he," "they" or "it" cause confusion because the reader does not know what they mean:

In the far North, *they* do very little in winter. *They* stay inside *their* shelters because the weather can kill.

Here the pronoun "they" has no antecedent. Does "they" refer to polar bears? To First Nations people? To Southerners stationed in the North? To those who live off the land? Or to those who search for oil, gas or minerals? *The easiest way to correct such confusion is to replace a vague pronoun with a noun:*

In the far North, *prospectors* do very little in winter. *They* stay inside *their* shelters because the weather can kill.

Now the pronouns "they" and "their" make sense, because they can refer to the noun "prospectors." Of course if the author had placed the "prospectors" in the sentence before, or maybe even earlier, we would have an antecedent to explain the pronouns. But *the antecedent should not be very far away.* The noun "prospectors" at the opening of an essay will not explain the pronoun "they" in the tenth paragraph!

• Sometimes a pronoun merely *seems* to have an antecedent, as in this example from a student essay:

Smoking is an expensive habit. *It* burns away as soon as a person lights *it* up, even when *it* is not being smoked.

Can "smoking" burn away, be lit up or be smoked? By substituting the noun "smoking" for the pronoun "it," we find that "smoking" has only disguised the lack of a real antecedent. Now let's add one:

Smoking is an expensive habit. A *cigarette* burns away as soon as a person lights *it* up, even when *it* is not being smoked.

Here is another typical way of misusing a pronoun:

In the newspaper, *it* says we will have a spring election.

"It" seems to refer to "newspaper"—until we check it by substituting the noun:

In the newspaper, the *newspaper* says we will have a spring election.

Since a newspaper can hardly be *in* itself, we see that there is in fact no antecedent. Let's avoid the problem by removing the pronoun:

The newspaper says we will have a spring election.

• Note that *the pronoun "I" needs no antecedent*, because it refers to the person writing. "We" should be explained, though, so readers know who else is included.

• Note how *the pronoun "it" is sometimes used in a general sense without an antecedent:*

It snowed last night.

It takes two hours to eat a good French dinner.

No one but the writer knows how difficult *it* is to fill up blank pages day after day.

B. **A singular pronoun should not refer to more than one antecedent.** The reader feels uneasy having to guess at the meaning of a sentence such as this:

I watched the old man walk out to his car, open the door, start *it* up and drive away.

What does he start up and drive away, the *door*? Though common sense tells us this is ridiculous, we waste effort having to interpret the message—because there are two possible singular antecedents, "car" and "door," and the second one is closer to the starting and driving.

One common way around this problem is to replace the unclear pronoun with the noun:

I watched the old man walk out to his car, open the door, start the *car* up and drive away.

Now what happens is clear, but the word "car" occurs twice, weakening the style through repetition. Let's find a different noun, then:

I watched the old man walk out to his car, open the door, start the *ignition* and drive away.

• *Be especially careful to make the pronouns "which," "that" and "this" refer to only one specific antecedent.* Since these pronouns can refer to many things—from a single noun to a group of words to a whole sentence or even a paragraph—they must be used with precision. Is the following passage clear?

> My boss accused me of taking extra breaks. *This* was ridiculous, because all day long the store was packed with customers.

Which was ridiculous, the employer's accusation or the author's taking extra breaks? We can only guess. Now let's look at a clearer version of both possibilities:

> My employer's accusation that I took extra breaks was ridiculous, because all day long the store was packed with customers.

OR

> My employer called my extra breaks ridiculous, because all day long the store was packed with customers.

C. **The pronoun "who" refers to a human antecedent. The pronouns "which" and "that" usually refer to nonhuman antecedents.** Most of us do not make this distinction when we talk, but in the space of an essay we are expected to be more exact: do not refer to a human as a nonhuman or a nonhuman as a human. Here are some typical cases:

> A student *that* cheats may not have a good self-image.

> People *which* lack interest in exercise are lazy in their bodies and minds.

> A pup is easier to train than an old dog, *who* cannot learn new tricks.

In essays, let's substitute the more exact pronouns:

> A student *who* cheats may not have a good self-image.

> People *who* lack interest in exercise are lazy in their bodies and minds.

> A pup is easier to train than an old dog, *which* cannot learn new tricks.

NAME_____

Pronoun Reference: Diagnostic

Put an "X" in the blank beside each passage that contains unclear pronoun reference, and underline each faulty pronoun.

Example: Using the word processor is easier than writing <u>it</u> out on paper.   _____X_____

1. Today employers like to hire an applicant that can speak either Cantonese or Mandarin.

2. When a thorn scratched my knee, it became infected with gangrene.   _____

3. In the travel brochures, they will say anything to convince you to go to their resort.   _____

4. In Quebec City it is very romantic.   _____

5. A computer does what it is told.   _____

6. By talking, it will bring emotions into the open.   _____

7. I had to have my car towed by a truck who was waiting nearby after he saw the accident.   _____

8. After the city health department did many studies, it decided to ban smoking in bus terminals, subway stations, airports and governmental offices.   _____

9. In my country, the children grow up totally dependent on their parents even after they are married.   _____

10. If I won a million-dollar lottery, there are several ways I would spend it.   _____

11. There are many athletes who would risk their lives to use steroids, in order to win.   _____

12. Many dog owners feel they are real companions.   _____

13. Once the grapes are chosen, the next step is to crush them with the grinder.   _____

14. The people that really get me are those that run up the escalators.   _____

15. At every high school they have a guidance counsellor.   _____

16. Women have been sending a clear message to men that they are as good as they are.   _____

17. In the United States they have a yearly event called the Super Bowl.   _____

18. An underground economy is created when prices are so high that people cannot afford it.   _____

19. Unions are dreaded by large companies, and they do everything in their power to keep them out.   _____

20. The coffee table matches the side table except that it is wider and longer.   _____

21. When reaching out for help, many women are turned away by shelters who have no room.   _____

22. Teachers should tell students how to be more responsible when they sit behind the steering wheel. _____

23. When writing a report, it should be totally clear. _____

24. Shy people are often misunderstood, because they do not express their opinions. _____

25. Every year in the United States more than 800 000 heart attacks occur, and of those only 300 000 survive. _____

26. Crack addicts may kill their parents because they refuse to give them money for their drug habit. _____

27. When the health authorities came to inspect the restaurant, they told Myra and Carol that they needed special permits to operate. _____

28. Do most people who buy homes actually own them? _____

29. Sometimes if parents have to discipline their children at home, they feel threatened by them. _____

30. Some people will cash their pay cheques and spend it all on lottery tickets. _____

31. The individual that wants to be successful must have a dream. _____

32. Public transit is readily available to anyone who wants to ride it. _____

33. The pensioner and his sister hid from their neighbours because they were afraid they would see how poor they were. _____

34. Children's drawings are very important to some child psychologists because, to them, they are signs of their mental and emotional states. _____

35. Plumbing was a profitable trade, but I didn't want to be one all my life. _____

36. Why do some people have back problems while others do not? Let us consider them. _____

37. The government are cutting back programs right and left. _____

38. The next generation of parents will probably be the same as their parents unless they learn from their mistakes. _____

39. In British Columbia, trees are their main resource. _____

40. If there is civilization elsewhere in our galaxy, they might be advanced beyond our imagination. _____

NAME _____

Pronoun Reference: Worksheet, Level 1

Most of the passages below are unclear, because pronouns are used inaccurately. Substitute pronouns that make more sense. Where this would create a repetitious style, though, revise the whole sentence in the space. If a passage is already clear, write "Correct" below it.

Example: At hundreds of airports t̶h̶e̶y̶ *guards* have dogs sniffing out illegal drugs or bombs.

1. Hong Kong lies in the subtropical zone. They have never dealt with snowstorms or vehicles stuck in drifts. How lucky they are!

   _____

   _____

   _____

2. Parents are completely in charge of their children's lives until they reach some maturity.

   _____

   _____

3. Consumers will be the ones that suffer from higher prices.

   _____

4. At the hospital they put ten stitches in my head.

   _____

5. For consumers, credit cards are useful because they do not have to carry large amounts of money.

   _____

   _____

6. During the snowy season, it can make life hard for country dwellers.

   _____

   _____

7. Many students, like my sister, have been working on multiplication since grade three and still don't know them.

   _____

   _____

8. By building tall buildings, it can save space.

   _____

9. Under current law, homeowners that use their firearms to defend themselves can be arrested.

   _____

10. There are still companies that are pessimistic about robots.

    _____

11. Parents need to inform their teenagers that they can always come to them for help.

_____

_____

12. In big cities the traffic is unbelievable! They drive recklessly. They disobey rules, don't stop at red lights, and speed as if to win an award.

_____

_____

_____

13. Not all people who diet have an eating disorder.

_____

14. The English promised the French that if they joined them they would give them the same powers, but they didn't.

_____

_____

15. People are becoming unemployed because now a computer can do it faster and better.

_____

_____

16. Have you ever asked yourself why they manufacture products that fall apart?

_____

_____

17. Teenagers will make decisions based on how they will be perceived, instead of the result it could have.

_____

_____

18. Men no longer have to open doors or light cigarettes for women, because they are equal.

_____

_____

19. During the final exam, a guy sitting in front of me took a pack of cigarettes out of his pocket and lit it up.

_____

_____

20. Suddenly, out of nowhere, a car came swerving around the corner before their light had changed to green.

_____

_____

NAME _____

Pronoun Reference: Worksheet, Level 2

Revise all faulty pronoun reference below. In some cases you can just substitute a clearer word, while in other cases the whole passage needs rewriting. If a passage has no errors, write "Correct" below it.

Example: In earlier times, children were the only security parents had ~~when they became old and helpless.~~ *in old age*

1. When crimes are committed by young people, they are usually placed in a detention centre or group home.

2. We turned on the radio to find out what was happening. There was a tornado warning and it was coming in our direction.

3. The easiest way for the average person to reduce pollution is not to litter. This is one of the most vile and disgusting of habits.

4. After World War II the soldiers that returned home gave rise to the "baby boom."

5. Montreal has many different styles of architecture. They do not yet have the computerized "Lego" neighbourhoods that Toronto does.

6. Quebec nationalism can be traced to historical roots, when the society was linked to the French empire. For example, they had a distinct dialect called "Canadien" as well as the French civil code of law.

7. The rent of the store site was extremely expensive, since it was located in the centre of Vancouver.

8. The maid of honour and best man carry the rings to be exchanged by the couple as a token of their love.

9. In New York a teenager was stabbed to death for trying to save his parents from thugs who were stealing their money.

10. By adding a camper to a pickup truck, it can be used for summer enjoyment.

11. Many people choose to have a dog as a pet because they are good companions.

12. After 30 minutes in the oven, the cake is tested by sticking a knife into it. If the knife blade remains clean, then the cake is done. If the knife blade has some batter on it, then it needs cooking for another ten minutes.

13. Under the Duvalier dictatorship they had employed up to 55 000 civil servants, who had little to do but took up 80 percent of the country's budget.

14. Some people think television programs are garbage, but we cannot ignore them just because they don't solve the problems in our society.

15. In order for the cars behind us to pass the accident, they went into the opposite lane and stared at us as they drove by.

16. Buyers can expect brand-name computers to cost 10 to 15 percent more than clones, because of the support service, the name, and the quality that they will guarantee.

17. It rained all night and, as a result, caused the tent to collapse.

18. In Quebec City they have buildings that attract crowds of tourists, because they are hundreds of years old.

19. Miss Scatcherd accused Helen of not washing her fingernails, which was impossible to do since the water was frozen.

    _____

    _____

20. Most parents want their children to have their own licences as soon as possible because they do not want to drive them everywhere. If they have their licences, they will not have this kind of trouble. However, they have the responsibility of driving with them for at least a few weeks once they get the licences.

    _____

    _____

    _____

    _____

21. Take politics, for example. Most of them can warp language to their advantage, because they can word campaign promises to solicit a variety of interpretations.

    _____

    _____

    _____

22. In football games I have been in fights to prove that my team is stronger and better than the other team, even though it is wrong.

    _____

    _____

23. In _Brave New World_, they turn on a loudspeaker while the children are asleep. It continually repeats things, so that when the children awaken they are implanted in their minds. By doing this they can teach what they want, when they want it and how they want it. In this way they condition them to turn out the way they want them to.

    _____

    _____

    _____

    _____

24. Poverty, homelessness, child hunger, unemployment, exploitation of children in the workplace and increased crimes are all alarming issues that seem to be a part of our daily lives, but what is being done about it?

    _____

    _____

    _____

25. The Canadian immigration department in Singapore set an appointment with my parents to be interviewed. They asked them some general questions about employment, health and criminal records. Then they informed them that they would get in touch with them in a couple of weeks. When they did get back to my parents, they sent all of my family to various departments for medical and criminal clearance. After all the results were in, they then summoned my whole family for the final interview.

_____

_____

_____

_____

_____

_____

_____

EDITING FOR AGREEMENT

The English we speak and the English we write can be as different from each other as the clothes we wear to the beach and the clothes we wear to the prom. In editing for agreement, this contrast can grow so sharp that sometimes it almost seems that what is natural in speech is wrong on the page, and what is correct on the page is unnatural in speech.

But there is really no problem unless we blindly take speech as our model for writing. We would all *say* "Everyone ate their lunch," and our listeners would regard this as normal speech. But the same words in the more formal space of your essay would seem illogical, because "everyone" is singular while "their" is plural.

This could change. In fact, some newspapers and magazines already use the speech-like approach of the example we just looked at: "Everyone ate their lunch." In a few more years most readers may agree. For now, though, the customary approach to agreement is safer for those writing in school—because many readers, especially teachers, still perceive these newer conversational usages as errors. Especially in the more formal kinds of writing, such as literary papers or research papers of all kinds, stay with the techniques explained below.

Note: Of the ten parts that follow, items "A," "E," "F," "H" and "I" will cover about 90 percent of all cases. Pay special attention to the most useful technique of all, the *pluralizing* suggested at the end of item "H," for it helps you avoid the whole problem of informality vs. formality.

A subject and its verb must agree in number; that is, they must both be singular or both be plural. A pronoun and its antecedent — the noun to which it refers — must agree in number and in person.

A. *Make a verb agree with its subject, and a pronoun with its antecedent, no matter how many words separate them.* Sometimes it helps to imagine brackets around interrupting word groups such as dependent clauses, to make items that must agree easier to identify:

        S
My first *impression* [of downtown Toronto with

its noise, traffic jams, crowded buses and thou-
               V
sands of pedestrians] *was* frightening.

     S
The *slaughter* [of rare species, not to mention
                      V
many more species still undiscovered,] *is* still

continuing.

B. *Make related nouns, pronouns and verbs agree even when one or more is outside the independent clause:*

              N   V P
I took the job because the *company pays its* employees well. (Here the related noun, verb and pronoun are all in a dependent clause.)

                 N   V
The film left out many *parts* that *were* covered in the book. (Here a verb in a dependent clause is related to a noun in the independent clause.)

   N   P
A *factory* leaves its workers unemployed when *it* closes down. (Here a pronoun in a dependent clause is related to a noun that is the subject of the independent clause.)

C. *Make the subject and verb agree even when their order is reversed.* Occasionally the verb occurs first, which makes the subject harder to identify. Just remember that the subject is what the sentence is *about*, while the verb tells what the subject *does* or *is*. Once you identify the two, making them agree is easy.

          V   S   S
On the desk *are* [not *is*] the keyboard, monitor,
S   S
mouse and printer.

To double-check your sentence, think of it in the normal word order with the verb following the subject:

      S   S   S   S V
The *keyboard, monitor, mouse* and *printer are* on the desk.

D. *Singular subjects joined by* or *or* nor *take singular verbs and pronouns:*

Butter or margarine *is* [not *are*] fattening.

Neither salad nor fruit *is* [not *are*] fattening.

Of course if the items were joined by "and," they would form compound subjects that would call for plural verbs:

Butter and margarine *are* fattening.

Where two subjects are habitually treated as a unit, though, the two together are singular:

Bacon *and* eggs *is* my favourite breakfast.

E. *Collective nouns take singular verbs and singular pronouns when the group is regarded as a unit:*

The company *wants* [not *want*] to lower *its* [not *their*] costs.

The government *was* [not *were*] ready to defend *its* [not *their*] decision.

The team *loses* [not *lose*] more than it *wins* [not they *win*].

Although a company, a government or a team may be made up of many people, we are discussing one company, one government and one team. Therefore each is singular. *If the members of a group act separately, though, the group may be treated as a plural:*

The jury *were* arguing about the verdict.

F. *"Indefinite pronouns" are usually singular, even though some may seem plural.*

another	*everything*
any	*neither*
anybody	*nobody*
anyone	*no one*
anything	*nothing*
each	*one*
either	*somebody*
everybody	*someone*
everyone	*something*

Anyone who *is* finished may hand in *his or her* [not *their*] essay.

Someone *has* left *his or her* [not *their*] notebook.

Everyone *is* going with *his or her* [not *their*] friends.

Note: Traditionally the pronoun "he" represented people in general (as in a group that includes both males and females). Today, though, many people view this as unfair to women. Therefore in the examples above, we have used "he or she" instead of the singular "he" (remember that "he or she" is singular, because both pronouns are joined by "or").

See further solutions to this common problem in the next section, "Editing for Equality of the Sexes in Language."

G. FOR ESL STUDENTS: If you are not sure whether a verb is singular or plural, remember that *although the final "s" makes a noun plural, it makes a verb singular:*

SINGULAR
    N V
The bird flie*s*.

PLURAL
    N V
The bird*s* fly.

If you are still in doubt about the number of a verb, apply the "it-they" test. Place the words "it" and "they" before the verb. If singular "it" sounds right with the verb, the verb is singular; if plural "they" sounds right, the verb is plural:

SINGULAR   PLURAL

H. *Be consistent in pronoun use.* Do not change in the middle of a passage from "he or she" to "they":

WRONG

The sensible drinker will have only one or two beers, so *he or she* will not lose *their* self-control.

The student who wrote this sentence forgot that singular subjects joined by "or" take singular verbs and pronouns. Other writers grimly exchange bad grammar for bad style by repeating pronouns:

The sensible drinker will have only one or two beers, so *he or she* will not lose *his or her* self-control.

As was said in the box, the traditional "he" or "his" is no longer the solution. It may be less repetitious than "he or she" and "his or her," but it implies that women do not exist:

The sensible drinker will have only one or two beers, so *he* will not lose *his* self-control.

A better solution is to rewrite the sentence so as to avoid all problems of grammar, style and prejudice:

The sensible drinker will have only one or two beers, to avoid losing self-control.

Note how the statement now has no pronoun problems because it has no pronouns at all! Solutions like these are very direct but not always possible. You will find that the most widely useful solution of all is to *pluralize* from the beginning. Use this method often:

Sensible *drinkers* will have only one or two beers, so *they* will not lose *their* self-control.

I. *A pronoun and its antecedent must agree in person:*

FIRST PERSON

I, me, we, us

SECOND PERSON

you

THIRD PERSON

he, him, she, her, one, it, they, them

In speech and informal writing, the second-person "you" is often used to mean people in general. Yet "you" is in the second person while "people" is in the third person. "You" may even be understood by the reader to mean herself or himself, personally:

In the two years *I* worked at the restaurant, *I* was always given a meal, a break and all the pop *you* could drink.

Unless the reader is the person who drank the pop, the writer should stay in the first person:

In the two years *I* worked at the restaurant, *I* was always given a meal, a break and all the pop *I* could drink.

Note: There is no such word as "*themself*" or "*ourself*," because "them" and "our" are plural, while "self" is singular. Instead, write the logical and standard terms, "*themselves*" and "*ourselves*."

J. *The words "media," "phenomena" and "criteria" are plural; their singular forms are "medium," "phenomenon" and "criterion." Examples:*

PLURAL: Television, radio and the other mass *media* are turning Canadians into Americans.

SINGULAR: Film is a *medium* of great cultural power.

PLURAL: Centrifugal force and centripetal force are two opposite *phenomena*.

SINGULAR: The falling of snow is a *phenomenon* that most of the world's population has never seen.

NAME _____

Agreement: Diagnostic

Put an "X" in the blank beside each passage that contains at least one fault in agreement. (Remember that the informal way we speak may not seem correct in the more formal space of an essay.)

1. The streets was filled with people. _____

2. In Canada the teenager has great freedom to do whatever they want. _____

3. I take pride in my car. It is great to have my own transportation for my convenience. _____

4. If one is short, they may want to choose a short skirt to make them look taller. _____

5. To take the oath, every person must raise his or her hand and repeat what the judge says. _____

6. Neither the cold virus nor the AIDS virus have cures. _____

7. Although eating and drinking is forbidden in the library, many students break that rule. _____

8. American movies and television programs dominates our Canadian society. _____

9. At the foot of the bed are a desk and a chair. _____

10. To help you stick with your budget, one has to look closely at all the impulse buying we do. _____

11. The mass media are very popular today. _____

12. Today's young generation have one goal in mind, to receive their driver's licence. _____

13. Society must clean up its act. _____

14. The *Sun* fills their classified section with 20 pages of ads for cars, houses and jobs. _____

15. The cost of car insurance range from $2500 to $6000, depending on the type of car and age of the driver. _____

16. Everyone has their ups and downs. _____

17. We attend years of school, studying for the one field you wish to conquer. _____

18. Every day someone behind you pushes and shoves their way into the subway car. _____

19. If an individual receives numerous traffic tickets, he is considered a high risk for accidents. _____

20. Travelling is a great way to learn about ourself. _____

21. Unfortunately, our society teaches teenagers that success, beauty and power comes from being slim. _____

22. Hockey provides unpredictable events that leaves the audience at the edge of their seats, biting their nails. _____

23. Food rich in proteins and fats are more expensive than starchy food. _____

24. Research into the effects of our population on the environment is extensive and necessary. _____

25. For a few minutes of happiness in gambling, one can lose the fortune which they have built all their lives. _____

26. The streets of Montreal was very busy. _____

27. My impression of the Ontario landscape was of hilly and rocky terrain. You could see trees for miles around. _____

28. When an older person retires, his or her income is usually cut in half. _____

29. If anyone tried to wander from the camp, they were imprisoned or shot. _____

30. In the main office are a dispatcher, a sergeant and a staff sergeant. _____

31. To make yourself heard, one must speak up to their peers and let everyone know your opinions. _____

32. I have both a high school diploma and a community college diploma, but neither of them have helped me get a job for the summer. _____

33. The number of common-law marriages has risen. _____

34. Sixteen is a trying time in one's life. The pressure of friends has a strong influence on your thoughts and your actions. _____

35. In prison I dared not pick a quarrel with anyone, because they could beat me at any time. _____

36. Computer viruses can duplicate themself and move to another system, then duplicate themself again. _____

37. If a person wants to work after 65, he or she should be entitled to. _____

38. Every résumé should have a brief covering letter which shows the company that you know something about them. _____

39. A pregnant person would start asking themselves questions such as "Is it a girl or a boy?" _____

40. Give a famous musician any song and they will make it popular! _____

NAME _____

Agreement: Worksheet, Level 1

Though many of the choices below would sound natural and correct in conversation, circle only those most appropriate for the essay writer.

1. Each of us (*is/are*) unique.

2. Sarah's family (*have/has*) a history of diabetes.

3. Speed, precision and efficiency (*is/are*) required in a factory.

4. The electronics industry (*is/are*) advancing rapidly.

5. Lying is something that everybody does at some point in (*his/their/his or her*) life.

6. One's home is (*his/her/their/his or her*) private place.

7. Today the price of houses (*are/is*) falling.

8. Everyone dreams of owning (*his/her/their/his or her*) own home.

9. To me, friends are essential. Without them (*you/I*) would be unable to function normally.

10. The Jewish faith (*have their/has its*) holy day on Saturday.

11. Neither a husband nor a wife (*are/is*) free to break marriage vows.

12. Jack's entire family (*was/were*) overweight.

13. Nobody wants to have a dump in (*his/her/their/his or her*) neighbourhood.

14. Anyone who denies that (*he or she has/they have*) ever flirted just isn't telling the truth.

15. The fastest growing segment of the population (*is/are*) senior citizens.

16. It took Canada too long to realize that (*they/we/it*) needed Quebec.

17. Across the street (*was/were*) an emergency hydro truck, two fire trucks, three police cars and an ambulance.

18. The merchandise in New York City, such as stereos, cameras and other electronic equipment, (*are/is*) cheaper than in Toronto.

19. In the big city, everyone (*is/are*) for (*themself/themselves/himself or herself*).

20. In Canada a criminal is eligible for parole after (*they have/he has/he or she has*) served one-third of (*their/his/his or her*) sentence.

21. The purpose of the pyramids (*is/are*) still unknown.

22. One will often spend more with a credit card than (*he/she/he or she*) really (*have/has*) to spend.

23. Neither money nor power (*provide/provides*) true happiness.

24. One of the car's lights (*were/was*) burned out.

25. Our family (*is/are*) planning to move.

26. To avoid criminal attack, we must think of methods to reduce the chance of its happening to (*you/us/ him or her*).

27. The orchestra (*was/were*) playing quietly in the background.

28. Quebec just wanted to be recognized for (*their/its*) importance in Canadian culture and tradition.

29. Today the cost of living makes me think twice. Should (*I/you*) move out, or stay with (*my/your*) parents?

30. The rapid activity, unpredictable events, and exciting violence of hockey (*leaves/leave*) a spectator standing on the seat.

NAME _____

Agreement: Worksheet, Level 2

Though some of the following passages might seem natural in conversation, many, through ignoring the principles of agreement, would be too casual and inexact for your essays. Wherever you find such a weakness, cross out the problem words and write your correction in the blank.

Example: The number of white-collar crimes h̶a̶v̶e̶ risen sharply.   *has*

1. Is there a person among us who is not haunted by how society tell them to look?   _____

2. A dictatorship can try to put out all the fires of democracy, by terrorizing, killing and beating all who believe in it, but they cannot wipe out hope.   _____

3. As soon as I open the machine shop door, the smell of burning steel and oil rushes into my nose and makes me cough. The constant harsh noises hit you like a car.   _____

4. The use of politically correct terms is becoming predominant today.   _____

5. I will be more careful in choosing a partner for my next relationship. I want someone who can take the initiative in telephoning me, showing their feelings about me and just showing they care.   _____

6. One can almost believe that they are actually part of the film, as the Dolby stereo sound of an explosion trembles right through your body.   _____

7. At one end of the room are the tuner, speakers, CD player, and two shelves of CDs.   _____

8. Television is not the only media that reinforces society's obsession with being thin.   _____

9. I have been to Montreal several times. I like to travel on their subways because it's clean and attractive.   _____

10. The number of hotels in the Emirate of Dubai has more than doubled since 1994 to meet the increase in demand.   _____

11. Being a night person, I can't understand how anyone can function properly if they have been awake since 7 a.m.   _____

12. The next time you walk by a homeless person, do not treat them like an animal. Give them the dignity and respect they deserve.   _____

13. When I go out at night in Vancouver, I make sure to take a cab home rather than walk, because you are less likely to be attacked when locked within the safety of a moving vehicle.   _____

14. Just because little green creatures with ten eyes have not invaded earth does not mean that life on other planets does not exist.   _____

15. It's true the city never sleeps, but why can't they stop emptying the huge garbage bins at one o'clock in the morning?   _____

16. The number of people wearing contact lenses are increasing.   _____

17. All too often, either injury or death is the result of drunk driving.

18. What makes hockey bloodier than other major sports is the fact that for 60 minutes of playing time, each of the players carries a large weapon in his hands, a stick that measures five feet in length and has a pointed tip, the better with which to jab your opponent in the gut.

19. As I grew older and was very attracted to men, the idea of committing yourself to one person for the rest of your life still didn't turn me on.

20. Trust me, never give your new boss your exact time schedule for school. They will put your work hours right after your school hours, literally giving you no time at all to do anything.

NAME _____

Agreement: Worksheet, Level 3

Revise all the weaknesses in agreement, either adding changes above the line, or, if you need to rework a whole passage, in the spaces below. See if you can identify the one passage that has no error at all.

Example: Everyone on the boat, including myself, ~~were~~ *was* very nervous about the storm.

1. The only time we hear about pit bulls are when they have done something wrong.

    _____
    _____

2. As a cashier we come in contact with every customer. If their visit was pleasant we hear about it, and if not we are especially sure to hear about it.

    _____
    _____
    _____

3. The passionate screams, the cries for help, the pushing and shoving, the smell of rubber and asphalt, the noise of horns and the impact of the crash stands out vividly in my mind.

    _____
    _____
    _____

4. Watching a championship game in which the home team is involved brings the spectators together not only for the moment but also for years to come, whenever the great play or game is mentioned and replayed in our minds.

    _____
    _____
    _____
    _____

5. With age and experience comes reason.

    _____

6. When a person comes home from work or school, the first thing they do is throw off their shoes and sit on the couch, with their zapper in their hand. When you turn the television on, you change from station to station and finally settle on a program. It could be a comedy or a drama, but how many times is it Canadian?

    _____
    _____
    _____
    _____
    _____

7. Since the government is able to find out how much money a person makes, they have the ability to determine the amount of money you are eligible for on your student loan application.

_____

_____

_____

8. How can a teenager resist wanting to look as great and as happy as the models in magazines? They view the success and contentment of these models as the direct result of their beauty and skinniness rather than hard work and experience acquired over years. In their hope to look and feel the same way, they pursue crash diets, hoping the weight loss will bring about these wonderful changes.

_____

_____

_____

_____

_____

_____

_____

9. To obtain a handgun in the United States, a person undergoes only a quick police check to ensure that they are not already a wanted criminal. Then they can buy a handgun. The gun does not even have to be locked up. It can be stored in a drawer in your home or the glove compartment of your car, or even concealed on your body. It can be stored anywhere a person might need it in order to protect themselves.

_____

_____

_____

_____

_____

_____

10. As a potential alcoholic walks down the street and sees the terrifying life of skid-row panhandlers, complete with their wine sores and filthy clothes, they confidently say that this would never happen to them because they are different. They do not realize that just a few years ago, the person they are looking at probably had a good job and a happy home life! Then something happened that they couldn't handle, and the drink which had always rescued them now turned out to be their worst enemy.

_____

_____

_____

_____

_____

_____

_____

_____

EDITING FOR EQUALITY OF THE SEXES IN LANGUAGE

One of the main social changes of our time has been the rising status of women. Not only do most Canadian women now work outside the home, but increasing numbers have entered professions once dominated by men (such as law, medicine and business), and more and more women have taken management positions.

Since language reflects society, some traditional aspects of English now strike most of us as sexist—biased against women. To say "policeman" ignores the fact that today we also see women patrolling the streets and driving squad cars. It is only natural that more and more people now say and write "police officer" instead of "policeman," for this more neutral term reflects an equality of the sexes.

Though some traditionalists still think the earlier usages are acceptable, almost everyone else now views sexism in language as a social and political blunder. Does it appear in your own writing? If so, consider and try out the following suggestions:

A. *Avoid terms that unnecessarily differentiate female from male:*

AVOID	TRY
businessman	business person, entrepreneur, manager
chairman	chairperson, chair, head
housewife	homemaker (can signify either a male or female)
maiden name	birth name
mailman	letter carrier
man, mankind	humanity, humankind, humans, the human race, people
man-made	imitation, synthetic, artificial
poetess	poet
policeman, patrolman	police officer
salesman	salesperson, clerk, sales clerk
stewardess	flight attendant
waitress	server, attendant
woman doctor, lady dentist, woman lawyer	doctor, dentist, lawyer

B. *Use forms of address that reflect equality of the sexes.* Traditionally we have called a woman either "Miss" or "Mrs.," signalling whether she is single or married. By contrast, we have used the less specific term "Mr." for all men. Some women still prefer the traditional terms; in these cases respect their wish to be called "Miss" or "Mrs." But call other women "Ms.," so they will not resent the unnecessary scrutiny of their private lives.

In the past, a woman was often addressed by her husband's full name:

Mrs. Pierre Tremblay
Mrs. Albert Tsang

Avoid this practice, for it implies that a woman's identity is derived only through a husband. Instead, use the woman's own first name, preceded by "Ms."—unless she prefers "Mrs.":

Ms. Jocelyne Tremblay
Mrs. Elaine Tsang

(Of course specify her own last name if she does not use her husband's.)

C. *The pronoun "he" should refer only to males.* This idea may seem to be self-evident, but remember the old practice of using "he" for a person or persons of unspecified gender ("Everyone paid for *his* own dinner"). In cases like this, the "his" or the "he" implies that males are more important than females; in fact, it almost implies there are no females at all. Another example:

A lawyer has little time for *his* family. (Unspoken assumption: lawyers are all men.)

One alternative is "his or her" (to be fair, use "her or his" half the time):

A lawyer often has little time for *his or her* family.

One problem with this approach, though, is its clumsy repetition and wordiness:

A lawyer has not only too little time for *her or his* clients, but also for *her or his* family.

In reaching for a style free of repetition, many people create new errors, this time in agreement (see pages 155 to 157):

A lawyer has not only too little time for *his or her* clients, but also for *their* own family. (While "his or her" is singular, "their" is plural.)

A better solution is to use plurals all the way:

Lawyers have not only too little time for *their* clients, but also for *their* own families.

An even cleaner solution to this and other pronoun problems is sometimes just to rewrite the sentence with no pronoun at all:

A lawyer has too little time for either clients or family.

> At first it may seem hard to free your prose of gender bias while still maintaining good style. But remember that there are almost always other ways to word your thoughts. Seek them through revision, as in these examples.

D. *Stereotyping the sexes is a form of bias. Avoid it.* Consider alternatives such as these:

BIASED	NEUTRAL
A welder must protect *his* eyes. (In other words, welders are men.)	Welders must protect *their* eyes. (Use plurals to avoid "his.")
A nurse must respect *her* patients. (In other words, nurses are women.)	A nurse must respect patients. (Remove the pronoun.)
	OR
	Nurses must respect *their* patients. (Use plurals.)
There were too many *guys* at the party and not enough *girls*. (In other words, females are only girls.)	There were too many *men* at the party and not enough *women*.
	OR
	There were too many *boys* at the party, and not enough *girls*. (Imply equality by using parallel terms.)

NAME _____

Equality of the Sexes in Language: Worksheet

Most of the passages below contain expressions or attitudes that are unfair to women. Remove all forms of sexism, either crossing out and replacing terms, or revising the whole passage in the space. Write "unbiased" under any passage that needs no work.

1. All the executives and their wives came to the party.

   _____

2. Within a decade, man will be on Mars.

   _____

3. When I regained consciousness, a lady doctor was taking my pulse.

   _____

   _____

4. There are 23 girls in my class but only seven guys.

   _____

5. Our neighbourhood is crowded with young girls and boys.

   _____

6. The chairman tabled the committee's report.

   _____

7. The guests were Mr. and Mrs. Edward Turnbull, Mr. Peter Chen, Miss Nancy Donnelly and Mr. and Mrs. Antonio Santos.

   _____

   _____

   _____

8. A good foreman is fair to his workers.

   _____

9. A good secretary keeps her desk neat.

   _____

10. Forty police manned the roadblocks to catch the fleeing gunmen.

    _____

    _____

11. After a day on the oil rigs, you crave a man-sized dinner.

    _____

    _____

12. Are there limits to the amount of knowledge man can obtain?

    _____

13. If he studies each day's work on time, the student will have no trouble with exams.

_____

_____

14. Vacuum cleaner salesmen intimidate housewives by accusing them of having filthy carpets.

_____

_____

15. It takes more than just size to be a policeman.

_____

16. How much should we tip the waitress?

_____

17. What was your mother's maiden name?

_____

18. The farmer often makes too little to cover his own costs, while the middleman in the city grows rich.

_____

_____

19. The candidates are Mr. Frank Johnson, Miss Lise Gagnon, Mr. Joseph Horvath and Mrs. Barry Rossiter.

_____

_____

20. My neighbour is a police officer.

_____

21. Every soldier knows how to maintain his rifle.

_____

22. Any person who skips breakfast is endangering his health.

_____

_____

23. Most of Canada's top businessmen think government spending is out of control.

_____

_____

24. Man now has the capability to create human life by artificial means. Perhaps man has obtained more knowledge than he was ever intended to have. In his quest for knowledge, man must set limits in his journey, both for himself and all of mankind.

_____

_____

_____

_____

25. The more time a person puts into developing his career, the richer his life experience becomes. He gets advancement in his job. He enjoys every day of his life. He gets full satisfaction out of his work experience and seems content and happy with his life. Advancement in his career also brings in more money and hence a luxurious life that everybody dreams of. He feels that he has got all that he ever wanted in life.

_____

_____

_____

_____

_____

_____

_____

_____

EDITING TO AVOID MISPLACED MODIFIERS AND DANGLING MODIFIERS

A MODIFIER is a word or word group that explains another word or word group. Place a modifier right next to what it explains; otherwise, it may seem to explain the wrong thing.

UNCLEAR

Most people like to relax after a hard day's work *in front of the TV.*

CLEAR

Most people like to relax *in front of the TV* after a hard day's work.

Often a misplaced modifier creates a ridiculous meaning, as above where people seem to do a hard day's work in front of the TV. Other times, a misplaced modifier just makes the passage hard to understand. The carelessly worded first sentence below was supposed to mean what the second one actually says:

UNCLEAR

I *only* eat out once a week.

CLEAR

I eat out *only* once a week.

See how, in the first version, "only" seems to explain the word "eat"—as if eating is all the person ever does. But in the second version, "only" now limits "once a week"—to correctly show that our author does not eat out every day.

"Only" is the most often misplaced modifier in our language. Note below how the meaning changes each time "only" moves to a new position:

Only I saw the robbery in Saturday. (No one else saw it.)

I *only* saw the robbery on Saturday. (I saw it but did not hear it.)

I saw *only* the robbery on Saturday. (I saw nothing else.)

I saw the *only* robbery on Saturday. (There was no other.)

I saw the robbery *only* on Saturday. (I did not see it any other day.)

A DANGLING MODIFIER is not connected at all to the word or word group it was meant to explain. Thus it seems to explain the wrong thing. Dangling modifiers are tough to fix: they cannot just be moved, but instead, part of the sentence has to be rewritten to make the connection.

UNCLEAR

While reading this essay, four people will die of starvation and 24 babies will be born somewhere in the world.

If the author of this statement had specified a reader, the ridiculous idea of dying and newborn persons reading the essay would not occur to us.

CLEAR

While you read this essay, four people will die of starvation and 24 babies will be born somewhere in the world.

CLEAR

In the time it takes the reader to finish this essay, four people will die of starvation and 24 babies will be born somewhere in the world.

UNCLEAR

When driving, the most important part of the car is the brake. (Is the brake driving?)

CLEAR

To drivers, the most important part of the car is the brake.

Not all dangling modifiers are as silly as these; others are harder to detect and fix:

UNCLEAR

At home, *when doing my homework*, there aren't any noisy parties to bother me, as there are in the dorm.

Since the author has said "*my* homework" and "to bother *me*," we may not imagine a noisy party doing the homework. Yet the sentence gives us an uneasy feeling that we are guessing at its meaning. If our author had openly used the word "I," and moved "the dorm" closer to the "noisy parties" that occur there, all would be clear:

When I am at home, the noisy parties at the dorm cannot distract me from my homework.

NAME _____

Misplaced and Dangling Modifiers: Diagnostic

Write "MM" in the blank beside each sentence that contains a misplaced modifier, and underline the misplaced modifier.

1. Drinking is said to be a bad habit by many doctors. _____

2. Active sports, such as soccer, involve a lot of competition. _____

3. Some children are forced to learn their first language by their parents. _____

4. Pills are virtually used for everything. _____

5. I was discouraged from speaking the truth by my lawyer. _____

6. After being hired, the manager teaches the newcomer his or her duties and responsibilities. _____

7. I only bought five items but had to wait in line more than 20 minutes. _____

8. We are only young once. _____

9. It takes my mother only three minutes to drive to work. _____

10. In the past, stores were only allowed open on Sundays during the holiday shopping season. _____

11. Since I was an only child, my parents wanted to protect me. _____

12. Hailstones only reach 2.5 cm in diameter. _____

13. I moved to Bayside with my parents when I was 13 years old from the city of Ottawa. _____

14. In the past, even an unimportant disease could kill the victim such as measles, whooping cough or diphtheria. _____

15. All students are not necessarily the same. _____

16. If you are like most people, a mortgage will be the largest debt of your lifetime. _____

17. A limited company takes responsibility for its actions, not its human directors. _____

18. When I was a kid I lived with my grandmother, a lovely lady who would let me do anything I wanted to, for a few months. _____

19. As a child, my father told me that the world is a cruel place to be in alone. _____

20. Children flock to see Santa Claus by the dozens. _____

Write "DM" in the blank beside each sentence that contains a dangling modifier, and underline the dangling modifier.

1. When driving in a big city like Montreal, parking is always a problem. _____

2. Once in the vehicle, the car doors should be locked. _____

3. After waiting two hours in the lobby, the doctor spent less than two minutes on me. _____

4. Dogs make good household pets because they are used for protecting the house while away for the day. _____

5. Living on the farm in southern Ontario, winter tends to be cold and harsh. _____

6. Looking at my nephew watching television, he seems to be in a trance. _____

7. When you are living as a family, housework needs to be done. _____

8. After a few months of cleaning a dentist's office, the dentist recommended me to her book-keeper, so I was able to clean the bookkeeper's office too. _____

9. When turning on the stereo system, the sound quality inside a car is great. _____

10. After eating a whole pizza, my stomach begins to feel strange. _____

11. After writing tests and quizzes, the board of education agreed to let me attend Grade 12 at York Memorial High School. _____

12. Being an ESL student, I had a hard time understanding the teachers. _____

13. Going through Grade 12, the teachers began to demand more work. _____

14. After spending three hours shivering and trying to stay warm, the storm subsided and we quickly headed for camp. _____

15. By recycling paper, thousands of square kilometres of forest will be preserved. _____

16. Dressed in secondhand clothing with long messy hair, his appearance was anything but cleancut. _____

17. Loose bindings will cause the skis to fall off while standing up and skiing. _____

18. The English language is always changing. Travelling from place to place, this change can be seen. _____

19. When feeling lonely and depressed, a dog is always at your side wagging its tail. _____

20. By simply putting on a pair of glasses a person's appearance can be transformed dramatically. _____

NAME _____

Misplaced and Dangling Modifiers: Worksheet, Level 1

Revise these sentences, correcting all misplaced or dangling modifiers. If a sentence has no error, write "Correct" in the space.

Example: ~~As~~ *When I was* a teenager, Agatha Christie was my favourite novelist.

1. Entering the park, the smell of hot dogs and peanuts filled our nostrils.

   _____

   _____

2. After finishing breakfast, the house is straightened up.

   _____

3. Peering through the windows, the computer lab looked full.

   _____

4. Many items we eat on a regular basis are full of empty calories, such as jam, mayonnaise and ketchup.

   _____

   _____

5. By simply repeating commands, my dog eventually understood what I wanted him to do.

   _____

   _____

6. Speaking from experience, large families are wonderful.

   _____

7. I only lost my first game.

   _____

8. There should be only one system of weights and measures.

   _____

9. In living common-law, a child is considered illegitimate.

   _____

10. Barrie is a quiet town when browsing through the main street.

    _____

11. Glasses can be a burden, especially when competing in hockey or football.

    _____

12. Now old people are told by their children what to do.

    _____

13. When raining, the motorcyclist can easily have an accident.

_____

14. Now at the age of six months, we take the dog everywhere we go.

_____

_____

15. At the age of four, my parents separated.

_____

16. Standing on the beach, the water gently rippled over my toes.

_____

17. While downhill skiing, your expenses can run into the hundreds of dollars.

_____

_____

18. Consumers are the ones who suffer from higher costs, not the producers.

_____

_____

19. Walking along Robson Street, a major thoroughfare like Yonge Street but half the length, the trendy shops sell the latest fashions and souvenirs for tourists.

_____

_____

20. As a member of the "X" generation, television is a very big part of my life.

_____

_____

NAME _____

Misplaced and Dangling Modifiers: Worksheet, Level 2

Revise these sentences, correcting all misplaced or dangling modifiers. If a sentence has no error, write "Correct" in the space.

1. After living in the old-age home for six months, I began to see a change in my grandfather; he was getting weaker and weaker every day.

   _____

   _____

   _____

2. When watching a one-hour show, as many as six food commercials can come on.

   _____

   _____

3. Although too young to watch restricted movies, the government allows many young teenagers to drive a lethal machine.

   _____

   _____

4. Nearing the top flight of stairs, my nostrils detected the familiar stale stench of the gym.

   _____

   _____

5. After the man received his money, he rushed out of the bank and vowed that he would never return.

   _____

   _____

6. Roughly estimated, my parents pay about $4000 in property tax and about $500 in house insurance.

   _____

   _____

7. Sitting on the bus, tears came to most peoples' eyes as they thought back to the joyful life they had led before the rebels took over the country.

   _____

   _____

   _____

8. I called the personnel manager on the phone, and by making a good first impression she called me for an interview.

   _____

   _____

9. Meeting my unit supervisor was next, who coordinated the ward's daily activities.

   _____

   _____

10. Sitting in the waiting room, looking through an old coverless issue of *National Geographic,* the dentist approached me.

_____

_____

11. The diameter of a capillary is only large enough to accommodate one red blood cell.

_____

_____

12. In the Canadian League, teams are only allowed three downs to get a first down.

_____

_____

13. Most students employed during the school break are able to work only three or four months.

_____

_____

14. In prison one is only allowed a certain amount of time to go outside into a yard surrounded by a fence, or else to sit and read in the cell.

_____

_____

_____

15. Reviewing the statistics, wife assault crosses all socio-economic barriers.

_____

_____

16. With suburban car purchases increasing by the thousands annually, should the use of cars be reduced when commuting to the city?

_____

_____

_____

17. Living at the corner of Jarvis and Carleton, the growl of engines, screech of tires and shriek of horns blend together in a roar so loud that at times it shakes the windows.

_____

_____

_____

18. The bride had long white gloves made of lace on her hands.

_____

_____

19. By the time I had spent an hour underwater, the cold was setting in.

_____

_____

20. Being out of the house most of the day because of school, and evenings because of dancing, my parents became aware that I was growing up.

    _____

    _____

    _____

21. In the late eighties, after being released from prison, the regime took away my rights to an education or a government related job.

    _____

    _____

    _____

22. While observing all the fascinating shapes of coral in the water, odd peeping fish began to crowd around my feet.

    _____

    _____

23. At the age of 16 my only responsibility was to leave my street hockey game when my parents called me in for dinner.

    _____

    _____

24. Many myths have surfaced through the years concerning rape which will be discussed later.

    _____

    _____

25. Being a wealthy city, crimes such as mugging and robbing are rare.

    _____

    _____

26. It seems that when reading the newspaper today, a story can always be found on a large company being caught for polluting the environment.

    _____

    _____

    _____

27. The music on the album was both recorded on stage and in the studio.

    _____

    _____

28. Racing into a high-speed curve at 150 kilometres per hour on a motorcycle, many things are going through the biker's head.

    _____

    _____

29. I'm not only dependent on my family financially but also emotionally.

    _____

    _____

30. At last the clerk told the audience to stand up and receive the judge, who was wearing a long black coat, coming from the side door.

_____

_____

_____

EDITING FOR PARALLEL FORM

Closely related parts of a sentence should fit harmoniously together. Like a red fender on a blue car, the wrong kind of word or word group in a sentence can ruin the effect of the whole. Consider this example:

> My boss was furious. She wanted to know why I was late, why I hadn't phoned, and *you'd better get serious about this job!*

While we can guess that the person who must get serious about this job is the author, not "you" the reader, this sentence would be clearer and the style more harmonious if we made a change:

> She wanted to know why I was late, why I hadn't phoned, and *why I wasn't serious about this job.*

Now we have a series of three indirect questions, rather than the start of a series interrupted by an independent clause. We have a sentence written in *parallel form*.

A. *Items in a series should be parallel in form.* For example, if one is a noun they should all be nouns; if one is a verb they should all be verbs; if one is in past tense they should all be in past tense.

WEAK

Three ways to control stress are having an active social life, eating a balanced diet and regular exercise.

BETTER

Three ways to control stress are *having* an active social life, *eating* a balanced diet and *getting* regular exercise. (All present participles ending in "–ing.")

BETTER

Three things that control stress are an active social *life*, a balanced *diet* and regular *exercise*. (All nouns.)

BETTER

Three ways to control stress are *to socialize* often, *to eat* a balanced diet and *to exercise* regularly. (All infinitives beginning with "to.")

If the items of a series are *parallel in form*, they should also be *related in logic*. One person wrote this:

Santa Claus, an old Christmas legend, is a reality to young children. He is an old gentleman in a red suit, black boots, white beard, a big belly and eight flying reindeer pulling a sleigh.

Well, Santa Claus may be an old gentleman *in* a red suit and *in* black boots, but is he *in* a white beard? Is he *in* a big belly? Is he *in* eight flying reindeer? Let's revise:

He is an old gentleman *in* a red suit and black boots, *with* a white beard and a big belly. Eight flying reindeer pull his sleigh.

Split up a list, as above, if the items are not closely enough related to be parallel in form.

B. Word groups that are paired by *contrast, alternation* or *another relationship* are strongest when parallel:

WEAK

I thought *I would save my money* but instead *a financial loss occurred.*

BETTER

I thought *I would save my money* but instead *I lost it.* (Note that "it," a pronoun, parallels "money," a noun. Note also that putting a paired statement in parallel form can make it more concise as well as more direct.)

WEAK

The advantages of public transit are *low fare* and *the environment is saved.*

BETTER

Public transit helps us *to save* money and *to protect* the environment. (Both infinitives beginning with "to.")

BETTER

Public transit *saves* us money and *protects* the environment. (Both verbs.)

C. "You can't compare apples and oranges," the old saying tells us. *In comparisons, parallel form is especially important.* Do you want to write "faulty comparisons" like this one found in a student essay?

The heart of a child beats faster than an adult.

In other words, a *heart* is beating faster than a *person.* Let's add the pronoun "that" to parallel the noun "heart":

The *heart* of a child beats faster than *that* of an adult.

When you look hard at this next comparison, does it really make sense?

An airplane takes a shorter time reaching its destination than by driving a car.

In case we picture not humans but an airplane driving the car, let's cut out all the unparallel items:

An airplane is faster than a car.

Finally, does this one make sense?

What fascinates me about New York is the size of the buildings and the people.

Unless New Yorkers are very large indeed, why not take "the buildings" and "the people" out of parallel so we will not compare them with each other?

What fascinates me about New York is the people and the size of the buildings.

NAME_____

Parallel Form: Worksheet, Level 1

One item in each series is not parallel to the other items. Cross it out, then substitute an item that is parallel.

Example: eating
drinking
~~talked~~ *talking*
sleeping

1. see
   hear
   feel
   touching
   taste

2. tall
   wide
   thick
   heaviness

3. to write
   speaking
   to read

4. confidence
   authority
   skilfully
   judgement

5. yellow
   large
   green
   red

6. frying
   baking
   to roast

7. steer
   shifted gears
   park
   accelerate

8. lack of exercise
   excess of food
   drinking too much

9. newspapers
   books
   magazines
   going to the movies

10. to skate
    skiing
    swimming
    dancing

11. Spain
    France
    Italy
    Ireland
    London

12. under the table
    after dinner
    in the closet
    behind the chair

13. Monday
    Wednesday
    April
    Saturday

14. honesty
    intelligent
    integrity
    loyalty

15. beaten
    vanquished
    overpowered
    losing

16. to plough the soil
    planting the seeds
    to cultivate the earth
    to harvest the crop

17. Chevrolet
    Ford
    Harley-Davidson
    Oldsmobile

18. love
    hate
    jealousy
    friendliness
    angry

19. hockey
    football
    playing tennis
    basketball

20. spring
    June
    fall
    winter

NAME_____

Parallel Form: Worksheet, Level 2

Most of these passages, from actual student essays, violate parallel form. Edit them, using the method of revision that seems best for each. Make the improvements either by crossing out and adding, or by rewriting in the spaces. When you find a passage already parallel in form, write "parallel" in the blank.

Example: In my free time I listen to records, go to movies and *take* long walks.

1. At the school cafeteria, the pop and juice cost the same as most corner stores.

   _____

   _____

2. My brother prefers luxuries like eating good food and nice clothing.

   _____

   _____

3. We have many stereotypes of "bike" riders: black leather jackets, big black boots, long thick chains and of course tough and mean.

   _____

   _____

   _____

4. Clearly, the speed and cost of using e-mail are much better than the traditional mailing system.

   _____

   _____

5. My favourite newspaper is *The Toronto Sun*: it is small, easy to read, the horoscope and the sports section.

   _____

   _____

6. Rugby is played on a field similar to football.

   _____

7. My office position requires me to answer phone calls, filing charts, using the computer to assist me in reaching the information that I need, and to retrieve charts for nurses and doctors.

   _____

   _____

   _____

8. As a small child I was very spoiled: I was the only daughter, the only granddaughter and the only niece.

   _____

   _____

9. Unlike the United States, a Canadian cannot carry a gun in public.

   _____

   _____

10. Japanese cars are usually more expensive than an American car.

_____

11. Although the feminist movement has called for equality between men and women, females continue to occupy low-paid positions such as sales, receptionists and junior clerks.

_____

_____

_____

12. Having the luxury of your own car gives you many privileges: car radio, control of the temperature, and you may eat and smoke.

_____

_____

_____

13. Men's shoes are made for comfort and made to last longer than women.

_____

_____

14. Research shows that most violent youth come from a broken home, impoverished neighbourhoods, poverty, alcoholism, racism and illiteracy.

_____

_____

_____

15. Like many of the schools in Trinidad, we all had to wear uniforms.

_____

_____

16. Narrow-minded people still look down on a woman who lifts weights, works on a car engine or speaking her thoughts freely.

_____

_____

_____

17. Some people feel that to lose their job is to lose their life.

_____

_____

18. The population of New York City is much larger than Toronto.

_____

_____

19. In Canada we have snow, rain, sun, cloudy, wind, warm and cold.

_____

_____

20. High-society people have the best of everything. Even the clothes they wear are of higher quality than the average person.

    _____

    _____

21. Unlike the big city, people in a small city take time to talk to you and even bake you cookies.

    _____

    _____

22. The rent of newer buildings is much higher than older buildings.

    _____

    _____

23. Today there are three types of parents: permissive, strict and wealthy.

    _____

    _____

24. The Sunday paper, unlike the other days of the week, has many entertaining articles about interesting people, which is a welcome change from the regular auto accidents and disasters.

    _____

    _____

    _____

25. I feel that an exciting essay can be written by being prepared, writing about a topic that interests both you and your audience, using many examples, don't repeat yourself, don't use flowery words and have a well-structured essay.

    _____

    _____

    _____

    _____

    _____

26. In Singapore, the pedestrians were actually walking faster than the cars.

    _____

    _____

27. In renting a condominium one is faced with certain restrictions: no pets, no overnight visitors, need for permission to do decorating and the noise level should be kept low at all times.

    _____

    _____

    _____

    _____

28. The price of brand-name computers is about 25 percent higher than clones.

    _____

    _____

29. There are computers in the banks, on our desks at home and at work, they are in the television set, in the car, in the supermarket and even in the kitchen.

_____

_____

_____

30. Everyone looks for distinctive qualities in a career: how much money it brings, how long will it take to get, what are the benefits, is it compatible with one's lifestyle, and the list can go on forever!

_____

_____

_____

_____

EDITING FOR SPELLING AND RELATED MATTERS

A couple of generations ago, many teachers and students believed spelling to be one of the main writing tasks. It seemed almost as important as the argument, itself—despite the fact that some major authors, such as Keats and Hemingway, had been terrible spellers.

Today we realize that fixing spelling is a relatively minor task. After the main work of focus and development has been done in the early draft or drafts, we check over the spelling as a kind of "quality control"—much as the manufacturer of a well-engineered car looks over the paint job to make sure there are no scratches to mar the finish.

We also realize now that attention to spelling belongs at the *end* of the writing process. Why invest the work earlier, when later you may cut out whole passages from your argument, and with them the effort put into spelling?

Or, if like most people you are now computerized, it may indeed make sense for your spell check to clean up the mess as soon as your discovery draft is done; with almost no labour on your part, this will make early drafts seem cleaner and easier to work with.

However, as we will see later on, spell check is not perfect. You still need to look over your spelling by hand, to catch what the relatively crude software missed. And that step still comes at the end of the writing process, for the same reason given above: so you do not waste your precious time on sections that may later be thrown out.

Though we know spelling is less important than the quality of the argument, why do we still devote time to it? Because poor spelling can quickly ruin the best of essays, by giving your audience a poor overall impression. Would you take seriously, for example, the sports essay one student wrote about the "Superbowel"? And how about these items that appeared in other essays?

bathtube	*pair tree*
Cuban missal crisis	*soup opera*
deadicated	*suck-seed*
drink a bear or two	*supperpower*
escapegoat	*toe truck*
law biting citizen	*viscous circle*
low self-steam	*well fear cheque*
the Mid-Evil age	*who nose?*

Whether such errors make the reader laugh or cry, one thing is certain: they will distract the reader from your message.

Commonly Confused Words

Note that all the above bloopers occurred when one word was confused with another. Not every error is made this way, but the worst and most frequent are. *Make sure that you know the difference, then, between the following commonly confused words.* (The worst trouble-makers are boldfaced.) Definitions are not given here, because you have a dictionary.

accept/except	***its/it's***
advice/advise	*know/no/now*
affect/effect	*lead/led*
are/our	*loose/lose*
bare/bear	*moral/morale*
brakes/breaks	*passed/past*
breath/breathe	*peace/piece*
buy/by	*personal/personnel*
capital/capitol	*principal/principle*
clothes/cloths	***quiet/quit/quite***
coarse/course	*right/wright/write*
council/counsel	*role/roll*
desert/dessert	*sight/site*
do/due	***than/then***
emigrated/immigrated	***their/there/they're***
farther/further	*thorough/threw/through*
hear/here	***to/too/two***
heroin/heroine	*weather/whether*
hole/whole	*were/we're/where*

"Strange how all six of your previous employers left the 'C' out of the word 'excellent.'"

Herman © Jim Unger/dist. Laughingstock Licensing Inc.

NAME_____

Commonly Confused Words: Worksheet

Circle the correct choice in the parentheses.

1. A person must (**accept**/except) all that life has to offer, both good and bad.

2. Mom warned us not to eat all the candy, but we ignored her (**advice**/advise).

3. Oil slicks in the ocean have a devastating (affect/**effect**) on wildlife.

4. The presence of parental love can (**affect**/effect) the child's ability to love others.

5. How do dreams change (are/**our**) lives?

6. I am so attached to my cat that I cannot (bare/**bear**) to part with it.

7. Some people get all the (brakes/**breaks**).

8. When oil is applied to the water, increasing the surface tension, the mosquito larvae can no longer poke their tubes up into the air to (breath/**breathe**).

9. A beginner will go to the nearest sports shop and (**buy**/by) every piece of equipment in sight.

10. Saint John's is the (capital/**capitol**) of Newfoundland.

11. One of the most important preparations for cross-country skiing is selection of light (**clothes**/cloths) that can be worn in several layers.

12. By the time I finished high school, I had never had a (coarse/**course**) in art.

13. A municipal (**council**/counsel) tends to be divided into prodevelopment and antidevelopment factions.

14. Large parts of Africa are turning into (**desert**/dessert).

15. Let's give credit where credit is (do/**due**).

16. In 1991 my parents (emigrated/**immigrated**) to Canada.

17. I swam laps in the pool till I thought I could go no (**farther**/further).

18. Old people feel isolated because they cannot (**hear**/here) well.

19. Desdemona is a tragic (heroin/**heroine**).

20. My sister ate the (hole/**whole**) pizza.

21. A dog is faithful to (**its**/it's) owner.

22. You never (**know**/no/now) what can happen.

23. Through the example of their parents, children are (lead/**led**) to cheat in society.

24. To (*loose*/*lose*) a game is to learn a lesson.

25. Police associations say that even the most disciplined force cannot function well if the (*moral*/*morale*) is low.

26. A year (*passed*/*past*) before Stephen Leacock found himself teaching at Upper Canada College.

27. I wanted a (*peace*/*piece*) of the action.

28. Three days after I was hired, the (*personal*/*personnel*) manager called me to her office.

29. I was not one of those troublemakers who were always sent to see the (*principal*/*principle*).

30. The hours past midnight are best for studying, because everything is (*quiet*/*quit*/*quite*).

31. At university, students have to (*right*/*wright*/*write*) exams as long as three hours.

32. Professional athletes are (*role*/*roll*) models to thousands of children.

33. Many students lose (*sight*/*site*) of their goals.

34. Skinheads dress differently (*than*/*then*) others their age do.

35. (*Their*/*There*/*They're*) stood my husband with the knife firmly in his hand, waiting to plunge it into the intruder.

36. The police are hard workers. (*Their*/*There*/*They're*) not out on the streets slacking off.

37. My friends and I used to go on trips (*thorough*/*threw*/*through*) the wilderness.

38. More and more coaches and athletes take a friendly match of football (*to*/*too*/*two*) seriously.

39. (*Weather*/*Whether*) to take a part-time job depends on many factors.

40. When students (*were*/*we're*/*where*) asked to name the prime ministers of Canada, some of them mentioned John Kennedy.

Your Own Spelling List

If you are like most people, 90 percent of your spelling errors may be the same 20 or 30 words gone wrong every time you write them. While over the long term the best way to spell better is to read extensively, *the most direct way to improve your spelling right now is to list all words you misspell in assignments, then study the correct spellings till you have mastered them.*

Have a friend test you on your list, then again on the "short list" of those words that still give trouble. You may be surprised at how far your spelling performance goes up in your next paper.

A Hundred Words Often Misspelled

Every English teacher has observed the mysterious fact that the same words are misspelled by large numbers of people. Here are most of the culprits, with the worst troublemakers boldfaced. Before you start memorizing, have a friend test you on these words—then study only a "short list" of the 10 or 20 that may need attention.

accommodate	*disappear*	*persistent*
achievement	*disappoint*	*piece*
acquaintance	*disastrous*	*playwright*
acquire	*dominant*	*possess*
across	*embarrass*	*predominant*
adequately	*emperor*	*preferred*
a lot	***environment***	*prejudice*
all right	*even though*	*prevalent*
among	*exceed*	***privilege***
analyze	***existence***	*pronunciation*
argument	*experiment*	*psychology*
athlete	*fascinate*	*quantity*
attendance	*fiery*	***receive***
basically	***government***	*resistance*
beneficial	*heroes*	*rhyme*
category	*imagination*	*rhythm*
committee	***independence***	*seize*
compatible	*knowledge*	*separate*
completely	*laboratory*	*similar*
conceive	*leisure*	*sincerely*
condemn	*loneliness*	*studying*
conscience	*maintenance*	*subtle*
consistent	*material*	*surprise*
controversy	***necessary***	*tendency*
convenient	*noticeable*	*tomorrow*
deceive	*obedience*	*tragedy*
definite	***occasion***	*truly*
dependent	*occurred*	*unnecessary*
description	*opponent*	*villain*
desirable	*perceive*	*weird*
destroy	*permanent*	
dining	*perseverance*	

Canadian Spelling

Everyone who reads much knows that the British spell certain words one way, the Americans another, and that Canadians are torn between the two.

Many Canadians, especially in the middle and eastern provinces, continue to use the mainly British spellings they were taught in school. Thus they work in *centres* such as the Toronto Dominion Centre. They get paid by *cheque*. After they *labour* they watch their *colour* television set or perhaps go to a *theatre*.

Yet when some Canadian newspapers write the words *center*, *check*, *labor*, *color* and *theater*, Canadians may not sense those spellings as "foreign," even though they are American. Though some newspapers do use American spelling, *The Globe and Mail* has recently changed back to Canadian spelling, because readers wanted it. Most Canadian book publishers also continue to use Canadian spelling, and so does the federal government in its publications.

So what is the college or university writer to do? Though some teachers mark American spellings as errors, calling American spelling wrong is no more logical than saying that English is better than French, or vice versa. Rather, the spelling you employ is mostly a cultural matter. Both systems are "correct," so the choice is yours.

If you are exceedingly concerned with saving a letter here and there (like managers of some newspapers who like to save a hundredth of a cent any way they can), then you may prefer the sometimes shorter American spellings. Even then, some equivalents, such as "centre" or "center," are the same length.

On the other hand, if tradition means something to you, and if Canadian spelling "feels" better just because you have always seen it, you will probably wish to stay with the usage you learned in school.

Many students who wish to do so have complained that some American software used here contains spellers that actually show Canadian spellings as errors. The easiest way to fix this, in about half an hour, is to systematically enter into the "add" function of your spell check all Canadian spellings that differ from American spellings (referring to the chart on page 197). Now "colour," "centre," etc. will be recognized as correct, along with "color" and "center." If you feel like taking things a step further, your software may also permit removing words (the American spellings) from its central list.

Whatever your view of this whole matter, remember that neither American nor Canadian spelling is "wrong": the only editing error is in mixing "correct" forms. *Be consistent: do not write* colour *and* color *in the same paper.* Here are three more principles to observe:

• Avoid the common error of extending Canadian forms to words in which they are not used, as in writing *authour* for *author* or *amoung* for *among*.

• Observe the limits to the *-our* form in Canadian usage: *honour, honourable* but *honorary; labour, labourer* but *laborious; vigour* but *vigorous* and *invigorate*. When you are in doubt, consult the list that follows.

• Although "Canadian" forms are based on British spelling, do not let avoidance of American forms lead you to use British forms that are eccentric in Canada. Avoid spellings such as these: *amongst, whilst, connexion, gaol, kerb, tyre* and *waggon*.

To help you apply consistently the system that you choose, here is a list of the most common differences between Canadian and American spelling. Try to use only one side or the other, and give some thought to your choice.

The dictionary has always been a key tool for writers, giving data on those building blocks of all speech, words: how to spell them, which ones to choose, and even the fine points of feeling carried by each. Though the good old book dictionary is still more complete and still deserves a place on your writing desk, your computer's spell-check system has one powerful new advantage: speed.

Now that we can whip through the spelling of a thousand-word essay in a couple of minutes, we are even changing the point at which we do the job; though parts may be chopped in later editing, the work is now so easy that it makes sense to spell check even the first version—to make it cleaner and easier to work with.

(You have surely noted, too, that you can count words swiftly through spell check, in case you have a word limit to reach or not to exceed.)

Despite its blinding speed, though, you have also surely noted the major flaw of this still crude software: since spell check works by comparing your spellings to the spellings in its own word list, it can do only one main thing: point out a word it does not recognize.

Thus you need never again write "recieve" for "receive" or "enviroment" for "environment"—but if you confuse "to," "too" and "two," the software thinks you are right. **The fact is that you must still always check spelling by hand, near the end of the editing process.** (So that you can do so, be sure to master the "words commonly confused" earlier in this section.)

See also p. 33 on using the electronic thesaurus, which also performs some functions of the traditional dictionary.

CANADIAN USAGE	SHARED USAGE	AMERICAN USAGE
armour		*armor*
behaviour		*behavior*
colour, colourful		*color, colorful*
favour, favourite		*favor, favorite*
fervour		*fervor*
flavour, flavourful		*flavor, flavorful*
harbour		*harbor*
honour, honourable	*honorary*	*honor, honorable*
humour, humourless	*humorist, humorous*	*humor, humorless*
labour, labourer	*laborious*	*labor, laborer*
neighbour, neighbourhood, neighbourly		*neighbor, neighborhood, neighborly*
odour, odourless	*odoriferous, odorous*	*odor, odorless*
rigour	*rigorous*	*rigor*
vapour	*vaporize*	*vapor*
vigour	*vigorous, invigorate*	*vigor*
calibre	*calibration*	*caliber, calibre*
centre	*central*	*center*
fibre	*fibrous*	*fiber, fibre*
litre		*liter*
lustre	*lustrous*	*luster, lustre*
manoeuvre		*maneuver*
metre	*metric*	*meter*
spectre	*spectral*	*specter, spectre*
theatre	*theatrical*	*theater, theatre*
mould (for casting), moulding, moulded		*mold, molding, molded*
mould (fungus), mouldy		*mold, moldy*
smoulder		*smolder*
defence, defenceless	*defensive*	*defense, defenseless*
offence	*offensive*	*offense*
cheque, cheque book, chequing account		*check, check book, checking account*
plough, ploughing		*plow, plowing*

Five Spelling Rules

Although at first the study of individual words is the fastest and most direct way to fix your spelling, the technique works less well once you have cut out the most frequent errors. You simply use too many words to study them all.

A partial solution is rules. Some languages, such as Spanish, have a logical system whose universal principles ensure correct spelling of almost any word, even a new one. We are less fortunate. English is such a mixture of other languages that some spelling rules contradict each other, and most have exceptions. Learning the rules may improve your spelling—but not very much. Besides, the task of applying lengthy principles to every tenth or twentieth word will probably not help you finish your essay by midnight.

In hopes that they may help, though, here are five of the clearest spelling rules. If you would like more, whole books about spelling can be found in any bookstore. You would do better, though, to take seriously the advice on page 208 about reading being at the heart of improvement in spelling.

A. Put **i** before **e**, except after **c**
    Or when sounded like **a**
    As in **neighbour** or **weigh**.

    Examples of **i** before **e**:
    belief, chief, piece, priest, relief

    Examples of **e** before **i**:
    ceiling, deceive, eight, receive, their

    Exceptions to the rule:
    either, foreign, height, neither, seize, weird

B. When you add a **prefix**, do *not* change the spelling of the root word:

    dis + appear = **dis**appear
    dis + satisfy = **dis**satisfy
    im + possible = **im**possible
    im + moral   = **im**moral
    mis + lead   = **mis**lead
    mis + spell   = **mis**spell
    un + afraid   = **un**afraid
    un + noticed = **un**noticed

C. When you add a **suffix** beginning with a vowel to a word root that is accented on the last syllable or that has only one syllable, and if the root ends in a single consonant preceded by a single vowel, then double the final consonant of the root:

    bat   + **ed**   = bat**ted**
    begin   + **ing** = beginn**ing**
    control + **ed**   = controll**ed**
    occur   + **ence** = occurr**ence**

    omit   + **ing** = omit**ting**
    prefer + **ed**   = prefer**red**
    rap   + **ed**   = rapp**ed**
    run   + **ing** = runn**ing**

D. Drop the final **e** when the suffix begins with a vowel:

    lose   + **ing** = los**ing**
    come   + **ing** = com**ing**
    use   + **ing** = us**ing**
    imagine   + **ary** = imagin**ary**
    separate + **ion** = separat**ion**
    ice   + **y**   = ic**y**

    Exceptions (to keep **c** or **g** soft): advantageous, changeable, enforceable, outrageous, noticeable

    Exceptions (to avoid mispronunciation): eyeing, hoeing, mileage

    Keep the final **e** when the suffix begins with a consonant:

    achieve + **ment** = achieve**ment**
    excite + **ment** = excite**ment**
    live   + **ly**   = live**ly**
    lone   + **ly**   = lone**ly**
    sincere + **ly**   = sincere**ly**
    use   + **ful** = use**ful**

    Exceptions: argument, probably, truly, wholly

E. A plural is normally formed by adding **s**, but **es** is added when another syllable results:

    ### ONE SYLLABLE

tree	trees
lake	lakes
cloud	clouds
star	stars

ONE SYLLABLE	TWO SYLLABLES
ash	ashes
branch	branches
fox	foxes
match	matches

Apostrophes

We'll discuss the apostrophe here, because, although it is a punctuation mark, its misuse is felt as a spelling error. Hardly an essay is written that does not contain one such error, and some contain dozens. Remember these principles:

A. Use the apostrophe to show **contraction**:

I am = I'm
you are = you're
he is = he's
we are = we're
they are = they're
it is = it's
do not = don't
cannot = can't
should not = shouldn't
I would = I'd

B. Use the apostrophe to show **possession**:

• In a singular possessive, the apostrophe goes **before** the final **s**:

The single parent's responsibility is doubled.

• In a plural possessive, the apostrophe goes **after** the final **s**:

Most parents' greatest concern is for their children's happiness.

Note how the word "children" above is already plural without an *s*. In such cases the apostrophe follows the plural ending, and an *s* comes last to show how the word is pronounced: *children's*. Two more common words that work this way are *women* (*women's*) and *men* (*men's*).

• The possessives **its** and **whose** never take an apostrophe, although the contractions **it's** and **who's** do. Many errors are made by people who ignore the difference:

POSSESSION

The snake reared *its* head.
Not: The snake reared *it's* (*it is*) head.
I know *whose* work this is.
Not: I know *who's* (*who is*) work this is.

CONTRACTION

It's snowing (*It is* snowing.)
Who's there? (*Who is* there?)

C. The apostrophe is *not* used with every word that ends in *s*. Avoid the knee-jerk reaction of thinking that, since the apostrophe sometimes goes with the final *s*, it always does so.

• The apostrophe does *not* form a plural:

ERROR

Student's from high school's, college's and university's were looking for summer job's.

CORRECTION

Students from high schools, colleges and universities were looking for summer jobs.

• The apostrophe does *not* form a third-person verb:

ERROR

A politician make's new promises whenever election time roll's around.

CORRECTION

A politician makes new promises whenever election time rolls around.

To Contract or Not To Contract ...?

Finally, should contractions be used at all in academic writing? You surely had high school teachers who said to avoid them all. Were those teachers right or wrong?

Like most pieces of advice, this one contains some truth but not the whole truth. Yes, in the kind of formal research essay explored in our final chapter, you should avoid all contractions—such as "didn't" or "wouldn't"—because they are too informal, too conversational. For the reader to believe in your scholarship, not only should your quotations and referencing be good, but your tone should be dignified and objective—not like a lunchtime conversation in the cafeteria. Even in other kinds of writing where a formal tone is expected (a literature paper, a business report, a lab report), contractions should be avoided.

On the other hand, in informal personal essays and certainly in things like letters to friends, a total absence of contractions would be too formal, too stuffy, too intimidating. In much of this everyday writing a contraction here and there is a good thing, a device to make language more direct and natural. Do continue to avoid contractions in academic writing, but in less formal assignments try to "feel" the style: if writing something out seems awkward or stuffy, then go ahead and use the contraction.

NAME _____

Apostrophes: Worksheet

Whenever you see an apostrophe error in these passages from student essays, write the correction, with the word in which it occurs, in the blank at the right. Write "C" after any sentence that is correct.

Example: The sun's ~~ray~~'s become more direct in spring.   *rays*

1. All pet's should receive more sympathy than they do.   _____

2. For entertainment Oshawa has movie theatres, ice rinks, roller arena's, night clubs and all sorts of gym's to work out at.   _____

3. The Beatles influence and popularity will live as long as rock and roll exists.   _____

4. The present art of producing with an assembly line system has come a long way since it's introduction.   _____

5. As I plunged into the water, its cold temperature chilled every bone in my body.   _____

6. Its exciting to see a great horse thundering down the track.   _____

7. The only way to reduce student's financial problems is to increase their grants and loans.   _____

8. Students who are 18 and over are the one's who need money the most.   _____

9. Thousands of people fish Ontario's lake's and river's each year, but how many will take a minute to consider the result's of fished-out waters?   _____

10. Driving a motorcycle give's one a sense of independence, because the rider know's people are watching.   _____

11. People who have no confidence in their own work will try to use others ideas.   _____

12. Politic's is what get's everyone talking and moving in this world.   _____

13. Parent's moral values are passed on to the next generation.   _____

14. My parent's emigrated from Greece.   _____

15. The Rolling Stones' music was unique for its time.   _____

16. After each goal the team that was scored against get's possession of the ball behind it's net.   _____

17. Its a holiday to escape from work and see who can catch the most fish.   _____

18. It's my parent's duty to take care of me; they are legally required to.   _____

19. She see's only his good qualities.   _____

20. What drains peoples' energy is the accelerating rate of change.   _____

21. Solar system's have a sun and various numbers of planet's. _____

22. Are Canadian's ashamed of their own country? _____

23. A person who's on LSD may see the ceiling of the house crash in. _____

24. There are many owner's club's for most sports cars. _____

25. Newtons Second Law of Motion helps the swimmer to conserve energy. _____

26. Illness can be the minds expression to withdraw from lifes stress's and strains. _____

27. We'd go to my grandparents house each year because it wasn't really Christmas anywhere else. _____

28. The four-cycle system is what most automobile engine's are based on. _____

29. When Nick sees the Buchanan's reaction to Myrtle's death, he develops a sense of moral responsibility. _____

30. Animals such as rabbit's, monkey's and cat's are being used for meaningless experiments. _____

31. The arteries' main function is to carry oxygenated blood. _____

32. It was Labour Day when all the delayed thought's of moving from my parents finally hit home. _____

33. When children see their favourite player's using sticks to jab and spear other players, the next thing you know, the children are imitating. _____

34. Anyone who has run for a few year's on the road has no doubt experienced a deterioration of the knee's. _____

35. Elizabeth realized the faults of her parent's marriage. _____

36. At colleges and universities, drinking has become part of the system. _____

37. True punk rockers wear safety pins through their nose's or cheek's. _____

38. A newborn child see's the light for the first time. _____

39. My mothers parent's don't travel at all. _____

40. All over the world we are confronted with the same problems in womens lives. _____

Capitals

Since capitals, like apostrophes, tend to be sensed as an aspect of spelling, we'll discuss them here.

Though everyone knows the main uses of capital letters, some fine points are not so well known—or may just be forgotten in the rush to finish assignments. Look over the principles below, in case there are any you have been ignoring.

A. Use a capital to **begin a sentence, a word group standing for a sentence**, and **a line of regular poetry**:

Our big cities are no longer safe.

Yes. Of course. No doubt about it.

Western wind, when will thou blow,
The small rain down can rain?
Christ, if my love were in my arms
And I in my bed again!
—anonymous

B. Capitalize the beginning of a **direct quotation** if it is a sentence or a word group standing for a sentence:

According to Aristotle, "Poverty is the parent of revolution and crime." (The quotation is a sentence.)

He shook his head and said, "Over my dead body." (Though the word group is not a sentence, it is meant to function as one.)

"I'll have roast duck," she said, "with fried rice." (The "with" is not capitalized, because it does not begin a new sentence.)

Ben Jonson wrote that Shakespeare knew "small Latin and less Greek." (The "small" is not capitalized, because the quoted words are only part of Jonson's original sentence.)

C. Capitalize **proper nouns**:

• Names of persons, nationalities and languages:

Céline Dion	Scottish
Rudy Wiebe	Spaniard
Canadian	speak French
Australian	an English course

• Academic courses whose names are not derived from languages are normally not capitalized:

psychology		English
history	BUT	French
calculus		Latin

• Specific places:

Calgary	Yonge Street
Saskatchewan	Cabbagetown
Canada	the Maritimes
the Fraser River	the North (referring to
the Rocky Mountains	a region, not just a direction)

• Names of organizations:

Seneca College
Mennonite Brethren Church
Bruce Trail Association
Parliament
Gennum Corporation

BUT

a community college
went to church
a hiking club
parliamentary procedure
a high-tech corporation

• Days of the week, months, and holidays, but not seasons:

Tuesday	Chinese New Year
Saturday	Ramadan
January	spring
August	winter

• Titles of books, magazines, newspapers, plays, films, musical compositions, poems, short stories, articles and essays. Capitalize the first word and all others except for connecting words (such as *a, an, the, and, or, but, in, on, by*) that have no more than five letters:

Book: *The Stone Diaries*
Magazine: *Maclean's*
Newspaper: *The Vancouver Sun*
Play: *Hamlet*
Film: *King Kong*
Song: "Yesterday"
Poem: "Fern Hill"
Short story: "The Painted Door"
Article or essay: "Exaggeration as a Comic Device in the Novels of Mordecai Richler"

(Names of periodicals and titles of books, plays and other *long items* are symbolized by italics or underlining. On the other hand, titles of *short items* such as songs, poems, short stories, articles and essays, are not italicized or underlined, but are put in quotation marks as above.)

• Words of family relationship when used as names or with names:

I congratulated Mother.
There was Father.
Uncle Ivan
Aunt Mary

BUT

I congratulated my mother.
There was our father.
My uncle was named Ivan.
Mary is my aunt.

• Titles appearing before a name, or used alone as a form of address:

Professor Serrano
Doctor Vaudouris
Captain Tremblay

Hello, Professor.
Thank you, Doctor.
I agree, Captain.

BUT

a professor
my doctor
an army captain

NAME _____

Capitals: Worksheet

Add the missing capitals wherever necessary, but avoid creating unnecessary ones.

1. a friend of mine, frank, once told me that he had been behind a mac's store smoking a cigarette when all of a sudden a police officer approached and asked him where the pot was hidden.

2. during the hockey game, the mother of one of the opposing players stood up from her seat and yelled as loudly as she could, "kill that little worm!"

3. in the first year of the program, students have to take accounting, economics, geography, mathematics, english, management, business law and psychology.

4. canadians have long been concerned with developing the north, but only recently with protecting it.

5. my parents bought a house north of the business district, within a five-minute walk of an elementary school, a middle school, a high school, a mac's milk store and a shopping centre.

6. on a bright summer morning, the first monday of july, we got in our canoe and started down the missinaibi river.

7. who has seen the wind?
    neither you nor i;
  but when the trees bow down their heads
    the wind is passing by.
    —christina rossetti, 1872

8. in high school one of my english teachers spent two months on *hamlet*.

9. in addition to containing beef and/or pork, wieners may contain water, flour, milk solids, salt and preservatives such as sodium nitrite, which has been known to cause cancer in laboratory animals.

10. cruise ships have many facilities such as bedrooms, swimming pools, lawn tennis courts, dancing halls, movie theatres and bars.

11. lady macbeth, a strong-willed character who was capable of influencing macbeth to murder his king, brought about her breakdown and death by her own ambitions.

12. john osborne was born on december 12, 1929, in london, england.

13. in today's modern society, people's morals and values are changing, so divorce, birth control and abortion are more easily accepted.

14. j. d. salinger's best short story, "for esmé—with love and squalor," shows how destructive war is to human feelings.

15. when i began high school i really got involved in soccer.

16. i arrived in trinidad on monday and began my search for a job on tuesday.

17. stephen leacock once wrote, "the essence of humour is human kindliness."

18. in his *biographia literaria*, coleridge refers to "that willing suspension of disbelief for the moment, which constitutes poetic faith."

19. mackenzie king said, "the promises of yesterday are the taxes of today."

20. blaise pascal called humans "the glory and the shame of the universe."

21. the driver stopped the bus to jump out and take a look. he was immediately followed by the spaniard, two mexicans, hugh, geoffrey and yvonne.

22. when the canadian dollar sank in value, foreign automobiles such as the volvo, volkswagen, toyota, subaru and honda rose sharply in price.

23. the national hockey league rules committee brought in new rules that prohibited players from being overly aggressive.

24. my mother speaks french, portuguese and english.

25. i have noted that math teachers do not dress as well as english teachers.

26. to depict their toughness, hockey players are given names such as "hammer," "battleship," "tiger" and "bull-dog."

27. one of the fastest-growing religions in the world is islam.

28. in each of mordecai richler's earlier novels, *the acrobats, son of a smaller hero* and *a choice of enemies*, the hero is an artistically inclined canadian with a deep dislike of canadian culture and a conviction that the society he lives in is a fraud.

29. as a faithful expression of the theme found in the play, the movie *fortune and men's eyes* was the epitome of success.

30. "well, doctor," i said, "since you agree with the other doctors, i suppose we had better go ahead with the operation."

Abbreviations

Don't overdo the abbreviations. When you write a.m. and p.m. instead of *ante meridiem* and *post meridiem*, you help your readers by saving their time. But when you cram into your essay every abbreviation you can think of (Can., Alta, N.S., Tues., Feb., GT, CB, ASA, LCBO, PC, PCV, etc.), you are only confusing them. To figure out all these letters takes much longer than to just read the original words.

See if you can put the words to the following common abbreviations into the blanks. (The answers are on page 239.) If this activity gives you trouble, you can see how abbreviations would also give your reader trouble.

1. CEO _____

2. CPI _____

3. GIC _____

4. GST _____

5. ICU _____

6. NDP _____

7. RAM _____

8. R&D _____

9. RN _____

10. SASE _____

Do use abbreviations to avoid repetition. For example, after naming the United Nations Educational, Scientific and Cultural Organization in your first paragraph, have mercy on your reader by referring to it the next ten or 20 times as UNESCO.

Also, if you are writing a technical report for specialists to read, such as "Shear Flow in Closed Single-Cell and Multi-Cell Systems," do use any abbreviations customary in the field, especially in tables and charts.

But in the kind of general classroom writing expected in courses such as English, history and philosophy, use abbreviations only where you can hardly avoid them. Here are some principles to guide you:

A. Abbreviate these titles before a name: *Mr., Mrs., Ms., Dr., Rev.*

Mr. Violi
Ms. Vasquez
Dr. Chen
Rev. Sung

Such titles are spelled out, though, when used in place of the name:

Well, Doctor, what are my chances?

Other titles are usually not abbreviated, even before a name:

Mother Teresa
General Montcalm
Sir Nigel
Professor Beauchemin

B. Abbreviate names of private or public organizations if the abbreviation is well known and customarily used. Do write out the full name, though, the first time you mention an organization, with the abbreviation just after in parentheses.

RCMP	UN
ITT	INCO
TSE	BBC
CIA	YWCA
NAFTA	CBC

C. Abbreviate academic degrees:

B.A.	B.S.
M.A.	M.B.A.
M.S.W.	M.D.
D.Ed.	Ph.D.

D. You may abbreviate certain geographical names:

U.K.   U.S.A.

Other geographical names (countries, provinces, counties, cities) are not abbreviated except in addresses.

E. Abbreviate certain terms from the Latin:

• Words that specify time periods:

a.m.	p.m.
b.c.	a.d.

• Certain terms used in academic writing:

cf. (compare)	i.e. (that is)
e.g. (for example)	q.v. (which see)

• That overused term, *etc.* Use *etc.* only to signal actual items that you know but choose not to include—never to hide what you do not know. Avoid abuses like this:

The major crops of British Columbia are apples, etc.

Symbols and Numbers in the Metric System

Although the traditional Imperial system of weights and measures is still used in some areas of our daily lives—as when we tell our height in feet and inches, or our weight in pounds—the metric system has become the norm in Canada for most other uses. Even when we write an essay, we may need to know the standard metric abbreviations, officially called "symbols," and how to use them.

When numbers are spelled out, terms of measurement used with them are also spelled out; when numbers appear as figures, the terms of measurement appear as symbols.

Thus in technical writing or in any charts and tables where a great many numbers are used, you will probably use figures and symbols. But where numbers occur less frequently, as in most essays, you will probably write out both numbers and terms of measurement.

EXAMPLES:

A piece of steel 0.25 cm thick, 1.75 m wide and 3.15 m long is welded to the frame.

The average fingernail is about one centimetre wide.

The following table gives the most common metric terms and the symbols for them. The symbols are identical in both singular and plural uses, and unless they occur at the end of a sentence, are written without a period.

LENGTH

kilometre	km
metre	m
decimetre	dm
centimetre	cm
millimetre	mm

AREA

square kilometre	km²
hectare	ha²
square metre	m²
square decimetre	dm²
square centimetre	cm²

VOLUME

cubic metre	m³
cubic decimetre	dm³
cubic centimetre	cm³
kilolitre	kL
litre	L
millilitre	mL

MASS

tonne	t
kilogram	kg
gram	g
milligram	mg

TEMPERATURE

degree Celsius	°C

Our traditional 24-hour day and its parts are of course not metric, but are wisely being retained:

TIME

day	d
hour	h
minute	min
second	s

The metric system specifies certain principles for the use of numbers:

• A zero is put before a decimal fraction:

0.9144 m

• A space, rather than a comma, separates groups of three digits. Numbers of only four digits are not separated:

1 000 000 g   1000 g

• Only numbers 10 and over are expressed in figures:

five kilograms   75 kg

Reading: The Key to Spelling

On the average, North Americans read less than one book a year, perhaps because they watch four hours a day of television. By the time they graduate from high school they have spent more hours in front of the "tube" than in the classroom. They may know a great deal about how to catch a bank robber, apply a half nelson or estimate the price of a refrigerator, but one thing they may not know well at all is how to spell.

By contrast, people who have read a book or two a month (or an hour or two a day of magazines or newspapers) from childhood to adulthood have seen each word so many times that, with rare exceptions, their own spelling is automatically correct.

Reading is the long-term solution to spelling problems and to most other writing problems as well. The great majority of people who read regularly will eventually become much better in spelling, grammar and style than those who do not.

Although the process takes several years, it is the only way to improve profoundly your writing. Therefore, *if you do not have the reading habit, consider acquiring it now.*

Subscribe to a magazine or two in a field that interests you. Read a newspaper every day. Keep a couple of good books by your TV chair. If you don't have the time now, start during the holidays or the summer break. And if you have not enjoyed reading in the past, don't let that stop you. With every hour you read, you are a better reader; and as you improve, the reading will become more fun.

Some Recommended Canadian Books

(novels except where noted otherwise)

As For Me and My House, Sinclair Ross
Away, Jane Urquhart
Black Robe, Brian Moore
The Book of Secrets, M. G. Vassanji

A Casual Brutality, Neil Bissoondath
A Certain Mr. Takahashi, Ann Ireland
A Discovery of Strangers, Rudy Wiebe
A Dream Like Mine, M. T. Kelly
The English Patient, Michael Ondaatje
A Fine Balance, Rohinton Mistry
My Father's House (memoir), Sylvia Fraser
Fifth Business, Robertson Davies
In Transit (stories), Mavis Gallant
La Guerre, Yes Sir!, Roch Carrier
Alias Grace, Margaret Atwood
Klee Wyck (autobiographical sketches), Emily Carr
Lives of Girls and Women, Alice Munro
Lives of the Saints, Nino Ricci
Microserfs, Douglas Coupland
Never Cry Wolf (semi-autobiography),
   Farley Mowat
Obasan, Joy Kogawa
The Stone Angel, Margaret Laurence
The Stone Diaries, Carol Shields
Volkswagen Blues, Jacques Poulin
The Wars, Timothy Findley

Part Five

The Research Essay

The process of writing a research essay is both like and unlike the process of writing the "short essay," which we discussed earlier. A research essay rests on the same foundations, but of course has a larger and more detailed structure.

One difference can be length. Though a research paper is sometimes as short as 5 or 6 pages, it's often 10 or 12 or even longer. Another difference can be the level of objectivity. While a "short essay" often relies on our own thoughts or experiences, a research essay is a more objective and formal argument: a methodical sifting of evidence to arrive at a valid conclusion. And in referring to this sifted evidence, it uses the scholarly devices of quotations, name-page references, and list of works cited.

Yet these differences do not change the fact that both the "short" and "research" essays need original ideas, a thesis statement that gives focus and direction, unified development by example and argument, and some serious revision. Since these foundations underlie the process of writing both essays, we won't go through the whole thing again here. Instead, we'll focus mostly on the special challenges and special rewards of the research paper.

If you haven't already studied "Process in the Short Essay" (pages 1–31), you might want to do so now, as preparation for the more specialized essay we are investigating now.

SELECTING AND FOCUSING THE TOPIC

What will you write about? Often a teacher makes it clear by giving a very specific assignment: you will compare the imagery of two assigned poems by Margaret Atwood, or analyze the Family Compact as a cause of the 1837 Rebellion, or describe how a hamburger chain selects a certain corner for a business site.

When you are given a ready-made and specific topic like one of these, part of your work has already been done. You may not know much about the subject, but you do know the direction your research will take, and you'll waste no time on side issues.

More troublesome at first—but often more rewarding in the end—are the more open assignments meant to be narrowed down so they fit limits of scope and size. For example Amy, a student in Communication 210, has a teacher who is giving a list of very broad subjects so students will get practice shaping their own topics. "I don't want anybody writing on what you see here," he is saying, pointing to the list on the assignment page, "these subjects are only the beginning."

Looking at the page, Amy sees that to do her research essay she could investigate "pollution," "family violence," "health," "language" or "employment." The last one almost gives her a shiver, because her brother, who graduated two years ago with a degree in geography, is still slinging hamburgers in a fast-food restaurant and always talking about his "McJob."

"I don't want that one," she thinks, "It's scary." But a minute later she is still looking at it on the page, and thinking: "So it's scary. Maybe that's *why* I should do it. This might teach me something, because someday *I* want to be employed."

Now Amy also realizes that both she and her brother are fans of the Canadian writer Douglas Coupland, who in novels like *Generation X* and *Microserfs* describes the frustrations people in their twenties have these days in finding a meaningful job and career. In fact, it was Coupland who thought up the word "McJob," which her brother always uses. "Maybe," Amy thinks, "I've already begun my research."

Before writing the first word, Amy already sees that an important aspect of doing her research paper is present: motivation. To increase your writing performance, be sure to give some thought to the relative importance and interest of topics on a list, and make sure, like Amy, to choose one significant to *you*.

At this point Amy has picked her subject, but how is she to cut down its size so she can write, as her instructor says, "more about less"? The possibilities are mind-boggling. A person could write on factors like job training, education, the booms and busts of the economy, the expanding or contracting of business sectors, NAFTA and world trade, or for that matter on totally different employment-related issues such as safety on the job or even the techniques of a particular occupation. The approach of a research paper on employment could be historical, psychological, geographic, technical, economic . . . you name it.

In fact, Amy *does* have to name it.

Certainly she could write a few lines on a couple of dozen matters related to employment and claim she had discussed the topic. But a superficial treatment is worthless: why should anyone read generalizations that everyone already knows? To be satisfying, to be interesting, to be instructive, an essay must reach a certain depth. And unless we write an essay as long as a book, that depth is reached only by focusing the topic. To write about employment, then, Amy needs to select *one* piece of the subject and explore it in detail.

But how will she choose? She still can't stop thinking of her brother, an intelligent and popular guy who got decent grades, who graduated—but then with all the budget cutting and layoffs taking place, could not find a job in his field. The whole family often sits around at dinner analyzing why, and trying to come up with solutions. "Isn't this the real heart of the matter?" Amy asks herself. "What can students actually do to move from school into a decent job? *This is what I want to know, and if I want to know it, then my readers will want to know it too.*"

Taking Time, to Save Time

REMEMBER: When the topic is general, take time to find the right subtopic. Later, as you write the essay, your heightened interest and motivation will repay you that time as well as increase the quality of your writing.

GATHERING AND ORDERING INFORMATION

Most of us can write "short essays" on topics we already know, without any research at all. But the major essay in a course is often a research paper meant to teach us about subjects we're just now learning. This means some library work before the writing begins.

The trouble is that libraries can have a paralyzing effect. Surrounded by more books and magazines and microfilms and CD-ROM disks than they could read in a lifetime, people feel their heart beating faster and they ask themselves, "Where do I begin?" If you don't have the answer, try this plan of action:

1. **Read just enough to focus the subject.**

2. **Try a tentative thesis statement.**

3. **Do the main research, taking notes.**

4. **Try a short outline.**

5. **Write the essay.**

Now let's follow Amy through each of these steps.

STEP ONE: READ JUST ENOUGH TO FOCUS THE SUBJECT

Amy believes she already knows something about her subject of how a student moves on from school to a decent job. "After all," she thinks, "why do people go to college or university? Why do we go to guidance counsellors? Why did I read that article just last weekend in *The Globe and Mail* on this very subject?"

That night Amy gets the old *Globe* out of the recycling box in the garage, and reads the article again. "Good material," she thinks, "but how about more?"

Back at the library the next day, she goes to the reference section and looks up her topic in those big hardbound volumes of the *Reader's Guide to Periodical Literature.* Then she moves to a CD-ROM terminal to check out the *Canadian Index* (it can refer her to articles in around 300 magazines and seven daily newspapers). In these standard references she finds the dates and page numbers to locate a half dozen promising articles recently published in periodicals that her library has.

She finds most of them, and spends a couple of hours skimming them for ideas that relate to her subject. But today she takes very few notes. After all, once she nails down her exact approach, some of this preliminary material may turn out to be off topic.

As she checks these articles, and later at the gym as she is working out, a preliminary concept takes shape in her mind. Four or five pieces of advice she has seen in her readings really do make sense, and she would like to explore them further. In fact, a couple of them sounded like things her family had already said around the table. Now she could recommend them to her own readers—that is, after investigating further to make sure the advice makes as much sense as it seems to today.

"Is this the way to narrow down the topic? Will my instructor think I have focused enough, by concentrating on four or five good ways to get into a career?" she asks herself.

As you focus your own topic, you also will ask yourself questions like this. You do not want to be like the horseman who Canadian writer Stephen Leacock said "rode madly off in all directions."

On the other hand, is it possible to focus *too far,* saying too much about too little? A sociologist writing about, say, cults, might send off an article entitled

"The Practice of Exorcism among Upper-Middle-Class Social Groups in Southern California." Who knows, a scholarly journal for other sociologists might publish it. "That's not my situation at all, though," thinks Amy. "I want this essay to give practical, useful advice about how students like me can actually get a real job."

STEP TWO: TRY A TENTATIVE THESIS STATEMENT

At first this step bothers Amy. Will her argument come across as just a few miscellaneous suggestions, like a how-to-get-a-job article in a magazine, or will it hang together and be organized? We have seen, on page 8 of our chapter on the short essay, that a thesis statement needs to do two things, *limit the scope* and *focus the purpose*. But how can the writer choose just the right thesis now, before having done all the main research? What if the later research contradicts the thesis? What if the thesis Amy thinks up right now will later seem totally off?

Sure, that could happen, but look at the alternative: with no thesis at all, Amy would be the person who "rode madly off in all directions." Better to make a good guess at a thesis, then use it as a guide to doing the main research. Better to have a tentative thesis statement than none; after all, even the scientist in the lab follows a hypothesis, and a hypothesis is nothing more than a well-informed guess.

As Amy considers her subject, she realizes now that her advice will not be comfortable or easy to follow. It will be a challenge. This is the common thread in her argument. Realizing this way of "limiting the scope" and "focusing the purpose," Amy finds her thesis. Here it is (in the more polished version that ends up later in her final draft):

> The answer to the new employment questions is flexibility. Only by letting go of old certainties, only by welcoming new tactics for new times, can today's students move more surely towards a real and satisfying career.

STEP THREE: DO THE MAIN RESEARCH, TAKING NOTES

Though a few libraries still use the card catalogue or microfiche system, Amy's library and most others are now online. At a computer terminal Amy can find what books are available, can see more details about the ones that look good, can find out where they are in the library, and can see whether they are checked out right now or are on the shelf. This system is so easy to use, fast and complete that Amy goes straight to it to start her main research, *making a list of sources to consult.*

Instructions are normally posted by the side of these terminals, and librarians are also around for help. Like both the card catalogue and microfiche systems, the online system catalogues library books in three ways: by *author*, *title* and *subject*. Since Amy does not yet know authors or titles, she looks up subjects, trying out such terms as "employment," "unemployment" and "jobs." She quickly passes over titles of books that seem off her topic, or that seem overly technical, or that are out of date. For each book she does intend to consult, she accurately copies down these facts:

1. *author's full name*
2. *title of the book*
3. *place of publication*
4. *publisher*
5. *year of publication*

After trying to locate books through the online catalogue, Amy realizes that her library has only a couple of promising books on her topic, since the whole subject is so recent. So now she goes back to the *Readers' Guide to Periodical Literature* and *The Canadian Index*, to look more carefully and find more current sources.

Each time she finds an article that looks promising, she carefully notes down all these facts:

1. *author's full name*
2. *title of the article*
3. *name of the magazine or newspaper*
4. *volume number and date of the issue*
5. *page numbers of the article*

(All the sources she actually uses must appear in a list of "works cited" at the end of the essay. If she does not have these facts with her then, her carelessness will cost her a last-minute trip to the library.)

It does not take long to gather a list of sources: perhaps 5 or 10 for a short paper and 20 or 30 for a long one. If you have a long list, you may want to record each source on a separate filing card, for ease of organization. A short list like Amy's, though, is more easily kept on one page.

Amy's topic is familiar enough that she is able to locate numerous sources. For more specialized topics, though, keep two other research tools in mind:

• *Interlibrary loans*: Your librarian will supply you with request forms, or will show you how to order online. You give the title, author and other information about a book or a magazine article that you need but that your own library does not have. The library will then use its database system to see which other libraries do have the resource, and will order it for you. There may be a small fee. Large research projects can hardly be done without the resources of additional libraries, but remember that for books the process takes a week or two. (Journal articles may arrive sooner, if your library is part of a system that sends these electronically.)

• *CD-ROM* (Compact Disk—Read Only Memory): Most people have used CD-ROM resources on personal computers, whether at home or at a school lab. The advantage is that one of these disks can store huge amounts of data, such as a whole encyclopedia, or a whole year of text from a newspaper.

Most postsecondary and large public libraries have several useful CD-ROM indexes and other databases, which students can quickly learn to use. One favourite is *ERIC*, which indexes and abstracts the articles of around a thousand journals in the fields of education and the social sciences. Through a user-friendly menu and through dialogue boxes, the user chooses from a vast array of possibilities.

For example a "descriptor" (key word) such as "employment" can be entered, to call up a list of all publications that include this subject. To narrow down the search, more descriptors such as terms that specify *where* or *when* or *who* may then be entered. For example the key words "youth" and "Canada" might be added. The result is a "boolian search," which identifies only those sources in which the descriptors overlap—in this case articles about "employment" for "youth" in "Canada."

The bibliographical data and the descriptions of articles on screen can then be downloaded onto the student's own floppy disk, to be printed out at home. Some libraries provide printers to do this on the spot.

CD-ROM does have one major disadvantage, though: unless you are a student at a large university, the journals that have the articles you want are probably not in your library. Thus you must begin research early enough to request interlibrary loans, for paper sources, or you must arrange through librarians for online sources.

Most libraries have many databases such as *ERIC* or *The Canadian Index*. Some give the actual text of publications (such as whole newspaper articles), which students can download to study and use at home (see Seyed's story in the following computer text box). Students can conduct a boolian search for such materials, to find exactly what they need in a very short time.

Finally, at a fairly steep cost the researcher may conduct an online search of any one of hundreds of databases that his or her own library does not have. Librarians will aid the researcher who wishes to try this specialized task.

A True Story: How Seyed Researched His Essay

One student, Seyed, was fascinated by the return of Hong Kong to The People's Republic of China, and by the effects on the city and its citizens. To research his essay on the subject, he went directly to his library's CD-ROM full-text versions of two newspapers, *The Toronto Star* and *The Globe and Mail*, and got most of his material there (after all, such a current topic shows up in newspapers before very many books attempt to cover it).

First Seyed located about 500 articles on Hong Kong. Trying to sort these rapidly by just looking at the titles, he downloaded what seemed like about the best 50 onto his own floppy disk, then took it home to read on his own computer screen. But there was nothing on the disk! Back at the library, this time he asked the librarian exactly how to download from these resources, did the whole thing over, and this time got it right.

At home again, he now read his 50 articles on screen, and printed out the best in draft form. Next he highlighted the most useful passages in yellow, and, finally, from this information and these potential quotations, developed his essay.

Reference Sources

The on-line library catalogue, the *Reader's Guide to Periodical Literature*, and the *Canadian Index* led Amy to all the sources she needed for her essay, especially since most articles and books that she consulted referred her to other writings on the subject.

In researching longer essays, though, or any essay on a more specialized topic, you may need to look further. Thousands of other reference sources cover almost any field you can imagine. These are a few that students have found useful:

General Sources

The New Encyclopaedia Britannica. Detailed and authoritative.

The Encyclopedia Americana. More popular than scholarly.

The Canadian Encyclopedia. Covers Canadian history, culture, geography, commerce and public life.

Canadian Newsdisc. CD-ROM full-text edition of *The Toronto Star*, *The Ottawa Citizen*, *The Gazette* (Montreal), the *Calgary Herald*, *The Daily News* (Halifax) and the *Vancouver Sun*. Find stories through key words in the headline or text.

Canadian Periodical Index. Under the same title, both print and CD-ROM index to articles in over 400 English and French-language periodicals in many fields.

The Globe and Mail (Toronto). Full-text edition available on CD-ROM.

World Almanac and Book of Facts. Annual collection of statistics and other facts on many subjects worldwide.

Canada Year Book. A review by Statistics Canada of economic, social and political developments in the country. Many statistics.

Canadian Almanac & Directory. An annual collection of facts about Canada.

Corpus Almanac & Canadian Sourcebook. Annual collection of facts about Canada.

The Corpus Administrative Index. Telephone numbers of government agencies and officials (for access to information).

The National Atlas of Canada. Has maps and graphs giving geographical, climatic, economic and social information.

The New York Times Atlas of the World. Maps of all parts of the world. Gives facts on geography, agriculture, industry, business and society.

The New York Times Index. Lists news articles of *The New York Times,* classified by subject, persons and organizations. The annual index shows when a story broke. Then use that date to find articles on the subject from other periodicals as well.

The Canadian Index. A major research tool. Indexes articles from over 180 Canadian business magazines, over 100 general Canadian magazines, and seven Canadian daily newspapers. The CD-ROM version is called *CBCA.*

Facts on File: Weekly World News Digest with Cumulative Index. Comes weekly, in binders that each hold one year's indexing.

Canadian News Facts. An "indexed digest of Canada's current events."

Bulletin of the Public Affairs Information Service. International subject index of periodical articles. CD-ROM version is called *PAIS.*

Essay and General Literature Index. Author and subject index to books of collected essays "with particular emphasis on materials in the humanities and social sciences."

Book Review Digest. Excerpts from reviews of American books.

Canadian Book Review Annual. Concise reviews of Canadian books in many fields.

Bartlett's Familiar Quotations. Indexed collection of quotations on many subjects, from ancient to modern times. Available also on the Internet: <http://www.columbia.edu/acis/bartleby/bartlett>.

Colombo's Canadian Quotations. Indexed quotations by Canadians.

Dictionary of National Biography. Biographies of important persons in Great Britain, to 1900.

Dictionary of American Biography. Biographies of prominent Americans no longer living.

Dictionary of Canadian Biography. Biographies of prominent Canadians.

The International Who's Who. Short biographies of important people worldwide.

Who's Who in Canada. Concise biographies of prominent Canadians.

Science and Technology

Applied Science & Technology Index. Cumulative subject index to over 300 English-language periodicals in many technical fields. Also on CD-ROM, with same title.

Chemical Abstracts. A mammoth international work summarizing conference papers, books and articles. Indexed in several ways. Both paper and on-line versions.

Computer Literature Index. Annual index to articles, organized by subject, author and publisher.

Computer Select. On CD-ROM, contains full text of over 40 computer publications, plus summaries of articles from a hundred more.

Encyclopedia of Physical Science and Technology (15 volumes). Covers "physical science and related technologies."

The Engineering Index. A much-used monthly index to conference papers and the major articles of hundreds of periodicals in all engineering fields. Short version on CD-ROM is *Engineering and Technology Index;* full version is *Compendex*Plus.*

Index to IEEE Publications. Annual index to articles in many areas of electronics.

The McGraw-Hill Encyclopedia of Science and Technology (7th edition, 1992). Twenty volumes on the physical, natural and applied sciences. Index.

Pollution Abstracts. Published six times a year, it indexes and summarizes "world-wide technical literature on environmental pollution."

Science Citation Index. Multidisciplinary index to the world's scientific and technical literature.

Social Sciences and Psychology

The Social Science Encyclopedia. In one volume, surveys the major social sciences.

Psychological Abstracts. Summarizes articles from scholarly journals of many countries and indexes them by author and subject. Read the summaries to find which articles are worth looking up. A similar version, *Psychlit*, available on CD-ROM.

Sociological Abstracts. Summarizes articles from the scholarly journals of many countries and indexes them by author and subject. Read the summaries to find which articles are worth looking up.

Social Sciences Citation Index. "An international multidisciplinary index to the literature of the social, behavioral and related sciences" (annual). Also on CD-ROM.

Social Sciences Index. Author and subject index to English-language articles from many publications in anthropology, economics, geography, law and criminology, public administration, political science, psychology, social work and sociology. Also on CD-ROM.

ERIC. On CD-ROM, summaries of articles in a huge number of periodicals on education and the social sciences. Print versions are *Resources in Education* (*RIE*) and *Current Index to Journals in Education* (*CIJE*).

Business and Economics

Business Periodicals Index. Monthly subject index to articles in a great many English-language business periodicals. Also on CD-ROM, under same name.

The Canadian Index. Indexes articles from over 180 Canadian business magazines, over 100 other Canadian magazines, and seven Canadian daily newspapers. The CD-ROM version is called CBCA.

The Journal of Economic Literature. An international quarterly that has articles, book reviews, summaries of articles from other sources, and an index. Geared to theoretical economics rather than companies and trends.

PROMPT. Monthly index on current markets and technology.

The Humanities (Excluding Literature)

Humanities Index. International index to articles in some 350 periodicals in the humanities. Coverage includes language and literature, philosophy, politics, history, literary criticism and music. Also on CD-ROM under the same title.

Music Index. International author and subject index of articles in music periodicals, including reviews of books and records. Also on CD-ROM.

The New Grove Dictionary of Music and Musicians. Illustrated multi-volume work on composers, instruments, musical works, etc.

The Oxford Companion to Film. Discusses directors, actors, critics, individual films, techniques, etc. Illustrated.

Film Literature Index. A well-used index to many film periodicals.

The New York Times Film Reviews. Reviews beginning 1913. Indexed.

Art Index. Much-used international author and subject index to over 225 periodicals in all major fields of art. Also on CD-ROM.

McGraw-Hill Dictionary of Art. A concise five-volume study of world art from its beginnings. Heavily illustrated.

The Encyclopedia of Philosophy. Authoritative articles about philosophy and philosophers from the beginnings, worldwide.

The Encyclopedia of Religion. Published 1987 in 15 volumes.

The Cambridge Ancient History, The Cambridge Medieval History, The New Cambridge Modern History. Detailed and authoritative coverage of these periods.

Literature

A Dictionary of Literary Terms. A good first source for research on genres or on technical aspects of literature.

The Oxford Companion to Canadian Literature. A concise and authoritative first source for most topics in the field, though has not been revised since 1983. Covers authors, literary works, genres, criticism and more. Strong emphasis on Quebec.

Literary History of Canada, eds. Carl Klinck et al. Comprehensive and authoritative, but does not cover recent times.

The Oxford Companion to English Literature. Also in this series are *The Oxford Companion to American Literature* and *The Oxford Companion to Classical Literature*.

Literary History of the United States, eds. Robert Spiller et al. An authoritative examination of the subject from its beginnings.

The Feminist Companion to Literature in English, 1 volume, 1990.

MLA International Bibliography. For serious literary research. Also on CD-ROM and online.

Canadian Literary Periodicals Index. Twice yearly from 1992, with annual accumulation.

Index to Canadian Literature. Yearly index to the important quarterly *Canadian Literature.*

Canadian Writers and their Works. Large series of volumes with chapters on Canadian writers.

Contemporary Literary Criticism. Multi-volume work that gives excerpts from criticism of current literature.

Contemporary Authors. Multi-volume guide to current authors in all fields, including film and television.

The Oxford English Dictionary, second edition. The largest and most complete dictionary of English, now on CD-ROM. Gives the fullest information on meanings, spellings and origins of words, illustrated by quotations from many periods.

The Oxford Companion to the Theatre. Briefly covers playwrights and their works, major movements in the theatre and technical aspects of theatre. Illustrated.

Having gathered her list of sources, Amy then conducts her main research, using the following guidelines given her by her instructor:

As you begin the main research, be efficient. A couple of minutes spent checking a book's table of contents and index, and leafing through the relevant chapters, may save hours. There is nothing more aggravating than laboriously collecting facts that are scattered through one book, only to find them collected in a few pages of the next book or even reduced to a graph or chart. Another waste of time is to collect facts from an old issue of a magazine or newspaper, only to find a newer issue with more current facts that make your notes obsolete.

When you have selected the most likely sources, begin taking notes:

• The bulk of your notes should be a *summary* of facts or ideas you think you'll need. Don't just jot down isolated facts, but give some of their context, too, so later you can make sense of them.

• When you find a key idea stated so forcefully or eloquently that you couldn't possibly word it as well yourself, copy it exactly, putting quotation marks where the quoted words begin and end.

(As many as half the quotations given in student essays contain one or more errors: spelling, words left out, punctuation changed, etc. Teachers notice carelessness, and don't like it. Help yourself proofread better by putting a straight edge, such as a ruler or a three by five card, under the line in the book or periodical, and another under the line you copied. Now move your eyes back and forth from one to the other, to make sure the two versions are identical.)

Take steps now to save time later:

• Accurately record the page numbers of all summaries and quotations, because you'll need them later for the references. *If you do not get them now, you'll be back the night before the essay is due, leafing furiously through books and magazines.*

• As you take notes, mark the items that seem most important, perhaps with an asterisk (*) in the margin, or by highlighting in colour. Later this step will help you more easily select the main points of your outline.

• Though the main outline comes after the research, put together a *rough outline* of five or ten lines as soon as you can. It may save you hours by channelling your reading and note-taking into exactly those areas that you will cover in the essay.

• Use one of these systems for getting notes into order for an outline:

1. For very long essays: Write notes on file cards, one side only, with each subject labelled at the top. Don't waste time in recording all the reference information with each entry, but do list the author, the title—if you use more than one article or book by the same author—and the page number(s). Later, when writing the list of "works cited," you can look up the other data in your list of sources. When all the cards are eventually placed in the order required by your outline, you write the essay from them.

2. For shorter essays: Write notes on sheets of paper, one side only. As above, record the author, title and page number(s) with each entry, and write a subject label above or in the margin. Later you can cut each item apart from the others with scissors, and arrange the items like note cards according to your outline.

STEP FOUR: TRY A SHORT OUTLINE

Amy knows that a research essay, like a house, is made from a plan. An outline, though, is not a blueprint. While almost every detail of a house is decided in advance, so the builder won't put things like doors or windows in the wrong places, the writer of an essay sometimes gets the best ideas in the middle of the job.

Of course the outline of a research essay is somewhat longer and more detailed than the brief and tentative outline of the "short essay" discussed in our opening chapter. But even this longer outline should not be so complete that it paralyzes Amy's imagination as she writes, or so final that she cannot improve it if her discovery draft awakens valuable new ideas.

To begin forming her outline, Amy divides her notes into groups that seem to fit together. (She actually moves them into different combinations on the desk in front of her, like the pieces of the puzzle which they are.)

Now she looks at them. Are there two main groups, one pro and the other con? Or does one group *cause* the material in the other group? Are there three groups, and therefore three branches of her subject? Or are there four? Do her notes flow onward in time order from first to last, with divisions wherever one time period ends and the next begins? Or is a clear background needed for the actual points to be given?

If you examine your notes with an open and spontaneous mind, you will usually "find" rather than "choose" the form of your outline. Amy finds, for example, that first she needs a good dose of background information to show why the workplace today is difficult, before she can then give her solutions to the problem one by one.

AMY'S OUTLINE

I. Introduction
   A. Background: The security of many jobs in past decades
   B. Contrast: Problems in the job market today
      1. Layoffs because of technology
      2. Underemployment
   C. Thesis: New challenges require new approaches

II. Body: Five ways for students to use flexibility in the quest for worthwhile employment
   A. Get a co-op education
   B. Develop computer expertise
   C. Diversify
   D. Put liberal arts in your education
   E. Begin to invest

III. Conclusion: Playing it safe vs. taking risks

Amy's outline is indeed short, still tentative, leaving room for development rather than trying to blueprint every single detail to come. It does rough out an introduction, a body and a conclusion, the three traditional parts of an essay. It also attempts (successfully, it turns out) to predict the main points to come.

Now before we discuss the last step of actually writing the essay, please read "Students and the New Workplace" on the pages that follow, so we can refer to it as an example.

Sung 1

Amy Sung

Professor Giuliani

Communication 210

5 April ____

Students and the New Workplace

The world of employment is in rapid change.
When many students look back at their grandparents'
careers, they see nine-to-five jobs, years and
years with the same employer, holidays and health
benefits--and at the end of the road a pension.
Even many parents of today's students still live
this secure and steady life of decades past.

Today, though, more and more Canadians, both
older and of student age, see around them a society
that is casting off its employees like dead leaves
from a tree; a society in which too many people
have no job, while many who do are working far too
hard at thankless and repetitive tasks. Canadian
Douglas Coupland, in the title of his widely read
novel Generation X, named a whole generation
enduring the underemployment of what he calls the
"McJob: A low-pay, low-prestige, low-dignity, low-
benefit, no-future job in the service sector" (5).

It is true that the characters of his later
novel Microserfs are the lucky graduates with "good"
jobs in the computer software industry. Are they
really that much better off, though? These
talented "geeks," as they label themselves, have to
spend 371 pages fighting their way out of the

MLA format does not require
a title page. Instead, give the title page information on the first
page of your essay, in the form
you see here.

Your own title is NOT underlined, put in quotation marks,
boldfaced, or put all in capitals.

1

A quick look at the subject's
past can be a good introduction
to its present and future.

2

In the name-page system of
documenting, if the author's
name is given on the page, it is
then omitted from the reference.

3

isolation and repetition of their workaholic jobs and into real life.

4 Quotation marks distinguish the slang terms "Xer" and "geek" from the more objective language of the research essay. Amy would not have used these terms at all, if she were not quoting a source.

The "Xers" and "geeks" Coupland writes about are some years older than today's high school, college or university student, but their younger brothers and sisters face the same challenges. How in fact do today's students plan a decent career? How can they enter today's "lean and mean" workplace and succeed?

A series of questions is dramatic, raising the interest of the reader and leading up to the thesis.

5 THESIS STATEMENT.

The overall answer to the new employment questions is flexibility. Only by letting go of old certainties, only by welcoming new tactics for new times, can today's students move more surely towards a real and satisfying career. The rest of this essay first examines the new challenges, then explores five ways to overcome them through flexibility.

6

By showing here how severe the employment problems are, Amy will help us to view her later solutions as important.

It is clear that present employment trends are not good. Why have corporations such as banks and manufacturers been making hefty profits for their management and shareholders, while at the very same time laying off thousands of employees? Why does a company's share price often jump when new "downsizing" of workers is announced? Why do we now do our banking by machine, talk with voice mail instead of humans, and drive cars built by robots?

7

Jeremy Rifkin, president of the Foundation on Economic Trends in Washington, D.C., captures these new realities in the very title of his book, <u>The End of Work</u>. In his view,

Sung 3

The Information Age has arrived. In the
years ahead, new, more sophisticated software
technologies are going to bring civilization
closer to a near-workerless world. In the
agricultural, manufacturing, and service
sectors, machines are quickly replacing human
labor and promise an economy of near
automated production by the mid-decades of
the twenty-first century. The wholesale
substitution of machines for workers is going
to force every nation to rethink the role of
human beings in the social process. (xv)

In other words, in the ever more competitive world
economy, corporations keep trimming expenses to
boost the balance sheet, relying on their new
electronic "employees"--and of course hoping that
their former human employees still have some money
to continue buying the products.

The future envisioned by Rifkin is one in which
a few highly-paid "knowledge workers" organize all
the computers to profit corporations and
shareholders, while former workers are left in a
vacuum of inactivity and poverty. Unless good
solutions are found, he concludes, social unrest
and even violence will result.

At the same time that many jobs are being
eliminated, others are diminishing in desirability.
According to Edward Greenspon,

almost half the jobs created in Canada in the
past 20 years have been non-standard jobs

Quotations over four lines are
indented 10 spaces (or two
"tabs" on the computer), are
double-spaced like the rest of
the text, and have no quotation
marks (because indenting is
already a signal of quoting).

8

9

Sung 4

(part-time, temporary or contract) without pensions or security . . . . They also pay about $150 less than the same work done by non-temporary employees . . . . (A12-13)

10   As for the growing numbers of temporary workers, the jobs of 75 percent last less than six months, according to Chris Clark, policy analyst for the Canadian Council on Social Development. In the same vein, Andrew Jackson, senior economist for the Canadian Labour Congress, points out that these days only around 60 percent of Canadians work full-time all year long for one employer (Wells 15).

11   Finally, in the new economy it may be women who face the hardest challenges of all. Social critic Heather Menzies, in her book <u>Whose Brave New World? The Information Highway and the New Economy</u>, points out that

>   More and more women are being ghettoized in the new permanent part-time workforce, with few if any benefits, including training, and with a skills, credentials, and silicon ceiling preventing their mobility. They are also part of the growing trend towards home-based work, particularly in the female ghettos of clerical, sales, and service. (34)

12   If high quality employment is indeed threatened, as these critics are saying, and if a new leaner world of underemployment and unemployment is taking its place, what, then, can today's students do to

Sung 5

meet the challenge? What new attitudes and tactics are of more use than the rosy assumptions of the past? What will work right now and in the years to come?

One overall personal trait seems to lie behind the best answers given by analysts: flexibility. When times change, people must change. Only by shaking off the old assumptions, the old patterns and the old habits, can people begin to seize new opportunities. Only by rethinking business as usual can the new generation meet the new challenges.

13

The following pages explore five concrete ways for today's student to bring this flexibility to the quest for worthwhile employment.

Here Amy clearly announces her organization for the rest of the essay. **14**

Get a Co-op Education

One path to job success in today's world can be choosing a co-op program at college or university. "The most important thing," writes Gordon Betcherman, a leading Canadian authority on the future of work, "is to encourage forms of education that mix schooling with work experience-- internship, co-op programs and work-term efforts. These methods have been shown to be very successful." He points out that students in such programs "make connections with potential employers", that they "learn what is required to sell [themselves] to employers", and that they "learn how to do the work" (D2).

15

Here Amy fits choice bits of a longer quotation into her own sentence structure. The whole thing should sound natural, as though she had written all the words herself.

16   Many of these students also speak to so many employers that eventually a job interview seems like an everyday thing. Many co-op students on job placement also make a salary, which helps pay for their education, and then after graduation many are invited back to work for the same employer. Naguib Oman, of the University of Waterloo, is an example. As a computer science major, he had a work term with a small software company, and even before graduation was making so much money that he bought a new car. Since then he has held down a well-paid job with the same company, writing software for a wireless communication program that uses satellite data to map locations and destinations for automobile drivers. (Oman)

There is nothing like a concrete example—such as this case study of Naguib Oman—to help readers "see" your point.

17   A co-op education truly demands the recommended trait of flexibility: the student alternates frequently between school and work, leaves friends every few months, moves to other cities and finds housing, then takes a year longer to graduate. However, for many students the effort brings great rewards.

If you are computing, set your margins to be "justified left," leaving a ragged right-hand margin as if the paper had been typed.

Develop Computer Expertise

18   This path is probably the easiest for most students: become fluent in computing, including use of the Internet and its rapidly expanding World Wide Web.

19   Not that these skills automatically translate into a good employment life. A great deal of

Sung 7

computer-related work is low-level drudgery: for
example data entry, or many service-sector
applications such as food order systems in
fast-food restaurants. Even some "good" computer
jobs, as Coupland shows in <u>Microserfs</u>, can oppress
the individual. On the other hand, those who rise
to the ranks of programmers, systems analysts
and other "knowledge workers" will in many ways be
the winners of the future; they will create and
manipulate the artificial intelligence that will
then displace other workers who did not make it to
the top.

Heather Menzies underlines the growing role of
computer skills in the workplace:

> In mid-1995 Statistics Canada reported that
> nearly half of all workers (48 per cent)
> were working with or on computers, three
> times the figure of 1985. It also found
> that "the most elite class of workers,
> managers and professionals," were the most
> computer literate--with 75 per cent of the
> men and 61 per cent of the women in that
> group working with computer systems. (47)

As for the Information Highway, though many
students see it as entertainment, mastering its
ever-increasing functions can help the individual's
larger goals come true. Consider the example of one
student at York University, who used the Internet
to find a summer job in Italy. This experience
then led to a new career choice in design (which,
these days, also exploits computer skills). As she

20

21

**Another student example
makes Amy's point more
concrete.**

Since Friedman had sent these comments to Amy by e-mail, there is no page number to include in the reference. Her last name is given, though, because it does not appear above in the text. Note in the Works Cited how an e-mail message is listed.

puts it, "The whole thing was so easy. I just made the initial contact by e-mail, then sent the documents and references the company asked for, and in two months I was there working." (Friedman)

22   Another Ontario student, Dan Jordan, is studying International Business at Seneca College and expects to work in that field, but in the meantime his computer skills have helped him create home pages for companies. His advantage: instead of charging the $4000 that a commercial firm does for company home pages, he charges $400. Even at one tenth the fee, he makes $100 an hour because he can usually do the job in four hours. (Jordan)

23   Through their computer skills, these students gain in career flexibility. They are on their way to the future.

Diversify

24   A quick transition moves readers from the previous section to this one.

The example of Jordan leads into another technique of flexibility in today's job world: diversification. It is said that, in medieval times, fathers tried to teach their sons more than one trade. Then if demand for the one diminished, the son could change to the other and still put bread on the table. Have things really changed? Jordan may think he is heading into international business, but who really knows? What if it, like so many other fields, falls victim to automation and consequent downsizing of employees? He can then

shift to his other option, the world of computers.
Each student should look around, asking himself or
herself what the options are. These are usually
seen first in hobbies, pastimes, or in part-time
or seasonal areas of employment. Which of these
excite the person? Which relate to real tasks
done in the real world?

Often these alternate areas are entrepreneurial.
Does the person enjoy working outside? Then
someday, with a used pickup truck and some
lawnmowers, the person could start a landscaping
company. Is the person adventurous? Has he or she
explored Latin America and learned Spanish in the
process? Then the future may be some kind of
international business. Does the person like to
write? Then someday the scribbling might turn
into manuscripts for romances or crime fiction,
or for that matter company proposals and annual
reports. The flexibility of diversification is
the essence of being an entrepreneur, and in a
time of unemployment and underemployment, being
an entrepreneur may be the shortest path to a
career.

In a 1995 address on youth unemployment,
Al Flood, CEO of the Canadian Imperial Bank of
Commerce, summed up his view: "The overall task is
to show more of the new generation, new to the
workforce or not yet in it, how to be entrepre-
neurs." ("Business and Education Must Join Forces
to Combat Youth Unemployment, CIBC Chairman Says")

25

More examples help us
"see" Amy's point.

26

Where no author is named
for an article or other
source, the reference gives
the title instead.

Put Liberal Arts in Your Education

27

Each page is numbered at the upper right, with your last name just before it.

Ironically, an important path towards success in the new economy is an old-fashioned, well-rounded liberal arts education--the kind society has been devaluing for years in its quest for the bottom line. Who are the people who rise in a company? Is it possible that they are the ones who wrote good essays in school?

28

Here Amy embeds Foot's words into her own sentences, to make the whole passage "flow."

Demographer David Foot believes that "The decline of literacy has enhanced the value of the small minority who can write well and who are able to make effective oral presentations." He adds that "the successful worker of the future needs the kinds of skills that an old-fashioned liberal arts education still provides very well--the ability to assemble information, analyze it and think about it." (Foot and Stoffman D2)

Where there are two authors, both are named in the reference.

29

The student who seeks future success would do well to take courses in literature and in writing, to read some philosophy, to know some history--to systematically gain exposure to a wide variety of subjects. English teachers often complain that few people write well. Students who aim high in the world of employment might well want to join these few.

30

English may be important, but is it enough? Tim Reid, president of the Canadian Chamber of Commerce, himself an anglophone who mastered French to further his career, believes that today's students need other languages:

Sung 11

Business dealings today have moved beyond
our backyards and into the global arena.
The status quo of education requirements of
our generation mean nothing in a job market
filled with applicants from around the
world, not just around the corner. Our
children need every advantage we can give to
them so they can go out and create their own
opportunities for success. (1)

With the emergence of our global economy, and
with the North American Free Trade Act drawing
Mexico, the United States and Canada closer
together, many future employees will indeed have to
know languages. This means taking French or Spanish
in school. It means going to Quebec on a language
bursary, to Mexico on a student exchange, or
anywhere else that gives real-life experience in
major languages and cultures. It means openness to
other lifestyles and values--a difficult thing for
those who have never yet left home. For those who
grew up speaking another language, it also means
practising and protecting their skill in it, and
making sure they can write it as well as speak it.
The rewards can be great: when equally good
candidates compete for a job, the one who knows
other languages will more often be chosen.

31

Amy does not document this information, because it is from her general knowledge, not her essay research.

Begin to Invest

The fifth path to success in the new economy
demands even more flexibility and sacrifice than

Since the fifth "path" is hardest, it is put last where it will form a climax. 32

the others. It seems a cruel hoax to urge those lucky graduates who are finally making money in their first real job to delay buying the long-awaited sound system or car--and instead write cheques to the mutual fund company or stockbroker. What few realize is that the painful act of saving money early in life begins an economic snowball effect that can eventually augment and even replace salary. In a time of government cutbacks and a Canada Pension Plan that many believe will disappear, it is the ultimate safety net.

33

Suppose the new employee manages to save $2500 a year for four years. With this $10 000, he or she then invests in stocks (probably at first through the easier and safer means of a stock mutual fund managed by a professional). Suppose also that the investment gains the long-term stock market average of 12 percent a year. Anyone who can figure compounding on a scientific calculator will see that in ten years the $10 000 will on

Amy does not document these figures, since they come from her own calculator, and since her readers will come up with the same figures if they double-check.

average grow to over $30 000, in 20 years to almost $100 000, in 30 years to almost $300 000-- and in 40 years to almost a million.

34

This is not the place to discuss the many fine points an investor must learn, such as the differences in taxation between an RRSP (Registered Retirement Savings Plan) and a regular investment account, or the many techniques involved in choosing good mutual funds and good stocks, or the economic cycles that influence markets, or the art

Sung 13

of diversifying kinds of investment for safety. The person who wants to set the snowball rolling must invest a great deal of study time, as well as some money. One place to start is the book <u>Low-Risk Investing in the '90s</u>, by the well-known Canadian financial writer Gordon Pape.

After the sacrifice of saving and the work of financial study should come the benefits: once the snowball really gets going, the investor can cash in stocks to start a business, to boost a low salary, or to pay bills when between jobs. Ironically, if in the new economy the corporation is gaining power over the employee, the employee can also gain power over the corporation--by owning it.

As with the other paths to success in the new economy--getting a co-op education, developing computer expertise, diversifying, and studying liberal arts subjects like writing and languages--achieving financial security through investment takes flexibility, openness, and the ability to take risk. These are new times. To some people they seem risky times. The highest risk, though, to today's students planning a career, is to follow the comfortable old path of playing it safe.

To keep the essay moving, here Amy refers readers to another source, rather than getting bogged down in a mass of specialized details.

35

Most research essays have a summary near the end, leading into the conclusion. Keep your summary short, like Amy's, so the reader is not bored by repetition.

36

The closing should pack a punch, to send readers off inspired. This one ends on an ironic contrast, concluding that in our times, safety can be more dangerous than risk.

Sung 14

Works Cited

Betcherman, Gordon. "What Government, Business and You Can Do to Brighten the Job Future." The Globe and Mail 27 Apr. 1996: D2.

"Business and Education Must Join Forces to Combat Youth Unemployment, CIBC Chairman Says." 21 Sept. 1995. Canada NewsWire. CD-ROM.

Coupland, Douglas. Generation X: Tales for an Accelerated Culture. New York: St. Martin's Press, 1991.

---. Microserfs. Toronto: HarperCollins, 1995.

Foot, David K., and Daniel Stoffman. "The Great Canadian Job Funk." The Globe and Mail 25 May 1996: D1-2.

Friedman, Jana. E-mail to the author. 21 Mar. 1996.

Greenspon, Edward. "Economy Changing Faster than People." The Globe and Mail 20 Apr. 1996: A1+.

Jordan, Dan. E-mail to the author. 17 Mar. 1996.

Menzies, Heather. Whose Brave New World? The Information Highway and the New Economy. Toronto: Between the Lines, 1996.

Oman, Naguib. Telephone interview. 25 Mar. 1996.

Pape, Gordon. Low-Risk Investing in the '90s. Scarborough: Prentice Hall Canada, 1994.

Reid, Tim. "International Thinking Is a Reality of Our Youth." CPF National News 71 (1996):1+.

Rifkin, Jeremy. The End of Work: Technology, Jobs and Your Future. New York: Putnam, 1996.

Wells, Jennifer. "Jobs." Maclean's 11 Mar. 1996: 12-16.

Where the author is unnamed, start the entry with the title.

Where you list two works by the same author, the second entry begins with three hyphens instead of the name.

Where there are two authors, only the first is presented in reverse name order.

Only the first line of each entry is at the left margin, so readers can more easily see the alphabetical order of references.

Amy can add her own primary research to the list: telephone or personal interviews, or (see above) e-mail messages.

Put no punctuation between name and date of a periodical.

STEP FIVE: WRITE THE ESSAY

Since the research essay is longer and more fully planned than the "short essays" discussed in our opening chapter, it is written in a less experimental way. We might still call the first version a "discovery draft," for the act of writing almost always triggers new ideas. Yet the extensive reading, note taking and organizing done before the writing begins will strongly shape even the first draft.

Amy finds herself writing more slowly and deliberately than in the "short essays" earlier in her course. Now she takes fewer risks, staying closer to her outline, for any major shift of direction now would probably mean more new planning and research.

Yet if while writing she senses that the facts are working *against* her tentative thesis statement, showing it to be wrong, like a scientists's experiment disproving the hypothesis, the only honest response would be to interpret those facts all over, throw out the old outline and write a new one.

As Amy writes her first draft, she follows these guidelines suggested by her instructor:

• *Put your thesis statement into an introduction.* An essay about a very familiar subject might have a short introduction with the thesis statement in the first paragraph, while one on a less familiar subject might begin with several paragraphs of introduction. Amy's falls in between: she gives a moderate amount of introduction to the new problems of the new workplace, then at the end of paragraph 4 places her thesis statement.

In your introduction, whatever its length, try to *interest and prepare your readers.* Amy's references to two current novels widely read by people her age, and the threats to her generation's professional life which she presents in paragraph 4, are designed to involve her readers and get them thinking about the topic.

Other introductions use a quotation from a famous person, an amusing story, a scary statistic, or whatever else the author thinks will interest and prepare readers.

• *Connect the parts.* Just as the sentences of a paragraph are connected by transitions, so are the paragraphs of an essay. Use the transitions we examined on page 43, especially at the beginning and end of paragraphs. Note, for example, how the opening sentence of Amy's paragraph 24 moves us onward from the point just ended to the point just beginning: "The example of Jordan leads into another technique of

flexibility in today's job world: diversification." You may even use a whole paragraph, like Amy's paragraph 13, as a bridge between longer sections.

Finally, larger organizational devices can connect the parts and keep them moving on. For example, Amy uses a natural and logical time order, looking first at traditional employment in past decades, then at the problems of employment now. Then once she is giving her suggestions to solve the problems, she saves the hardest for last, rising to the momentum of a climax.

• *Write a meaningful conclusion.* Do not end with a mere summary, although most research essays, like Amy's, do have one near the end. Instead, try for a larger effect, as in musical compositions that rise at the end to a climax. (Note the placement of her suggestions, just discussed.) Also the very end should convey some kind of power, to leave the reader moved. Amy reaches for this through a contrast or paradox: she claims that in today's employment world, trying to be "safe" is actually riskier than taking risks.

Above all, do not end on some minor matter. Imagine the effect if Amy had closed on a sentence like this: "Finally, when a job interview does in fact occur, it can often be important to polish your shoes, press your clothes, and not chew gum."

• *Revise,* as the author of our "short essay" revised. Since we saw the whole process at work on pages 21–29, we will not repeat it all here. What you have just read is a final draft, revised, edited and proofread—the product of Amy's most careful work. It may still have flaws, but its writer sought to polish the argument as thoroughly as possible by "reseeing" it through several drafts.

In the last of those drafts, Amy scrutinized all suspicious-looking sentences and all words that just might be misspelled (since spell check doesn't catch everything!). It is in this final stage that she reaches for her guide to style and usage (why do this in the early stages, when paragraphs or even whole pages may later be cut?).

Putting the editing and proofreading last does not take away from their importance. Some readers, detecting a punctuation or spelling error, are like a hawk pouncing on a mouse. They just gloat over the fact that you were wrong and they are right. Don't let this happen: why distract a reader with things like this when what that reader should really be doing is paying attention to your argument?

Since research papers are long and are revised through several drafts, word processing is a powerful tool in writing them. A first draft can be stored, retrieved at any time for further work, or printed out in "hard copy" where you can see it better and edit on paper. Why not save all drafts, under different filenames such as "draft1," "draft2," etc.? Then if a newer version doesn't work out, you can go back to an earlier one.

Notes and potential quotations can of course be put into their own files as well. Keeping a running copy of the works cited, in its own file, is especially useful; at any time you can check it so far, add new items, delete items that were not used, or print.

As to format, the Modern Language Association (MLA) advises "justifying" left, leaving a ragged right-hand margin as in typed copy. As for underlining titles of works mentioned, it now advises that either the traditional underlining or the equivalent symbol of italicizing is acceptable.

Especially when writing a long assignment such as a research paper, be sure to "save" drafts onto a backup floppy disk; otherwise you could lose a week or more of work if your hard drive crashes. For any project over 20 pages or so, it is also good to make a third backup disk to keep in another building—in case of theft or fire.

FINAL FORM OF THE RESEARCH ESSAY

Few things are agreed upon by everyone, and essay form is no exception. If your teacher does not specify a particular style, though, follow the form of our sample research essay, which is based on the name-page method of referencing recommended by the Modern Language Association of America (MLA) in its *MLA Handbook for Writers of Research Papers* (fourth edition).

This widely-used way of documenting replaces the old footnote or endnote system. Now brief references in parentheses, in the text of the essay, refer directly to items in a list of "works cited" (formerly called the "bibliography") at the end of the essay. Footnotes or endnotes, now called "content notes," are used only for explanations too minor to appear in the essay itself. (Amy didn't use any at all in her paper.)

Title Page?

Though some teachers still ask for a title page, the MLA no longer recommends it. See whether your own teacher wants one, and if so, what should be on it. Otherwise follow MLA format, which replaces the title page with the following facts on the upper left of the first page of the essay:

your name
the teacher's name
course designation
date

The title appears just below this information, centred, and below it comes the first line of the essay. (See page 1 of Amy's essay for format and spacing.)

Page Format

Use standard-size paper, one side only, and leave standard margins so that your teacher will have room to write comments. If you type or use word processing, double-space. If you write by hand, ask your teacher whether single- or double-spacing is preferred. If the teacher requires a title page, do not repeat the title at the top of page 1. In the upper right corner of each page, put your last name and the page number (see Amy's essay for exact format). Indent the first line of each paragraph five spaces if you type (or, in word processing, one "tab"), and further if you write by hand.

Quotations

Of course whenever you repeat someone else's exact words, you must signal that fact so the reader will not think the words are yours. **Quotations of up to four lines are put in quotation marks and incorporated into the body of your text. Quotations longer than four lines, though, are indented 10 spaces all along the left margin, and are double-spaced.**

Note that quotation marks are not used in a passage of more than four lines, because the indented format already identifies the passage as a quotation.

• *A quotation and the sentence in which it appears must make grammatical sense together.* Avoid constructions like this:

> The author refers to the snow "It would fill the tracks in half an hour."

To correct this fused sentence, let's integrate the quotation with what comes before:

> The author says that the snow ". . . would fill the tracks in half an hour."

Note how the final quotation marks come after the period, not before. They would also come after a comma:

> The author says that the snow ". . . would fill the tracks in half an hour," making the search more difficult.

(*See also*: More explanation and examples of this matter on pages 112 and 113 of the section "Editing Out the Comma Splice and Fused Sentence.")

• *Where one quotation occurs inside another, enclose the inner one in single quotation marks:*

> Then I said, "If this is what you call 'natural food,' I'll go back to TV dinners."

• *You may omit unimportant material from the beginning, middle or end of a quoted sentence by substituting an ellipsis (. . .) of three dots with a space between each.* If the omission is from the end, add a fourth dot which is the sentence period. (See examples in paragraph 9 of Amy's essay.) The omission of one or more sentences from a passage is also signalled by four dots.

Even with omissions, the quotation as it appears in your essay must make sense. Don't attempt to save time by just quoting the beginning and end ("With a . . . it"), assuming your reader will find the rest in the book. Instead, the reader will just get lost!

Fairness to your source is equally important. An unscrupulous publisher might place on the back cover of a new paperback a quotation from a reviewer who said the novel is " . . . an excellent book. . . . ," when unfortunately the critic's full comment was " . . . an excellent book to throw in the garbage." An essayist who quotes out of context is falsifying as surely as if she or he had faked the whole passage in the first place.

• *You can sometimes make a quotation clearer by adding or substituting words in square brackets* (see the example in paragraph 15 of Amy's essay, where the added word "[themselves]" replaces the pronoun "yourself," which made less sense in her more formal, third-person style). Use square brackets sparingly.

Name-Page References

Quotation marks tell your reader when you are using another person's words, but not whose words they are or where the reader can find them in order to check the accuracy of the quotation or find more information on the subject. In a short informal essay it may be enough to introduce a quotation with a few facts: "As Margaret Atwood points out on page 75 of *Survival* . . . ." Your teacher will let you know if this is all the documentation expected.

But in a longer formal research essay, you need a fuller system of giving credit for quotations. The standard used to be footnotes or endnotes, followed on the last page by a bibliography. This system did the job, but wasted time: arranging and typing footnotes was laborious, and the notes and bibliography repeated too much of the same information.

For some years now, the Modern Language Association has recommended a modernized system that delivers all the same information but in streamlined form. If your teacher prefers this approach, as most now do, study the following directions and see Amy's research essay for examples of their use.

The main feature of the name-page reference system is the way you now refer briefly, in the body of the essay, to sources used. Instead of adding a numeral that refers to a note elsewhere, you simply place, after a quotation or other borrowed material, the author's last name and the page or pages where the information can be found. Note how both facts are put in parentheses, as in this example from paragraph 10 of Amy's paper:

> (Wells 15)

This brief reference is one part of your documentation of sources; the other is the corresponding entry in your list of works cited (formerly called the "bibliography") at the end of the paper. When we look there under the name "Wells," we find all the other facts we may need: the rest of the author's name, the title of her article, the fact that it appeared in *Maclean's*, the date and year, and the page numbers:

> Wells, Jennifer. "Jobs." <u>Maclean's</u> 11 Mar. 1996: 12–16.

Now we can look up the original article to check Amy's accuracy, or to find more information.

The exact form of the name-page reference and the form of the entry in our list of works cited will both vary sometimes, depending on several factors. Study the guidelines that close this chapter, as well as the examples in Amy's essay, so you know what to do in each case. But first let's discuss the main question of documentation more fully.

When Do We Reference?

Some people worry about documentation, gloomily expecting to make a mistake and be accused of plagiarism. But most teachers can easily tell the difference between accidental and intentional plagiarism. The few students who deliberately present others' words or ideas as their own, in order to avoid the work of thinking, are often caught and harshly punished—perhaps by failure in the course or even by expulsion from school.

As for the honest majority of essay writers, observing the following principles should cover most cases of documentation. Even if your performance is not perfect, your teacher will note your honesty and will probably recommend improvements rather than blame you for "stealing" information.

• *Reference whenever you quote an author's words or copy visual information such as a chart.* If the borrowed passage is only part of a sentence, or even just a key word or two, it is still put in quotation marks and referenced.

• *Reference whenever you summarize or paraphrase a source.* In high school some students think that doing "research" means finding good passages in the encyclopedia and copying them out into their essay, shuffling a few words around to avoid plagiarism. What they fail to see is that not only words, but also ideas, can "belong" to the person who wrote them.

For example James Higgins, in his essay "Gabriel García Márquez: *Cien años de soledad*," published in Philip Swanson's 1990 book *Landmarks in Modern Latin American Fiction*, states the following on page 157:

> The character with the acutest sense of life's futility is the disillusioned Colonel Aureliano. After undertaking thirty-two armed uprisings he comes to the conclusion that he has squandered twenty years of his life to no purpose and withdraws to his workshop, where he devotes himself to making the same little golden ornaments over and over again.

Suppose that a student doing an essay on the novelist García Márquez would write the following:

> Colonel Aureliano is the character who shows the most acute sense of life's futility. After his 32 armed uprisings he realizes that he has squandered 20 years to no purpose and retreats to his workshop, where he spends all his time making the same little ornaments of gold over and over.

Do these thoughts still "belong" to Higgins? Despite the shifting of phrases and substituting of synonyms, a comparison of the two passages shows the whole progression of thought to be unchanged. A name-page reference should obviously follow the new version.

Furthermore, small groups of words such as "thirty-two armed uprisings" are identical in both passages. The essayist must either change all such passages, to produce a total paraphrase, or put the borrowed parts in quotation marks to show who wrote them.

• *Reference whenever you take from your source a particular idea or fact that is not common knowledge and that does not appear in other sources.*

For example, the year of Shakespeare's birth is not such common knowledge that most people could give it when asked. But since it can be found in thousands of sources, do not reference it. However, if critic X discovers an old trunk in an attic, filled with mouldy documents that prove the year of birth to be not 1564 but 1565, and publishes an article about it, you must reference this information because it is the intellectual property of the author.

Kinds of Name-Page References
Reference to a Single Author

> As for the growing numbers of temporary workers, the jobs of 75 percent last less than six months, according to Chris Clark, policy analyst for the Canadian Council on Social Development. In the same vein, Andrew Jackson, senior economist for the Canadian Labour Congress, points out that these days only around 60 percent of Canadians work full-time all year long for one employer (Wells 15).

Note how the period ending the sentence is placed *after* the reference. Note also that no comma appears between the name and page number, and that the word "page" or "p." is not used before the page number. This name-page reference leads us to the alphabetized entry under "Wells" in the list of works cited, where more information is given. Finally, although the above passage is not a quotation from Wells, it is documented because it is Amy's close paraphrase of Wells' information.

Here is a common variation on the kind of basic name-page reference shown above: If you give an author's name in the text of your essay, then you need give only the page number in the reference:

> "The most important thing," writes Gordon Betcherman, a leading Canadian authority on the future of work, "is to encourage forms of education that mix schooling with work experience—internship, co-op programs and work-term efforts" (D2).

Note how often Amy does name her source in her own text; this procedure helps her essay "flow" by giving readers enough context that they are not tempted to interrupt their thoughts by always turning to the list of works cited.

A variation on the above mode of documentation is placing the page reference directly after the author's name in the text:

> Social critic Heather Menzies (34) believes that women are even more victimized than men by the spread of part-time work.

When Two or More Titles by the Same Author are Listed in the "Works Cited"

> Recurving is "Leaving one job to take another that pays less but places one back on the learning curve" (Coupland, Generation X, 24).

Since another of Coupland's novels, *Microserfs*, is also listed in the works cited, Amy avoids confusion in the above reference by naming the novel quoted. She also names the author, since he is not mentioned here in the text.

(By the way, see how in paragraph 2 of Amy's essay Coupland is quoted, but the reference gives only the page number. The reasons: his name is not needed because it was given a few lines earlier in Amy's essay, and the title does not appear in the reference either, because it, too, was mentioned above; thus we would not mistakenly go to Coupland's other book listed in the works cited.)

Documentation procedure may seem complicated, as in this case, but it is all based on reason: references give only the facts we really need to know.

A Work That Has Two Authors

> In the future, successful employees may well need the skills fostered by an education in liberal arts (Foot and Stoffman D2).

Titled but Unsigned Sources

> In a 1995 address on youth unemployment, Al Flood, CEO of the Canadian Imperial Bank of Commerce, summed up his view: "The overall task is to show more of the new generation, new to the workforce or not yet in it, how to be entrepreneurs." ("Business and Education Must Join Forces to Combat Youth Unemployment, CIBC Chairman Says")

List of Works Cited

Book

> Rifkin, Jeremy. The End of Work: Technology, Jobs and Your Future. New York: Putnam, 1996.

(Note how only the first line of the entry is at the left margin, while the rest is indented. This helps the reader find the right entry, because the last name of the author is the item alphabetized.)

Periodical Article

> Greenspon, Edward. "Economy Changing Faster than People." The Globe and Mail 20 Apr. 1996: A1+.

(Note where periods are used or not used. Also note that months are abbreviated. Finally, if an article appeared on more than one page, you may just specify the beginning page and add a plus sign.)

A Work by Two Authors

> Foot, David K., and Daniel Stoffman. "The Great Canadian Job Funk." The Globe and Mail 25 May 1996: D1–2.

(The first and last names of the second author are not reversed, since the last name of only the first author appears in the alphabetical order of the list.)

An E-Mail Source

> Friedman, Jana. E-mail to the author. 21 Mar. 1996.

An Internet Public Online Posting

> Statistics Canada. *Computer Use in the Workplace.* General Social Survey 12F0052XPE. Online. Available http/www.statcan.ca/Documents/ English/Media Rel/Social/gss.html. July 26 1995.

A CD-ROM

> *Oxford English Dictionary Computer File: On Compact Disc.* 2nd edition. CD-ROM. Oxford: Oxford University Press, 1992

A Telephone Interview

> Oman, Naguib. Telephone interview. 25 Mar. 1996.

Note: The above examples will cover the most common situations, but there are many more. For the fullest detail on MLA format, consult the *MLA Handbook for Writers of Research Papers*, current edition, published in New York by the Modern Language Association.

Further information on the MLA style of citation for electronic sources is also available on the world wide web at http://www.uvm.edu/~xli/reference/mla.html.

ANSWER KEY

Using a Little Craziness to Overcome Writer's Block: Worksheet (p. 7)
This activity is of course open-ended.

Limiting the Scope: Worksheet (p. 9)
This activity is open-ended.

Making Thesis Statements: Worksheet (p. 11)
This activity is open-ended.

Relating to Your Audience: Worksheet for In-Class Group Exploration (p. 15)
This activity is open-ended.

The "Main" Paragraph: Worksheet (p. 47)
Answers to the first set of five questions are of course open-ended. The topic sentence answers to the next set of five will probably be close to these in theme:

1. Fast food is not nutritious.
2. The means of trade have advanced steadily.
3. Driving harms the environment.
4. Many houses waste energy.
5. Clearcutting forests harms the environment.

Topic Sentences: Worksheet (p. 51)

1. B	2. C	3. C	4. C
5. A	6. C	7. B	8. C
9. C	10. A	11. C	12. A
13. C	14. B	15. B	16. C
17. B	18. C	19. B	20. C

There could, of course, be alternatives to these answers, depending on how the topic sentences might be developed.

Unity in "Main" Paragraphs: Worksheet (p. 53)
The revisions are open-ended.

Improving "Thin" Paragraphs: Worksheet (p. 55)
The revisions are open-ended.

Economy: Diagnostic (p. 63)
Only these items are free of wordiness or undesirable repetition: 8, 16, 24, 31, 39.

Economy: Worksheet, Level 1 (p. 65)
Here are the most obvious corrections of these self-repeaters:

1. astounded	2. in the future
3. industrial products	4. the result
5. advantages	6. feelings
7. cheap	8. fascinating
9. a fact	10. at that moment
11. unique	12. share
13. 8 a.m.	14. in the future

15. our environment
16. crucial
17. deaths
18. confidence in myself
19. etc.
20. $150
21. obvious
22. fascinating
23. miserable
24. self-esteem
25. reappear
26. moisture
27. obvious
28. 600 students
29. chaotic
30. crucial
31. rectangular
32. light green
33. impossible
34. in June
35. in 1998
36. light brown
37. unique
38. no alternative
39. competition
40. in my opinion

Economy: Worksheet, Level 2 (p. 67)

Only number 9 is "correct." Revisions, of course, could vary so much that there is no point in presenting them here.

Economy: Worksheet, Level 3 (p. 69)

No item is "correct." The revisions are open-ended.

Clichés: Worksheet (p. 73)

Only these items are "correct": 3 and 15.

Euphemisms: Worksheet (p. 79)

The answers are open-ended.

Euphemisms and Their Opposite: Words Biased Pro or Con: Worksheet (p. 81)

All answers are open-ended.

Jargon: Worksheet (p. 85)

This activity has no one set of correct answers.

Slang and Colloquialisms: Worksheet (p. 89)

These items are "appropriate": 10 and 23.
The revisions are open-ended.

Completing Sentences: Worksheet (p. 95)

A great range of answers is possible.

Complete Sentences: Diagnostic (p. 103)

Only the following items contain no sentence fragment: 4, 9, 14, 19, 23, 29.

Complete Sentences: Worksheet, Level 1 (p. 105)

Items 7 and 19 are complete. Also complete are items 4 (first word group), 9 (first word group), 13 (first word group), 15 (second word group), 21 (first word group), 22 (first word group), 23 (first word group), 25 (first word group).

Complete Sentences: Worksheet, Level 2 (p. 107)

Items 4, 14 and 17 are complete. Also complete are items 3 (first and third word groups), 5 (first and third word groups), 6 (second word group), 8 (first word group), 9 (first and fourth word groups), 13 (first word group), 15 (first word group), and 19 (first word group).

Complete Sentences: Worksheet, Level 3 (p. 109)

These items are complete: 4 (first word group), 5 (second word group), 6 (first word group), 7 (first word group), 8 (first and third word groups), 9 (first two word groups), 12 (first word group), 13 (first word group), 14 (first word group), 15 (first word group).

Comma Splice and Fused Sentence: Diagnostic (p. 115)

1. CS	2. CS	3. FS	4.
5. CS	6. CS	7. CS	8. FS
9. FS	10. FS	11. CS	12. CS
13. CS	14. CS	15.	16.
17. FS	18. FS	19. FS	20. CS
21. FS	22.	23. CS	24. CS
25. CS	26.	27. CS	28. CS
29. FS	30. CS	31.	32. CS
33. CS	34. FS	35. FS	36. CS
37. CS	38. CS	39. CS	40. CS

Comma Splice and Fused Sentence: Worksheet, Level 1 (p. 117)

Items 5, 12 and 23 are "correct." The revisions are open-ended.

Comma Splice and Fused Sentence: Worksheet, Level 2 (p. 119)

Items 2, 3, 11 and 16 are "correct."

Commas: Worksheet (p. 125)

1. As I put my coat on, the dentist and receptionist had a brief discussion.
2. Sharon flirted outrageously with Michael, and Kenny and Jason flirted with her. OR: Sharon flirted outrageously with Michael and Kenny, and Jason flirted with her.
3. My brother, grandfather and I had been going to the races since before I could remember.
4. North Americans believe in eye contact.
5. The fastest sports are soccer, hockey, football, rugby and basketball.
6. People in Istanbul seem to think that hamburgers and fries are not worth eating.
7. O.J. Simpson, the famous athlete, a hero to many, was an abusive husband.
8. Once I placed a couple of lines on the paper, some thoughts began to appear.
9. Players who fight during a game should be suspended for the whole season.
10. Our media, especially television, are to blame for sexism in society.
11. If you can, use cash or make your payments promptly.
12. While Dad was putting the lights on, my brothers and I started to place the star on the Christmas tree.
13. Adoption is an event that dramatically changes a child's life.
14. Children who were victims of their parents' violent outbursts may undergo mental illness or personality disorder when they grow up.
15. Our diet should contain dairy products rich in protein, and vegetables.
16. Correct.
17. Shopping malls, such as the Bay and Eaton Centre, attract tourists.
18. Marriage is a big commitment.
19. If you write a word without being completely sure of how to spell it, you may be making a mistake.
20. For hundreds of years English Canada had social and political control over Quebec.
21. Although stubborn, Hagar is one of Margaret Laurence's most admirable characters.
22. As I mentioned before, Ontario has a low level of education.
23. When planning your holiday, visit or phone the tourist information centre in your city.
24. Correct.
25. Photo radar fails as a true safety device on our roads, because the real problem, the driver who is weaving in and out of traffic cutting people off and causing accidents, is not being stopped.
26. Once the needle is in, the plunger is retracted to check for blood.
27. One thing that really bothers me is the idea of a large dog being kept in the city.
28. I love to play hockey, but studies come first.
29. Alcohol has become a problem for our schools, and teachers are deeply concerned.
30. The truth is that many alcoholics never seek help, resulting in their own destruction.
31. Correct.
32. Ham radio has become my obsession.
33. Correct.
34. Harsh lighting produces harsh photographs.
35. Correct.
36. One of my math teachers helped me learn to achieve my goal in the subject, by spending a great deal of time working with me.

37. When rivers lose their velocity, suspended particles of clay and silt are deposited, creating fertile soils in river deltas.
38. Brian McDonald, a youth worker in Vancouver, says one of the major reasons for school violence is the "slow response of a clogged court system."
39. The last step is to record the time, drug and dosage on the patient's chart.
40. I love to cook, myself, and eat at home.

Semicolon, Colon, Question Mark and Exclamation Point: Worksheet (p. 131)

These items are "correct": 9, 15, 22, 31.
The revisions are open-ended, since there is often more than one way to eliminate the errors.

Run-on Sentence: Diagnostic (p. 135)

Only the following items are not run-ons: 3, 9, 11, 15, 19, 25, 27.

Run-on Sentence: Worksheets, Levels 1 and 2 (pp. 137 and 141)

There are no "correct" items in these exercises. The revisions are open-ended.

Pronoun Reference: Diagnostic (p. 147)

Only the following items do not have a fault in pronoun reference: 5, 8, 11, 13, 28, 32.

Pronoun Reference: Worksheet, Level 1 (p. 149)

These items are "correct": 10 and 13.

Pronoun Reference: Worksheet, Level 2 (p. 152)

Only item 9 is "correct."

Agreement: Diagnostic (p. 159)

The following items are "correct": 3, 5, 9, 11, 13, 24, 28, 30, 33, 37.

Agreement: Worksheet, Level 1 (p. 161)

1. is	2. has	3. are
4. is	5. his or her	6. his or her
7. is	8. his or her	9. I
10. has its	11. is	12. was
13. his or her	14. he or she has	15. is
16. it	17. were	18. is
19. is, himself or herself	20. he or she has, his or her	21. is
22. he or she, has	23. provides	24. was
25. is	26. us	27. was
28. its	29. I, my	30. leave

Agreement: Worksheet, Level 2 (p. 163)

These items are "correct": 4, 7, 10, 14, 17.

Agreement: Worksheet, Level 3 (p. 165)

Only item 5 is "correct."
The revisions are of course open-ended.

Equality of the Sexes in Language: Worksheet (p. 169)

These items are "unbiased": 5 and 20.
The revisions are open-ended.

Misplaced and Dangling Modifiers: Diagnostic (p. 175)

1. Drinking is said to be a bad habit <u>by many doctors</u>.

2. Active sports, such as soccer, involve a lot of competition.

MM

3. Some children are forced to learn their first language <u>by their parents</u>.   MM

4. Pills are <u>virtually</u> used for everything.   MM

5. I was discouraged from speaking the truth <u>by my lawyer</u>.   MM

6. <u>After being hired</u>, the manager teaches the newcomer his or her duties and responsibilities.   MM

7. I <u>only</u> bought five items but had to wait in line more than 20 minutes.   MM

8. We are <u>only</u> young once.   MM

9. It takes my mother only three minutes to drive to work.   _____

10. In the past, stores were <u>only</u> allowed open on Sundays during the holiday shopping season.   MM

11. Since I was an only child, my parents wanted to protect me.   _____

12. Hailstones <u>only</u> reach 2.5 cm in diameter.   MM

13. I moved to Bayside with my parents when I was 13 years old <u>from the city of Ottawa</u>.   MM

14. In the past, even an unimportant disease could kill the victim <u>such as measles, whooping cough or diphtheria</u>.   MM

15. All students are <u>not</u> necessarily the same.   MM

16. If you are like most people, a mortgage will be the largest debt of your lifetime.   _____

17. A limited company takes responsibility for its actions, <u>not its human directors</u>.   MM

18. When I was a kid I lived with my grandmother, a lovely lady who would let me do anything I wanted to, <u>for a few months</u>.   MM

19. <u>As a child</u>, my father told me that the world is a cruel place to be in alone.   MM

20. Children flock to see Santa Claus <u>by the dozens</u>.   MM

1. <u>When driving in a big city like Montreal</u>, parking is always a problem.   DM

2. <u>Once in the vehicle</u>, the car doors should be locked.   DM

3. <u>After waiting two hours in the lobby</u>, the doctor spent less than two minutes on me.   DM

4. Dogs make good household pets because they are used for protecting the house <u>while away for the day</u>.   DM

5. Living on the farm in southern Ontario, <u>winter tends to be cold and harsh</u>.   DM

6. <u>Looking at my nephew watching television</u>, he seems to be in a trance.   DM

7. When you are living as a family, housework needs to be done.   _____

8. <u>After a few months of cleaning a dentist's office</u>, the dentist recommended me to her bookkeeper, so I was able to clean the bookkeeper's office too.   DM

9. <u>When turning on the stereo system</u>, the sound quality inside a car is great.   DM

10. <u>After eating a whole pizza</u>, my stomach begins to feel strange.   DM

11. <u>After writing tests and quizzes</u>, the board of education agreed to let me attend Grade 12 at York Memorial High School.   DM

12. Being an ESL student, I had a hard time understanding the teachers.   _____

13. <u>Going through Grade 12</u>, the teachers began to demand more work.   DM

14. <u>After spending three hours shivering and trying to stay warm</u>, the storm subsided and we quickly headed for camp.   DM

15. <u>By recycling paper</u>, thousands of square kilometres of forest will be preserved.   DM

16. <u>Dressed in secondhand clothing with long messy hair</u>, his appearance was anything but cleancut.   DM

17. Loose bindings will cause the skis to fall off <u>while standing up and skiing</u>.   DM

18. The English language is always changing. <u>Travelling from place to place</u>, this change can be seen.   DM

19. <u>When feeling lonely and depressed</u>, a dog is always at your side wagging its tail.   DM

20. <u>By simply putting on a pair of glasses</u> a person's appearance can be transformed dramatically.   DM

Misplaced and Dangling Modifiers: Worksheet, Level 1 (p. 177)
These items are "correct": 8 and 12.
The revisions are open-ended.

Misplaced and Dangling Modifiers: Worksheet, Level 2 (p. 179)
These items are "correct": 5, 13, 19.
The revisions are open-ended.

Parallel Form: Worksheet, Level 1 (p. 185)

1. touching
2. heaviness
3. speaking
4. skilfully
5. large
6. to roast
7. shifted gears
8. drinking too much
9. going to the movies
10. to skate
11. London
12. after dinner
13. April
14. intelligent
15. losing
16. planting the seeds
17. Harley-Davidson
18. angry
19. playing tennis
20. June

Parallel Form: Worksheet, Level 2 (p. 187)
These items are "parallel": 8 and 17.
The revisions are open-ended.

Commonly Confused Words: Worksheet (p. 193)

1. accept
2. advice
3. effect
4. affect
5. our
6. bear
7. breaks
8. breathe
9. buy
10. capital
11. clothes
12. course
13. council
14. desert
15. due
16. immigrated
17. farther
18. hear
19. heroine
20. whole
21. its
22. know
23. led
24. lose
25. morale
26. passed
27. piece
28. personnel
29. principal
30. quiet
31. write
32. role
33. sight
34. than
35. there
36. they're
37. through
38. too
39. whether
40. were

Apostrophes: Worksheet (p. 201)

1. All pets should receive more sympathy than they do.

2. For entertainment Oshawa has movie theatres, ice rinks, roller arenas, night clubs and all sorts of gyms to work out at.

3. The Beatles' influence and popularity will live as long as rock and roll exists.

4. The present art of producing with an assembly line system has come a long way since its introduction.

5. C

6. It's exciting to see a great horse thundering down the track.

7. The only way to reduce students' financial problems is to increase their grants and loans.

8. Students who are 18 and over are the ones who need money the most.

9. Thousands of people fish Ontario's lakes and rivers each year, but how many will take a minute to consider the results of fished-out waters?

10. Driving a motorcycle gives one a sense of independence, because the rider knows people are watching.

11. People who have no confidence in their own work will try to use others' ideas.

12. Politics is what gets everyone talking and moving in this world.

13. Parents' moral values are passed on to the next generation.

14. My parents emigrated from Greece.

15. C

16. After each goal the team that was scored against gets possession of the ball behind its net.

17. It's a holiday to escape from work and see who can catch the most fish.

18. It's my parents' duty to take care of me; they are legally required to.

19. She sees only his good qualities.

20. C

21. Solar systems have a sun and various numbers of planets.

22. Are Canadians ashamed of their own country?

23. C

24. There are many owners' clubs for most sports cars.

25. Newton's Second Law of Motion helps the swimmer to conserve energy.

26. Illness can be the mind's expression to withdraw from life's stresses and strains.

27. We'd go to my grandparents' house each year because it wasn't really Christmas anywhere else.

28. The four-cycle system is what most automobile engines are based on.

29. When Nick sees the Buchanans' reaction to Myrtle's death, he develops a sense of moral responsibility.

30. Animals such as rabbits, monkeys and cats are being used for meaningless experiments.

31. C

32. It was Labour Day when all the delayed thoughts of moving from my parents' finally hit home.

33. When children see their favourite players using sticks to jab and spear other players, the next thing you know, the children are imitating.

34. Anyone who has run for a few years on the road has no doubt experienced a deterioration of the knees.

35. Elizabeth realized the faults of her parents' marriage.

36. C

37. True punk rockers wear safety pins through their noses or cheeks.

38. A newborn child sees the light for the first time.

39. My mother's parents don't travel at all.

40. All over the world we are confronted with the same problems in women's lives.

Capitals: Worksheet (p. 205)

1. A friend of mine, Frank, once told me that he had been behind a Mac's store smoking a cigarette when all of a sudden a police officer approached and asked him where the pot was hidden.

2. During the hockey game, the mother of one of the opposing players stood up from her seat and yelled as loudly as she could, "Kill that little worm!"

3. In the first year of the program, students have to take accounting, economics, geography, mathematics, English, management, business law and psychology.

4. Canadians have long been concerned with developing the North, but only recently with protecting it.

5. My parents bought a house north of the business district, within a five-minute walk of an elementary school, a middle school, a high school, a Mac's Milk store and a shopping centre.

6. On a bright summer morning, the first Monday of July, we got in our canoe and started down the Missinaibi River.

7. Who has seen the wind?
   Neither you nor I;
But when the trees bow down their heads
   The wind is passing by.
      —Christina Rossetti, 1872

8. In high school one of my English teachers spent two months on *Hamlet*.

9. In addition to containing beef and/or pork, wieners may contain water, flour, milk solids, salt and preservatives such as sodium nitrite, which has been known to cause cancer in laboratory animals.

10. Cruise ships have many facilities such as bedrooms, swimming pools, lawn tennis courts, dancing halls, movie theatres and bars.

11. Lady Macbeth, a strong-willed character who was capable of influencing Macbeth to murder his king, brought about her breakdown and death by her own ambitions.

12. John Osborne was born on December 12, 1929, in London, England.

13. In today's modern society, people's morals and values are changing, so divorce, birth control and abortion are more easily accepted.

14. J. D. Salinger's best short story, "For Esmé—with Love and Squalor," shows how destructive war is to human feelings.

15. When I began high school I really got involved in soccer.

16. I arrived in Trinidad on Monday and began my search for a job on Tuesday.

17. Stephen Leacock once wrote, "The essence of humour is human kindliness."

18. In his *Biographia Literaria*, Coleridge refers to "that willing suspension of disbelief for the moment, which constitutes poetic faith."

19. Mackenzie King said, "The promises of yesterday are the taxes of today."

20. Blaise Pascal called humans "the glory and the shame of the universe."

21. The driver stopped the bus to jump out and take a look. He was immediately followed by the Spaniard, two Mexicans, Hugh, Geoffrey and Yvonne.

22. When the Canadian dollar sank in value, foreign automobiles such as the Volvo, Volkswagen, Toyota, Subaru and Honda rose sharply in price.

23. The National Hockey League Rules Committee brought in new rules that prohibited players from being overly aggressive.

24. My mother speaks French, Portuguese and English.

25. I have noted that math teachers do not dress as well as English teachers.

26. To depict their toughness, hockey players are given names such as "Hammer," "Battleship," "Tiger" and "Bulldog."

27. One of the fastest-growing religions in the world is Islam.

28. In each of Mordecai Richler's earlier novels, *The Acrobats*, *Son of a Smaller Hero* and *A Choice of Enemies*, the hero is an artistically inclined Canadian with a deep dislike of Canadian culture and a conviction that the society he lives in is a fraud.

29. As a faithful expression of the theme found in the play, the movie *Fortune and Men's Eyes* was the epitome of success.

30. "Well, Doctor," I said, "since you agree with the other doctors, I suppose we had better go ahead with the operation."

Abbreviations (p. 207)

1. CEO = chief executive officer
2. CPI = consumer price index
3. GIC = guaranteed income certificate
4. GST = goods and services tax
5. ICU = intensive care unit
6. NDP = New Democratic Party
7. RAM = random access memory
8. R&D = research and development
9. RN = registered nurse
10. SASE = self-addressed stamped envelope

Index

STUDENT REPLY CARD

In order to improve future editions, we are seeking your comments on

PROCESS AND PRACTICE, Fifth Edition

After you have read this text, please answer the following questions and return this form via Business Reply Mail. *Your opinions matter. Thank you in advance for your feedback!*

Name of your college or university: _____

Major program of study: _____

Course title: _____

Were you required to buy this book?   yes _____   no _____

Did you buy this book new or used?   new _____   used _____ ($_____)

Do you plan to keep or sell this book?   keep _____   sell _____

Is the order of topic coverage consistent with what was taught in your course?

Are there chapters or sections of this text that were not assigned for your course? Please specify:

Were there topics covered in your course that are not included in this text? Please specify:

What did you like most about this text?

What did you like least?

If you would like to say more, we'd love to hear from you. Please write to us at the address shown on the reverse of this card.

- *cut here* - - - - - - - - - - - - - - - ┐
                                                                                     |
                                                                                     |
                                                                                     |
                                                                                     |
                                                                             cut here
                                                                                     |
- *fold here* - - - - - - - - - - - - - - - |

Postage will be paid by

MAIL ⮞ POSTE

Canada Post Corporation / Société canadienne des postes

Postage paid If mailed in Canada	**Port payé** si posté au Canada
Business **Reply**	**Réponse** **d'affaires**
0183560299	01

0183560299-L1N9B6-BR01

Attn.: Sponsoring Editor
College Division

MCGRAW-HILL RYERSON LIMITED
300 WATER ST
WHITBY ON   L1N 9Z9